PILGRIMS WERE THEY ALL

Studies of Religious Adventure
in the Fourth Century
of our Era
by

DOROTHY BROOKE

" ... *a compaignye*
Of sondry folk by aventure y-falle
In felaweshipe, and pilgrimes were they alle."

FABER AND FABER LIMITED
24 Russell Square
London

First Published in September Mcmxxxvii
By Faber and Faber Limited
24 Russell Square London W.C.1
Printed in Great Britain
At The Bowering Press Plymouth
All Rights Reserved

ἀλλὰ τί μοι τῶν ἦδος; ἐπεὶ φίλος ὤλεθ᾽ ἑταῖρος,
Πάτροκλος, τὸν ἐγὼ περὶ πάντων τῖον ἑταίρων,
ἶσον ἐμῇ κεφαλῇ.

⋆ CONTENTS ⋆

★ INTRODUCTION ★

Centuries have sometimes an individual character so distinct that they cannot be regarded as arbitrary fragments of time; events in them seem to have had an arithmetical sense, and obligingly to have shaped themselves to suit the common chronology of historians. Such a century, with a small and pardonable time-lag, ran from 1815 to 1914, and such another was the fourth century of our era, which may be regarded as beginning in the year 311 with Galerius' edict intended to terminate the persecution of the Christians, or, if preferred, with the edict of Milan of about 313, and as having closed with the capture of Rome by Alaric in 410. There is in the course of history no more distinct or rounded period of time.

It was the first century of Christian liberty, the last of the Western Roman Empire. The two events which began and ended it, the edicts of Toleration and the sack of Rome, may not have had the connection which has been seen in them, in different ways, by Saint Augustine and others; and, of the processes which gave rise to these events, it is difficult, as with the hen and the egg, to say which was cause and which was effect, whether the new religion brought the empire down or whether the decay of Rome gave the new religion its chance. Perhaps both were secondary, and the cause of both was a change in the minds of men, who could no longer see their personal fulfilment in maintaining the fabric of a great imperial system, and demanded complete spiritual satisfaction for the individual, each for himself.

During the fourth century the Church, freed for the first
time from political oppression and from social contempt,
took possession of the entire fabric of society: pagans in
large numbers remained, but were becoming gradually a
survival, a curiosity. The Church could disregard them,[1] as
she herself had not been disregarded, and the legend of the
Milvian Bridge should be reversed, for it was not Constantine who conquered through the Cross but the Church
which conquered through the emperor, and won an
imperial, if also a terrestrial, crown.

The victory, like so many victories, trailed a cloud of
dust; the battlefield was haunted by the usual birds of prey.
In accordance with the first of historical platitudes, the
struggle had produced a semblance of unity; with peace
came the re-emergence of ordinary human feelings, in short,
there was quarrelling among the allies, and a century which
began with the persecution of Christian by pagan ended
with Christians persecuting one another. 'Religious love
put out religion's eye.'

The new realm that had been conquered proved a Promised Land indeed: it flowed with milk and honey, it was
rich in comforts and vanities for the body, in nectar and
ambrosia for the mind. The great men in religion, prelates
and high ecclesiastics, were now the great ones of the earth;
the poor fishermen of Galilee had been succeeded, somehow,
by mitred persons on thrones. And as the cultured classes
capitulated to Christianity, Christianity itself went to school,
to the university, and became rhetorical and metaphysical,
cultured and gentlemanly, acquired in fact that classical
education which it has never since been able to shake off.
That fusion was completed which had begun in the previous
century when Christianity, in contact with the Alexandrian
schools, encountered neo-Platonism, and acquired difficult

---

[1] There were sporadic anti-pagan outbursts, as at Alexandria, due
to occasional mob violence, not to organized oppression.

metaphysical concepts like the *Logos*, fireworks which, in unaccustomed hands, went off unexpectedly in violent explosions of controversy. Now rhetoric, too, was in the Church's hand, that art which in ancient times embraced eloquence and dialectic of all kinds, whether forensic or political. It had been the breath of life to the ancient democracies, a florid Sicilian thing in its origin, preached to the Greeks by its prophet Gorgias, frowned upon by the puritanical Plato. The Romans adopted it from the Greeks and, undeterred by Plato, loved it for its own florid sake, forgot, except in the law courts, the need for any content, and lost themselves in the joy of sheer word-embroidery. In the later empire nothing was left but the words, and the object of education was to use as many of them as possible, to say the same thing over as many times as possible and in as many ways, till the thought, if any, had collapsed under the burden and become as flat as a pancake.

The Fathers of the Church, the very greatest of them, advocated and pursued the ancient culture as a new weapon in the Church's armoury. But the weapon was dangerous to handle, and could play some unexpected tricks. The contact of theology with philosophy produced that dizzy whirl of speculation which was precipitated and crystallized in the controversies, and confusion was the more confounded by the rhetoricians, who drowned everything in a torrent of phrases and words, and gave both religion and philosophy a drenching from which they never recovered. Tertullian, quick to pick out flaws, had recognized the dangers of dialectic to orthodoxy; and to busy emperors, anxious only for unity and peace in their vast domains, the heresies and controversies seemed nothing but words.[1] To the puritans, a people who flourish in most ages and nearly every clime, the Church of that time seemed to have gone a-whoring

[1] See *Theodosian Code*, Section XVI, and the letters of Constantine in the Arian controversy.

indeed. Haunted by some vague imaginings of what Christianity should signify, they were aghast at the perversion, and from the luxury, the culture, and the power, from the mitres and the metaphysics, they fled to the wildernesses and became anchorites and monks, in numbers greater than had ever fled from the persecutions. Side by side with the new worldliness of religion arose that wild ascetic movement which is one of the most fantastic manifestations of the century.

It was an age of intense and varied human animation; and a religion which seemed to aim at liberating the soul from the dragging chains of materialism, at sublimating human passion to an angelic benevolence and calm, was tinged with every colour of the human spectrum. The many-coloured dome had been swiftly interposed before the too blinding white light, which reached the earth stained with all the colours of human passion, some of them bright and lovely, some just dirty; and one of them was that of blood.

There is tragedy in the spectacle, but also comedy, and very occasionally edification. The happenings of the fourth century are always interesting, often astonishing, sometimes amusing. The martyrs with their grim glory and their crowns are gone, their lives are already half legendary and their tombs are shrines; and with growing confidence and vitality a less dignified concourse crowds before us, hermits, heretics, preachers, prelates, monks, pilgrims, and scholars, with the variety and vivacity of Chaucer's pilgrims, each full to the brim of matter and eager to beguile the way with his story.

Their adventures were fantastic indeed, with the novel distinction that they were not encountered by chance, but courted and contrived deliberately. The fugitives from the worldly scene, the ascetics, climbed upon pillars and lived there or in caves and holes, or, imitating Nebuchadnezzar, they ate grass and mooed. Those who were ensnared and dazzled by the ancient culture fell to writing flowery orations which they called homilies, or composed hexameters, iambics, elegiacs, thousands of them, line upon line. The adventurous and the curious set out on the most delightful and extensive tours to visit, in the name of edification, the Holy Places, the shrines of famous martyrs, and the abodes of the hermits. For every one who knew how to use it religion opened up, as nothing had before, opportunity for personal development, for the indulgence of a natural bent.

Of the individuals who filled this busy scene we are in no dearth of information, for they were very ready, most of them, with the pen. It was a lettered age, if not an age of great literature; nearly everybody wrote, and those who did not, or wrote but little or but feebly themselves, admired and cherished the work of their betters. Much of what they wrote has been preserved, their most trifling letters, their most tedious homilies, the most unblushing of their flatteries addressed in letter or panegyric to other, greater men, their most shameless libels and attacks upon the people they disliked or disagreed with, as well as their more respectable and more fortunate performances. The long procession of vast tomes which comprises the Benedictine edition of the Fathers, both Latin and Greek, a great part of which comes from the pens of the fourth century, testifies to the value (often, it must be confessed, much exaggerated) set by their contemporaries, and by portions of posterity, upon every scrap of written matter produced in that age within the Church. And with the art of self-revelation, as expressed in letters and controversial writings, biography and autobiography come to life, the recording of the individual and his adventures, and inevitably the novel. The Lives of the Saints are emerging, a new and distinct form of literature which was to dominate the Christian world through many ages and can still find readers.

[15]

If they wrote industriously, these Christians of the fourth century, that was nothing to the way they talked.[1] Between the lines of their writing the talking is more than audible, it is a babel of tongues, a roar. Numbers of people seem to have had nothing in the world to do but write about religion and talk. The humble processes of earning a living are out of sight and out of mind. Asceticism is a help in this direction, of course, for the less a man eats or needs the less must he do to gain his necessaries, and to the desert hermit, who avoided the organized communities, all his time was his own. But the recluses were not the most active with tongue and pen. Much of the talk and of the writing comes from people who had not left the world; there was a most surprising extent of leisure in ordinary life. Its usual employment, upon endless discussions of religion and theology, which were inevitably involved with the profoundest problems of metaphysics and ethics and flourished the more for that, must command our respect, even if we have no wish to join in them. It must be admitted that it was a highly civilized century.

The fusion of the old and the new, the fresh life breathed by the new religion into the traditional, sophisticated forms of thought and speech of the ancient world, produced a rich and complex culture. The sacred buildings and artistic works of the time, scarce though they are, seem all of a piece with it; they derive directly from the past, with a difference. They have richness, imagination, gaiety almost; and the past they remember is not the pagan temple but the public meeting-places, the social centres, the basilicas, the baths. As for the people, excepting only the ascetics, they were quite at home in an age of transition and found no inconvenience in it; with their feet planted firmly in both worlds they extracted sustenance and savour from both.

[1] Except some few of the hermits who made silence their rule, and those who mooed.

Then, as time passed and the empire broke up into the Germanic kingdoms, there remained as the sole symbol of social unity, the sole repository[1] of the ancient culture till the Renaissance should dawn, the sole link that held, in the general disintegration, between earth and heaven, that strange phenomenon the Church.

[1] Except for the Arabs, whose conquest of some of the ancient seats of learning, such as Alexandria and Cæsarea, put them in possession of a good deal of ancient literature.

I
THE ASCETICS
Antony and Others

Εἰ μοναχοί, τί τοσοίδε; τοσοίδε δέ, πῶς πάλι μοῦνοι;
ὦ πληθὺς μοναχῶν ψευσαμένη μονάδα.

Every one, as Theodoret says in his *Religious History*, has heard of Saint Simeon Stylites,[1] the saint who dwelt in Syria upon a pillar, all the Romans, of course, and the Persians and Medes and Ethiopians and Scythians as well; and to these can now be added those nations to whom Lord Tennyson's roving historic fancy has made him a familiar name. He has certainly had his due of admiration, this fantastic pillar-dweller; already in his lifetime it was so lavishly bestowed that in his opinion it was the worst of all the trials which he had to bear. Long before he betook himself to the pillar's top he was a celebrated ascetic and holy man, and the pillar, at first, was not an ascetic device, but a desperate resource to evade the pressing contact of his admirers, who crowded round him wherever, on the earth's surface, he might flee to escape them, and not satisfied with crowding merely, must touch and kiss his holy person and carry off, as amulets and souvenirs, portions of his clothes. There had been saints who burrowed for themselves underground hiding-places to escape their public; Simeon chose to rise above it, and soon found that the pillar served a number of purposes, and that a pillar-saint may have the best of more than one world. So the pillar grew from five feet high to fifty, and the crowd round its base increased, tolerated and

[1] Simeon lived about 388 to 459. The reputed base of his column can be seen to this day, among the ruins of the magnificent monastic buildings which grew up around it. See G. L. Bell: *Syria: the Desert and the Sown.*

even encouraged by Simeon, who did not care how large it was now that he had found out how to be admired without being squashed. He would even indulge it with surprises; as the pillar lost its novelty there were variations on the principal theme. Could he remain standing through Lent without the support of the prop to which he had tied himself during the early stages of his pillar career? Apparently he could, for the prop was thrown away and to stand thus erect for weeks at a time became an oft-repeated, and to his public, at any rate, a favourite turn. Pilgrims flocked from all parts to see him, imperial persons[1] waited upon his words, his fame flew about the universe, and his portrait was on sale in every bookshop in Rome. He became so fashionable that a long line of pillar-saints sprang from his example, and took up their abode upon the pillars that stand about in the deserts of the Near East, the ruins, mostly, of Roman buildings, much as storks will come and build upon a chimney or a steeple and are regarded as picturesque and lucky neighbours, in spite of the damage they frequently do.

To many it may seem that life is full enough of trouble without that which is to be had by trying to live upon a pillar, but if their view were universal the world would be a duller place, shorn of a great deal of innocent entertainment provided by acrobats, parachute-jumpers, record-breakers of all kinds. Always they must strive for something which the ordinary person cannot do, and with them goes the professional ascetic,[2] whose very name implies the trained competitor in a contest, whom his contemporaries, in the hey-day of his profession, called the athlete of God.

Simeon was neither the first nor the greatest of the hermits, of that most curious race who, in what Crabbe calls a religious whimsy, forsook the world in the early Christian ages to live in deserts and in wildernesses in the most un-

---

[1] Theodosius II and the Empress Eudocia.
[2] Greek ἄσκησις, training or practice of an athletic kind.

likely and unwholesome abodes. He was, in fact, a climax rather than an originator, and his pillar was a symbol of the lengths to which a man may be compelled to go in order to cause a sensation in a crowded profession. Before his time the universe had already been ransacked for strange and surprising places in which to make a home. Tombs and holes in the ground, desert caves, cells without window or door, wind-swept islands in the seas, had become quite hackneyed. Feats of privation had been pushed to the very limit of human endurance, till a man would have to live without food or sleep at all to create a new record. Sometimes, when the solitudes became too crowded, and there was neither seclusion nor peace to be found, men of determination gathered themselves into a community and formed the first organized monasteries, where, with a wall to protect them from intruders and a rudimentary discipline to protect them from one another, they might at last find that peace which the wildernesses could no longer give.

By the close of the reign of Constantine seas and islands, deserts and marshes, in certain parts of Asia and Europe, were alive with hermits. There were thousands of hermits in Egypt alone, and by the end of the fourth century the district of Nitria in the Libyan desert, itself but a small part of the hermit-inhabited wastes, had its thousands of monks and hermits, the tales of whose wonderful lives and doings drew sight-seers from far and wide. From Britain, from the Atlantic seaboard, from Gaul and Italy they came to feast their eyes upon the holy men who ranked with the Holy Places themselves as goals of pilgrimage, and to revel in the thrilling spectacle of so many people indulging in a living death. Indeed, the constant intrusions of these admiring gazers and the obligation of providing for their refreshment in a desert place became a severe burden upon the resources of the holy men. In fact, the desert, like Arden, in respect that it was a desert, was a good life, but in respect that it was private was a very vile life, and the hermits must be forgiven an occasional lapse from their own standard of endurance in the indulgence now and then of a caustic remark or practical joke at the intruders' expense.

The sight-seers may have annoyed the hermits; to posterity they did the inestimable service of recording, occasionally, what they saw. They also recorded a certain amount that they did not see; if they heard or read a good anecdote, naturally they put that down too, but there is a certain consistency, in a general way, in their narratives which compels respect. There was Palladius, a monk of Asia, who spent about thirty years of his life, and ruined his health, investigating and trying to share the lives of the anchorites in Nitria and such places. He compiled at the request of Lausius, chief chamberlain to Theodosius II, what is known as the *Lausiac History*,[1] the result of his researches in the holy deserts, a good book, full of marvels of course, as becomes an author in the age of faith, but written in a style dry enough to be a guarantee, at least, of honesty. Palladius was an intelligent man, and he learned a great deal among the hermits, in particular that asceticism is for those who can stand it, and, in contradiction to the commonplaces of proverbial wisdom, that those who attempt the highest and fail may be in a worse case than those who have attempted nothing. Palladius is candid, too, about the failures, and he warns Lausius against the current exaggeration of the value of asceticism, against placing it above ordinary virtue. 'Neither eating nor fasting are anything in themselves; faith, by means of charity, shows itself in good works.'

---

[1] A great deal of ingenuity has been expended upon proving that Palladius was or, alternatively, was not the author of the *Lausiac History*. Dom Cuthbert Butler has concluded that the present version of this work is partly by Palladius, having been put together from Palladius' book and other (Coptic) sources.

[24]

There was a party of seven pilgrims, probably Greeks, whose visit to the Egyptian monks, about the years 390–400, is described in the *History of the Monks*, best known in the Latin translation by Rufinus of Aquileia.[1] There was John Cassian, a person of considerable ability and excellent common sense, who visited Egypt at the close of the fourth century to gather information about the organized communities or *cœnobia*, with the object of founding similar societies in Gaul.[2] There was Sulpicius Severus,[3] a Gallic presbyter, friend and biographer of Saint Martin of Tours, who in his *Dialogues* gives, in the person of *Postumianus*, an account of what seem to have been his own experiences among the hermits. And there are a number of lives of individuals, some, including those ascribed to Jerome and Athanasius, of fairly respectable origin, others too plainly remodelled and amplified in later centuries to suit an already established tradition. And there is Jerome's account of Nitria,[4] and his descriptions of his own life in the desert. These records, even the best authenticated of them, as the work of men of creative imagination inspired by religious zeal, should not be regarded as quite unvarnished tales; and it is idle now to attempt to distinguish in them between the fictitious and the true. Contemporary readers believed their stories, the Middle Ages regarded them as a principal part of Christian knowledge, as important—for they were quite as familiar—as the Bible itself,[5] and there are Christians living to-day who regard them as a pattern of true holiness, an example to be imitated by every Christian as nearly as he can. To the

---

[1] Once attributed to Jerome, also to Rufinus. Originally incorporated with the *Lausiac History* under various titles. See Dom Cuthbert Butler: Introduction to the *Lausiac History*, and Sir E. Wallis Budge, *Book of Paradise*: Introduction.

[2] See his *Institutes* and *Conferences*.

[3] About 363–420.

[4] Ep. XXII. *Life of Saint Hilarion*; *Life of Paul the Hermit*.

[5] See Caxton's *Golden Legend*.

[25]

hermits and their biographers, and to many others who believed everything they heard, the evidence for the marvels of the desert was quite as good, as Charles Kingsley has pointed out, as is that for the existence of China to most people, indeed it was rather better, and who shall maintain that any phenomena exist outside the human imagination?

Certainly there were extraordinary happenings in the deserts, and the saints who dwelt there performed astonishing feats. Their austerities and refinements of self-torture in their frightful dwellings were quite appalling. And they seem to have been endowed with powers which, if not always saintly, were of great assistance in their difficult lives. They could fly over rivers at need without wetting their robes; they were fed upon miraculous food laid by unseen hands at the doors of their cells. They could foretell events, cause water to flow at a touch of their holy hand, cure spells, and, better still, impose them. They communed with the beasts of the desert; and the wild gazelles, most timid of all creatures, would not flee at their approach. Nor did the hermits themselves fear the less timid, the predatory beasts, the lions and hyenas, and the aquatic monsters of the Nile, who not only did not harm them, but obeyed their bidding. For there were tame, obedient lions and crocodiles, and soft-hearted wolves with sensitive consciences, and even stranger things than converted, holy beasts. There were satyrs and centaurs galloping about the desert, shameless intruders from a quite different world, and little devils with hairy coats, and horns and hoofs, 'with colt-like whinny and with hoggish whine,' and larger and more dangerous devils with lovely, if occasionally dusky, bosoms and faces, and all the sirens' alluring wiles. The pilgrims bear witness to all these things, and even Palladius, with his matter-of-fact, blue-book outlook and style, faithfully records the whole phantasmagoria of beasts and marvels.

In the Egyptian deserts there seems indeed to be no escape

from the miraculous; it is scarcely even the miraculous in the accepted Christian sense. Merely the cumbrous chain of cause and effect is discarded, or in that clearer air things perhaps are visible which in other climates are obscured. Egypt had been too long an abode of mystery and magic to be a safe refuge for the strained ascetic, for the spiritually overwrought. She could hardly be expected to harbour a dense population of holy men without casting her magician's mantle over them. And as for the beasts, perhaps their long career of sanctity in that country had made them unfitted for the humble rôle of commonplace dumb animals. They are at least the equals of the holy men and share their lives and minister to and assist them in their holy careers, or, turning against them, give the devil and his minions shape and shelter in which to lie in wait for the saint inclined to trip, ready to weaken in his high resolve.

It is indeed a fairy world, almost a mediæval world, inspired not by reason but by holy desire. It is the direct and more vital successor of the Hellenistic fables and romances, the bridge between antiquity on the one hand, and Christian folk-lore and romance on the other. From it mediæval Christianity descended, its fairy part at any rate, with its dreams and voices, its temptations in alluring human form, and its horned shaggy devils with their mocking laughter and their unmistakable, characteristic, bad smell.

Perhaps the world cannot get on without some fairyland to look to, and now that the bright summit of Olympus was wrapped in clouds and its genial population lost to view, some refuge had to be found for human fancy, where it could forget human limitations and rise above dull actuality. So the wildernesses of the Nile were inhabited not only by hermits but by a *mélange* of beings derived from ancient mythology through the melting pot of Alexandrian literature, and from the ancient sanctities and magic of the old Egyptian world. Saint Antony himself, greatest of all the desert-dwellers, was cruelly tormented and delayed upon an errand of mercy by the attentions of a centaur, some fauns and satyrs, whom he knew by their heathen appearance to be informed by no good motives. Egyptian magic, potent and flourishing still, crops up over and over again; often the hermits have to contend with it, and if they are holy enough they can wield its powers themselves, they can cast spells and lift them. A case of the well-known binding-spell, which is found in the magic of many lands, is recorded by Palladius. A monk, who had been slandered by an erring lady as the father of the child she was about to bear, remained rigidly upon his knees at prayer, refusing to stand up or move, while the unfortunate lady, bitterly regretting her slander, to which she confessed, lay in protracted agony. Her friends besought the monk to forgive her, they banged upon his door, but he continued to kneel pitilessly, while the lady continued to suffer. At length the bishop, perfectly aware of what the monk was doing, bade him 'loose what he had bound'. The monk, compelled to obey his spiritual superior, rose at last from his knees and stood, and instantly the lady was eased and her child was born. A similar spell was cast by a famous hermit, John of Lycopolis, upon some robbers who approached his cell. They remained rooted to the spot, unable to move, and were about to be lynched by the holy man's disciples when he intervened and, with Christian forgiveness, released them.

Their relations with the beasts, perhaps, show the hermits in their most amiable light. An aged hermit of Tabenna in the Thebaid, a very holy man who never spoke to human kind for thirty years, communed instead with gazelles and ibexes, whose footprints were constantly seen around the mouth of his cave; another lived with a herd of buffaloes. The great Macarius, called the Egyptian, would employ a crocodile to carry him when he wished to cross the Nile to visit the holy men on the other bank, and the obliging creature would wait while the good man completed his business and carry him back again.

Lions, of course, always decorative and often tractable, were favourite associates of holy men, and their companionship came to be regarded, as lovers of painting know, as the proper sign of a well-conducted desert life. Saint Jerome's lion seems almost as inseparable from him as his writing-desk and his splendid large hat. A couple of lions appeared in the nick of time to help Saint Antony in the difficult task of digging a grave for the celebrated hermit Paul, in a remote part of the desert where he was unprovided with a spade; and two runaway slaves, who were in fact a holy monk named Mark and an equally holy virgin, who had been captured by Arabs and sold into slavery, were saved from death by a lion, who ate up their angry master when he pursued them with intent to kill.[1] He had been a kind master, and wishing to benefit them he had very inconveniently decided to join them together in holy wedlock, a state intolerable to both, especially as the virgin already had a husband elsewhere, to whom she had been married before she became enslaved. To avoid trouble and satisfy their master the two slaves maintained the appearance of a married couple, and eventually conspired together to escape, with disastrous results to their well-intentioned but ignorant employer.

A hermit and a lion shared in a friendly manner the dates which the hermit gathered daily from a palm. Every day the lion, unable to reach the fruit for himself, waited under the tree for the hermit's arrival, and having received his due portion, which he licked up shyly and gratefully, trotted quietly away into the desert. There was an unhappy lioness whose cubs had reached nearly their full size without open-

[1] Sir Ernest Wallis Budge, in his introduction to the *Book of Paradise*, notices scraps of local knowledge and colour in this story which prove that the narrator had a first-hand knowledge of the desert at any rate.

ing their eyes. Weeping copiously she sought the aid of a holy man from Nitria, who obligingly opened their eyes, and received in payment from the grateful creature a fine animal-skin for a cloak. Another beast, a she-wolf, showed remarkable evidences of a moral sense under the influence of the society of a saint. She used to come to his cell daily as a welcome guest, to share his simple meal. One day the monk failed to make his appearance at the usual hour, and the wolf, a creature of punctual habits, helped herself to some bread which was hanging in a basket by the door. Thereafter she was so afflicted by the pangs of a guilty conscience that she could not bring herself to visit the monk for a number of days. He missed his companion and prayed for her return. On the eighth day she re-appeared, but with downcast eyes and such an appearance of shame and repentance that any one could see how sorry and ashamed she was. She was forgiven, and assured that all was forgotten, by the present of two loaves for that day, twice the usual ration, and the happy companionship was thenceforth resumed.

II

Certain localities where physical conditions were peculiarly austere attracted large ascetic populations. Nitria, known to-day as the *Wadi Natrun* or soda valley, the valley of the Natrun Lakes, a shallow depression about twenty-two miles long in the desert north-west of Cairo and not far from the Rosetta arm of the Nile, became a celebrated centre of asceticism and harboured an enormous population of monks. It has always been a source of soda, and on the shores of one of its shallow reedy lakes, in ancient times, was an Egyptian glass factory. As a home for hermits it may have been inaugurated by Saint Frontinus and a group of refugees from persecution in the second century, but its proper career as an ascetic centre was initiated by Saint Ammon, who retired thither with a handful of hermits about the time of the Council of Nicæa.[1] Here the sins of the world, in the words of Saint Jerome, were daily washed away in the clean washing-soda of the monks' orisons. Here the gentle slopes of the sides of the *Wadi*, dry sand with loose stones and out-croppings of rock, became covered with hundreds, and then thousands, of cells, roughly built of stones by each hermit for himself, and thatched with rushes from the margin of the soda lakes. A little town, which still carried on its ancient glass-blowing industry, provided a market where the monks could sell the mats and baskets they made to purchase their few necessaries. Here some of the most

---

[1] A.D. 325.

famous and picturesque of the hermits had their abode, and
were products of what eventually became a highly competi-
tive atmosphere. There were the great saints called Macarius,
thought by some to have been three in number, by others
only two, so confused have their personalities now become:
in the Middle Ages they had the status, almost, of magicians.
There was old Father Ammon, the reputed founder of the
place, and his lesser namesake, who ate no cooked food and
cut off his own ear to save himself from a bishopric,[1] for
physical deformity, apparently, was not to be tolerated in
a bishop, and could save a man from the episcopacy. There
was black Moses, a reformed Sudanese sheep-stealer, who,
having been a robber himself, knew how to handle such
persons when they attempted to molest the hermits. And
there was Arsenius, who slept but one hour in the twenty-
four, and made a bad smell for himself to mortify his
squeamish nose, by keeping indefinitely the water in which
he soaked palm-fibres for his basket-making, till his neighbours, who had not themselves chosen that particular road
to salvation, entreated him to throw it away. And there was
the acute and somewhat rough-tongued Pambo, who accurately took the measure of the great Melania[2] when she came
to visit him, intending, in a grand renunciatory manner, to
make him a present of her family plate. She was determined
that her sacrifice should not, literally, be made light of, and
so desired him to weigh the silver in order to impress him
with its value. Pambo, who had no scales in his cell, told her
that the weight of the silver was already known to God, and
sent it away to be sold on behalf of the poor.

Quickly the hermitages multiplied; in Palladius' time
there were about five thousand in Nitria and many more in
the surrounding wildernesses. When visitors approached
they gave forth their hermits in swarms like bees from a

---

[1] See p. 249.
[2] See pp. 101, 203.

hive. Some were in solitary cells, some shared a rude hut
or tabernacle in twos and threes, and some were in communities, for walls in time grew up round various groups of cells,
for safety against bandits and also for privacy. These walled-
in groups of cells came to be known as 'lauras', and with
walls came more than privacy, a certain amount of organization and discipline and the apportioning of tasks. But there
was at first no rule and no obedience, no regulation of the
individual monk's spiritual life. He must attend certain
offices in church, perform certain necessary tasks, draw water
or hew wood, or cultivate the pot-herbs needed for holy,
frugal meals; but his religious exercises, his food or sleep
or abstinence therefrom, were his own affair, and each monk
made what pace he could, according to his capacity. In the
days of Palladius there were fifty lauras with considerable
equipment for organized existence. In one of them seven
bakeries, managed by monks, provided bread for the community, and there were even pastry-cooks. There were
brethren who had been doctors and surgeons in the world,
who plied their art among the ailing brethren: for though
wonders could no doubt be performed when a demonstration was desirable, not all the healing was done by miracles.
Churches eventually were built, and in the forecourt of one
were three palm-trunks of sinister purpose, with a whip tied
to each, a warning to casual bandits or unruly monks.

In time the pilgrims and visitors had to be provided with
special accommodation in a hostel apart, where they might
live during their stay without intruding upon the cells of
the resident monks. But they must not be a burden on their
hosts, so they might be given work to do in the gardens.
Or, if a visitor had intellectual attainments, a book might be
lent him to read, for there were books in Nitria; in fact by
degrees something like a library was gradually collected, for
not all the monks were entirely occupied with contests with
the devil or in seeing how little they could eat. Copying was

c

carried on by monks who were expert writers, a gift too precious to be sacrificed even to ascetic ends. Little is heard, in the records of these early monks, of their more intellectual activities, for those who indulged in them were naturally not the most celebrated ascetics, and our authorities, Palladius and the pilgrims, were interested in ascetic performances rather than in people carrying on more ordinary occupations, who could be seen anywhere else. And for all the fame of the ascetics, and the world of romance which they left behind them, it is to the obscure toilers with the pen that we are most indebted now; for in the surviving remnants of the great Nitrian communities, the tumble-down fragments of three or four monasteries inhabited by a handful of poverty-stricken, ignorant monks, were preserved what are now some of the oldest dated books in existence. The Syriac Gospels, the epistles of Ignatius, and other precious texts were discovered there in the nineteenth century by Robert Curzon[1] and by other astute travellers, in conditions in which it could hardly be believed that such precious and vulnerable objects could survive.

It has been suggested that the present aspect of these monasteries, many of which still stand about in the deserts, for all their decay and some subsequent rebuilding under Moslem influence, must preserve a measure of their ancient appearance. Even to-day there is a certain uniformity among them, so that 'to describe one is to describe all. In an unlimited waste of undulating sand-hills, lightly covered with gravel or rocks, a bare wall rises, some fifty feet high. Not a sign of life as you approach . . . your conviction is confirmed that no human beings can exist in so desolate a spot. You see a tiny iron-studded door; beside it a rope swinging

---

[1] *Monasteries of the Levant.* Curzon's story of how the MSS. were literally spirited away by the influence of sweet liqueurs upon an old, blind, but hard-headed Coptic abbot, is one of the best things in the book.

from a bell at the top of the wall. You toll the bell: five, ten, fifteen minutes pass, and high above you on the wall appears the head of a monk, who demands your business. On seeing visitors he quickly disappears, and you hear noises from inside, a hunt for the monk in charge of the postern, or for the wooden key which he has mislaid. Finally it opens and a number of monks welcome you effusively.' The door is seldom opened; the few ordinary transactions that usually require doors are carried on by means of a basket over the wall. Gates in fact are a quite modern and decadent innovation. Inside the wall is a kind of village of huts grouped round a central church, and but for a communal meal taken together on feast days the monks live quite independent lives. There is an abbot, but he is not always in residence. 'Vegetable garden, well, storehouse, bakery, some goats, beasts of burden, and chickens complete the picture, which must differ scarcely at all in essentials from the lauras that Palladius and the pilgrims saw.'[1]

Beyond the soda valley, though often included in it in a general way of speaking, in farther and more unredeemed deserts, was the district called Cellæ, or the Cells, a group of hermitages founded by those who found Nitria too worldly, too full of human traffickings. Here the cells were out of sight and earshot of one another. And across the soda lakes was Scetis or Scete, a further desolation, where Macarius the Egyptian first settled in a cell, and beyond Scete was Climax, the Ladder, the extremest region of desert solitude and discomfort, where there was no water at all nearer than eighteen miles. Few were the hermits who could endure its rigours or stay there for long; the pilgrims, even if they penetrated beyond Nitria to Scete or the Cells, hardly ever reached it.

In Upper Egypt, far from Nitria, was another hermit-

[1] E. H. Sawyer, *Antiquity*, vol. iv, no. 15. *The First Monasteries:* Permission to use the quotation kindly given by the Editor of *Antiquity*.

inhabited district commonly known as the Thebaid, some fifty miles north of Luxor, less accessible to pilgrims than Nitria, and not quite so populous, but equally famous. It was full of cells and hermitages, and here about the year 320 an ex-soldier called Pachomius founded at Tabenna a community of monks, with a strict discipline and a rule for the conduct of each day. It differed radically from the loose, free-and-easy asceticism of the lauras; it was in fact the first monastery proper in the Christian world, and the progenitor of the entire Christian monastic movement. What Pachomius set his hand to flourished. Already in his lifetime six other monasteries sprang up around the original foundation, and he had thirteen hundred monks under his rule. At the close of the century John Cassian saw seven thousand monks at Tabenna, or believed they were there. And Pachomius' sister gathered the scattered nuns of the surrounding district into something like a nunnery, at a discreet distance across the Nile but near enough to Pachomius to come within range of his disciplinary eye, which was needed, for we hear little of that nunnery but quarrels and hysteria and how Pachomius composed and punished them.

Soon there were few corners of the deserts of the Nile or the Red Sea unprovided with hermitages, lauras, or monasteries. Even the towns and villages of Egypt were crowded with monks. Oxyrrhynchus, when the pilgrims saw it, was a kind of holy city with anchorites in every nook and angle of the buildings or the walls, from which, it seems, both day and night, incessant hymns resounded. The local bishop boasted that he had ten thousand monks and twenty thousand nuns in his jurisdiction. The walls of the place positively bulged outwards, one witness tells us, so full it was with its holy men and women, and when he visited them he had such a warm reception that his clothes were nearly torn off his back.

If Syria became the home of some of the strangest

exhibitions of asceticism, Egypt was the accepted headquarters of the movement. From the community ruled by
Pachomius a monk who had been a sponge-diver carried the
movement into Mesopotamia. Travelling by means of the pilgrims and their tales, this strange manner of life spread over
the Near East, the Mediterranean countries, to Britain, Spain
and Gaul, till mountains, forests and vales, islets in rivers and
even in the western seas, were filled with hermits, in endless
succession, defying climate and privation and sometimes also
the disapproval and discouragement of civil or religious
authority. Anchorites and anchoresses, the poor holy men
and women who dwell in the forest and the wild, haunt
legend and literature in many ages. In the twelfth century
English bishops were driven to frame rules for anchoresses,
intended to discourage the too frequent adoption of this
mode of life, and to encourage respectable and correct conduct among those who were already in it. Anchoresses were
forbidden to keep anything but a cat, for there were some
who took to farming, or held land and took rents. But they
were not all worldly, and some who lived in the woods near
St. Albans were so determined to be unhindered in their
devotions that they complained to the bishop about the
disturbing noises made by the local, very numerous,
nightingales.

There have been great men in religion who from the very
outset have doubted the wisdom of the monks' way of life.
Palladius, Basil, Jerome, after considerable personal experience, disliked extreme asceticism, and asceticism pursued
for its own sake merely, and doubted whether the emaciated
half-crazed fanatic of the desert was indeed a credit to his
religion. Palladius warned Lausius not to be too greatly
moved by recitals of the hermits' feats of asceticism, and not
to emulate them: he is to train himself 'to be able to abstain,
and to be able to indulge, without excess'. 'Many have vowed
and have fallen through their morbid and extravagant at-

[37]

tempts at asceticism. Reason is the surest guide. It is better to drink wine with reason, than water with vain-glory and pride.' Basil, when he evolved his own system, rejected all forms of monastic life except that in a highly organized community under a closely defined and firmly enforced rule, without any ascetic extremes. He once complained of a Roman nobleman, unsuited to the religious life, who had done well enough in the world, but had been led away to become a monk, and had subsequently fallen. 'The world has lost a gentleman', he said, 'and not even gained a monk.' And an aged father called Moses, as recorded in John Cassian's book, arrived in his simple way at the gist of the matter. He decided that he was more in danger of the devil in the weak state to which he had reduced himself by mortification than if he had eaten and slept in a moderate degree.

From a public and civic point of view the monks were considered reprehensible. Isolated from ordinary life and out of reach of ecclesiastical and civil organization, they were a source of political trouble and a hot-bed for heresies. The Nitrian monks went a-whoring after Origen,[1] and after the Anthropomorphist heresy, the error of which was in picturing God in man's image, with nose and eyes and ears; and there were monks like those who have been a bad joke in all ages, just lazy, greedy, drunken and vicious. Roman civil administration hated them as outside Roman jurisdiction, a dead letter as regards civil and military duty and taxation. The monks had a solidarity of their own and formed a block of opinion which might suddenly affect the balance in a religious or political controversy. The Syrian hermits interfered to good effect to save the terror-stricken inhabitants of Antioch in the trouble about the statues.[2] Valens tried to bring the

[1] See pp. 201, 202.
[2] The Antiochenes in 387 smashed the statues of Theodosius and the empress, and hearing of the emperor's displeasure gave way to hysteria. See Chrysostom, *De Statuis*.

monks to heel by a decree, the success of which is uncertain, obliging them to undergo a period of military service.[1] Valentinian II, deciding that since they would not take their proper responsibility as citizens they should at any rate be prevented from interfering, forbade them in 390 to live in towns, where they had too many opportunities for meddling in matters which did not belong to them; they were to keep to 'desert places and the vast solitudes'.[2]

[1] Possibly never enforced.
[2] *Theodosian Code*, xvi, 3, 1. See also Ambrose, Ep. 41, § 27. The law seems to have been re-enacted two years later.

⋆ III ⋆

The hermits, Palladius tells us, would often argue among themselves as to who had been the originator of their way of life. In times of hardship and stress, long before the Edicts of Toleration of 311 and 313, there must have been settlements of voluntary exiles in remote places. There was Frontinus, who fled from persecution into the desert in the second century; there was Paul, who left Alexandria in the Decian persecutions[1] and became a most severe ascetic in the wilderness, to be buried eventually at the great age of one hundred and thirteen years, by a greater saint, Antony, with the assistance, as we have seen, of lions; and there was the imposing Ammon, reputed founder of the famous Nitrian settlement. But to Palladius, and to the mass of monks, their founder and leader was Antony, to all later ages the type and ideal of asceticism, the prince of all the dwellers in the holy wildernesses. 'Paul introduced the way of life, Antony made it famous.'[2]

The 'founder of asceticism' and 'model for monks', as his biographer Athanasius of Alexandria calls him,[3] is a person whom not even the fairy-tales which contemporary and mediæval Christianity wove around him can seriously belittle or disguise. Perhaps it is a safe rule that any personality that

[1] A.D. 250.
[2] Jerome.
[3] Probably this is the biography which was instrumental in Saint Augustine's conversion. Dean Farrar decided that Antony never really existed, and that Athanasius' biography of him was a novel.

can gather round it an aura of legend must be worth attention, and will repay the effort to find out something of what
it was really like. Myths and tales gathered round Antony
in plenty. He had the usual complement of miraculous gifts,
fantastic temptations, and ascetic feats. In all these he did
not, however, surpass the most celebrated ascetics of his
time, and he made no attempt to lead; rather he fled from
men, and he never sought an audience or a following. He
must have had the indefinable faculty of attraction which
belongs to some people, which nothing they can do in the
way of discouragement and rebuffs to others can counteract.
Wherever Antony went swarms of admirers followed him,
and the desert, whithersoever in it he might flee, was a desert
no more; his unwanted flock would still be after him. He
might shut himself up for twenty years, still a throng awaited
him the moment he emerged, and when he had gone for
a short time to Alexandria to succour the victims of persecution, the desert when he returned to it was fuller than
ever, and the flight began all over again. He was reduced to
disappearing in disguise with an Arab caravan; and when
he was at last rediscovered, he had to forbid his disciples
to come and feed him, for a messenger, even at long intervals, would bring in his train the usual swarm of sight-seers
and devotees. When he was over eighty he came at
Athanasius' request to Alexandria to preach against the
Arian heresy, but he was so mobbed in the streets by
enthusiastic crowds that he was forced to leave the city and
bury himself again.

He was born about the year 250, of wealthy Christian
parents, at the village of Coma, on the borders of Upper
Egypt. At eighteen years of age, six months after the death
of his parents, who seem to have died simultaneously like
those of the Babes in the Wood, he decided, like many of
his contemporaries, to take quite literally our Lord's advice
to the rich young man whom he loved, to sell all he had

and give to the poor. He included his sister's property in this renunciation and persuaded her, now penniless, to get her to a nunnery, or to what at that time was its equivalent, seclusion in some kind of cell or retreat under the care of a lady of discreet age. Anchorites were already numerous on the outskirts of villages and towns, and Antony at first tried to live in solitude near Coma, on bread and water, or on nothing at all, making baskets and mats for a livelihood.

In spite, as he thought, of his austerities, in fact because of them, temptations assailed him. They took all sorts of shapes, both frightening and alluring. Satan and his devils, disguised as hyenas and wolves, howled at him and menaced him; sometimes they took the guise of satyrs and centaurs, full of ribald pagan suggestiveness, and sometimes they were vaguer, far more obscene and terrifying imps and bogles. More agonizing still were the lovely faces and forms of women which haunted the solitudes and the night, and endeared the temptations of Saint Antony as a theme to the painters of the Renaissance. Farther and farther Antony fled into the wilderness. He tried a ruined tower in a terrible desert between the Nile and the Red Sea, but here the lovely shapes pressed closer round him, the wolves and hyenas howled more loudly, and the demons set upon him and beat him, and once nearly burnt him alive.

For nearly twenty years he endured the solitudes, and the temptations too, for like all the hermits he failed to guess that solitude is their dwelling place and the solitary their especial prey. Persistently he shut himself up, determined to brazen it all out alone. Sometimes he could be induced to preach to the throng of disciples waiting always at no great distance, but his horror of publicity was genuine, and the more they crowded round him, the more he desired to be alone.

But if ovations and admiration could not move him danger and suffering could, and during the persecution of Maximian he went immediately to Alexandria to work amongst the victims in the jails. Orders from the civil authority that he should leave the city could not be enforced; Antony just remained where he was as long as he pleased, and no one harmed him or took any step to turn him out. When the persecution was over he returned to his beloved desert, away from which he felt, as he said, a fish out of water, only to find his former solitude full of monks, pilgrims, and sight-seers. Again he fled, in disguise this time, with the friendly aid of an Arab caravan, into still remoter desert wastes that only the Arabs knew; and pagan though they were, they cherished and revered the saint, and kept his hiding-place a secret.

In the end his admirers were convinced that his apparent coyness was not a veiled invitation to pursuit, and his desire for peace was respected. As a safeguard for his solitude, to focus the attention of the inquisitive elsewhere, he per-mitted the establishment of a monastery about two hours' walk from his retreat, under the governance of an inti-mate friend and disciple, Macarius. Hither he would come for a talk with his friend, or with any one worthy who might be there. But, with the exception of his brief excursion to Alexandria in the Arian troubles, he never again stirred from the friendly wastes, in which he attained the magnificent age of one hundred and five years.

Such are the bare facts about Antony, through which we see a person of heroic stature, of charm also, as well as force. But he is incomplete without the fairy-tales; they tell us something about him, if only the feelings he inspired, we can believe them or not as we like. He could heal, he could foresee events, he conversed with angels, he had only to speak nicely to some gazelles and ibexes, which infested his corn, to stop their depredations, and he tamed some croco-diles which used to annoy and frighten people when they crossed a canal. He crossed rivers himself without wetting his clothes,[1] and he had a wonderful adventure with some lions. At an advanced age he walked a long way in the desert to visit the aged Paul, whom he found like to die, and demanding to be buried in a certain cloak which the great Athanasius had promised to give him. There were some preliminary *politesses* over Paul's provisions, a solitary loaf of bread, which the two holy men, to ensure precise bisection, pulled between them into two exact halves. Antony then set off to fetch the cloak, forgetting, in his haste, that other funeral requisite, a spade. When he reached Paul again, the old man was already dead, and the situation serious, for if Antony went off to fetch a spade the hyenas and jackals would have no respect for a deserted corpse. It was at this juncture that the lions appeared, a pair of them, rushing towards him with flying manes, but purring so loudly and wagging their tails so amiably that Antony saw at once that they were from God. Seeing Paul they roared alarmingly, but only, it seems, in grief, and then set to work to dig the grave, flinging up the earth with their paws. When a nice hole, just the right size, was ready in the sand, Antony dismissed his grave-diggers with a blessing, for there is no knowing how a hard job of digging may whet the appetite of even a holy lion, and they ran peaceably off. So he buried Paul, and went home to his own cell, giving thanks to God for the assistance of the kind and dexterous beasts.

Like many of the hermits Antony had a reputation for oracular wisdom. The Emperor Constantine and his sons wrote to him for advice, and there are signs that those who asked for his advice must follow it, for a sub-prefect of Alexandria who ignored a request to stop ill-treating Christians shortly afterwards fell from his horse and was killed. Conundrums, also, were sometimes put to him by

[1] As Egyptian fellahin commonly do, by carrying their clothes in a bundle on the head.

those who liked to collect *bons mots* and to see what smart
or sharp-edged answer he would give, for the manufacture
of repartee was a pastime in that rhetorical age, and to set
riddles, to place people in logical dilemmas and see how they
would extricate themselves, were still popular practices
among the sophisticated. Antony had never learned to read
(so his biographer Saint Athanasius tells us), but he was a
match for the sophistical nit-wits of Alexandria, of the
university or the clubs, who came to his retreat to see him,
and he forestalled their questions by asking them why they
had come. They replied: because they thought he was wise.
'Then if you think me wise,' said Antony, 'live as I do,
because it is foolish to perceive wisdom and not follow
it.' A variant of the favourite hen-and-egg question was
also put to him, whether the mind produced learning, or
learning the mind. 'Does not the naturally bright and
intelligent mind surpass that which is merely learned?' asked
Antony, who had no learning, giving the conversation an
awkward twist which the sophists could hardly be expected
to relish. We do not know their reply.

Visiting, that industry of the desert, was a scourge to
Antony. He valued good company when it was to be had,
but it was difficult to achieve without attracting the idlers
and busybodies who only wanted to have a gape at a great
man. When, at last, people of this kind were persuaded to
keep away from his cell, they used to hang about Macarius'
monastery, two hours' distance away, and take a chance of
catching a glimpse of Antony on one of his rare visits to
his friend. And so, when Antony approached the monastery he would call out to Macarius, whose head no doubt
popped up over the gate or the wall to see who was there,
and ask whether there were any visitors in the monastery
that day. If the answer was affirmative, he would call out
to Macarius 'Are they Egyptians or Jerusalemites?'—in accordance with an understanding between the two of them, that

by 'Egyptians' they meant simple innocent monks not worth a serious man's time, and by 'Jerusalemites' clever men whose company Antony would enjoy. If the answer was 'Egyptians' the poor simple monks were given a mess of lentils to eat and were bustled on their way without being allowed a sight of the great man. But if they were 'Jerusalemites' Antony would sup with them and they would sit up and enjoy profitable discourse through the night, for Antony was not a man to waste time in sleeping if there was good conversation to be had.

A friend and disciple of Antony's who made a great name and had many followers, especially in Syria, was Hilarion, whose biographer was no less than Jerome himself. Hilarion, as a lad, was sent by his parents to Alexandria for his education, and there he heard of Antony, and at fifteen years of age visited him in his remote desert abode, whence he returned resolved to lead a similar life. He betook himself to the Syrian desert, where the armies of Satan beset him in various forms, and he performed many miracles. Like Antony he was followed everywhere by crowds, and his example filled the deserts with monks and nuns. When Julian's anti-Christian activities made life difficult for the ascetics, and Hilarion's hermitage was raided and sacked, he fled to Egypt, and thence to Sicily, and wandered amongst the islands and coasts of the Mediterranean, performing miracles and scaring the heathen into belief. Eventually he came to Cyprus, where he abode in the ruined shrine of the Paphian goddess, preferring a place where the demons were especially numerous, and to be met at really close quarters. There at length he died, and though his body was taken to Palestine his name lingers in the Castle of Saint Hilarion built by the Lusignans, also called alternatively the Castle of the Goddess of Love.[1]

Contemporary and equal, almost, in importance to Antony

[1] Charles Kingsley, *The Hermits.*

among the desert Fathers, though not so highly esteemed outside the desert, or by posterity, was Ammon, the founder of the Nitrian settlement. Unlike Antony, who merely sought solitude for himself and had no thought to draw others after him, Ammon pointed the way to the desert and conceived of large concourses of monks, aloof from the world, grouped together for mutual support and encouragement.

His ascetic life began, rather unseasonably perhaps, upon his wedding night; either because he had failed to make up his mind before, or because of some histrionic instinct, so often displayed by the saints, which chose this occasion as likely to give his renunciation its fullest dramatic effect. The young lady seems to have been the choice of his uncle, who wished, in the place of his parents, who were dead, to see him suitably married. On reaching the nuptial chamber with his bride, Ammon read her Saint Paul's Epistle to the Corinthians, explaining it with such convincing force that she agreed to preserve her virginity and his, and to inhabit a cell for the remainder of her life. Palladius describes more vividly how the bridegroom jumped out of bed, and said to his wife: 'Madam, this marriage which we have contracted is nothing very special, we shall do well if henceforward we sleep apart, and recommend ourselves to God by preserving our virginity.' He then requested her to live in a separate dwelling. The lady at first refused to be dismissed from his home as well as from his bed, and the couple retained the appearance of holy matrimony, living together for eighteen years in chaste cohabitation, after which they parted, the lady to a nunnery, Ammon to the Nitrian valley, the fame of which was soon to be so great. Twice each year the parted couple paid one another a saintly visit, and Ammon, when he died, was seen by Saint Antony being transported by angels to heaven, in what is reputed to have been the one hundred and thirteenth year of his age.

[47]

Like many anchorites Ammon could see right through people, to their deepest motives and whatever guilt might be upon their consciences. A youth was brought to him, suffering from hydrophobia, to be healed. As the boy's relatives stood before him entreating for his aid, he looked them in the eyes and said: 'First make restitution of the value of the bull you stole from the poor widow and secretly slew, then I will heal the boy.' There was no alternative but to pay up, for holy assistance is to be had only at its own price.

Another great desert saint was Macarius the Egyptian, who dwelt in Scete, where the harshest asceticism only was practised. Hither Macarius had fled for refuge after an unnerving experience in the home of his youth. He had tried, in his native village, to follow the calling of an anchorite, but had been slandered by an erring village damsel as the father of her child. Macarius did not deny the accusation; with Christian patience he bided his time, and by dint of working very hard at his monkish handicrafts made enough money to support his supposed victim. When her time came, however, she was in great straits, and remained therein till she confessed her slander and told the truth, which immediately relieved her painful state. The village then came in a body to Macarius' cell to apologize to him for having believed the slander, but the cell was empty. Macarius had gone to Scete, glad to forego a petty triumph for the joys of a retreat beyond the reach of village maidens and village tongues.

He it was who disenchanted a lady whom a rejected lover had turned into a mare, thinking no doubt that her husband would turn her out of doors, or at least put her in his stable. The husband, however, who was a kind man, and in great distress because his wife would now eat no food of any kind, either human or equine, brought her to Macarius, who performed the magic necessary to restore her to human shape. Macarius took the opportunity of puzzling her husband and friends, perhaps to safeguard himself in case of failure, by saying, 'It is you who are horses, with the eyes of horses; this is a woman, unchanged except in the eyes of those who are deceived.' To this sophistical sally he added a warning that all the trouble was due to laxity about attendance at mass.

Macarius was a great abstainer from food and drink, of which he scarcely partook at all. 'Eat hay,' he used to say, 'wear hay, and sleep on hay, and thy heart shall be as iron.' He disapproved of wine, but occasionally took a little, in order that his spirit might be mortified and afflicted afterwards. At length his disciples, out of pity and affection for their master, took counsel together and decided to put away the wine, so that he might no longer afflict himself in this way. For bookishness he had some of Saint Antony's contempt, which he allowed to lead him to rather extravagant lengths. He ordered a monk who owned three books to burn them, as worldly possessions unworthy of a good monk. The books were of a perfectly edifying nature, greatly valued by their owner and frequently borrowed by the brethren, who derived much spiritual profit from their contents. But Macarius was inexorable and the monk had to obey. Like Saint Antony he too suffered from too many visitors, and as his reputation and the number of sight-seers grew he was obliged to make an underground passage for himself, half a stadium[1] long, leading from his cell to a little cave, and when visitors were sighted whom he did not wish to entertain, down he popped into his burrow till the intruders were gone. Twenty-four prayers he is said to have recited, both going and returning, in the underground passage, to beguile the way, and perhaps to ask forgiveness for his rudeness.

For sheer ascetic powers the great record-breaker was Macarius of Alexandria, originally, in his secular life, a seller of confectionery. His feats of abstinence from food and

[1] About one hundred yards.

drink and sleep were appalling, and there can be no doubt
that he indulged in them in a purely sporting spirit. He never
could hear of a great feat of abstinence without setting to
work to out-do it. When told that the monks of the Thebaid
ate no cooked food through the whole of Lent, his reply
was to dispense with cooked food for seven years; and having achieved that, and heard that a monk somewhere else
could live on nothing but a pound of bread a day, he needs
must crumble up his daily ration of biscuit and live on just
what he could pick up at one time in his fist. Only he added
the refinement of putting the crumbs in a narrow-necked
jar, into which he had to insert his hand to extract the
statutory handful; and when he tried to withdraw his fist
from the mouth of the jar, naturally he had to relax it, when
most of the crumbs escaped, leaving him a tiny daily ration
indeed. It sufficed him however for three years, with water
and a little oil.

He was the owner of several cells, each in a different
district, in Nitria itself, in Scete, and in Cellæ, each with its
peculiar and acute disadvantage, no light, or no door, or
insufficient room to lie down. From strength to strength
he went till at length he decided to commune with angels
and archangels and shut himself up for that purpose alone.
But this time he had gone too far. The devil, provoked at
last to reprisals, tried to burn down his cell, in fact
he succeeded to the extent of burning everything except
Macarius and the mat upon which he was kneeling. For all
his miraculous preservation Macarius was just a little scared,
and decided that his project of talking with angels and archangels was not altogether innocent of the sin of vainglory.

More than any one else, this Macarius must have elicited
Saint Jerome's remark that the monks seemed to make manifest their labours as if they were envious of one another.
When he was over eighty years of age, hearing of the great
ascetic feats performed at the monastery of Pachomius, he

crossed the desert on foot, disguised as a workman, from Nitria to Tabenna, a distance of over two hundred miles, in order to demonstrate to the monks, under their own eyes, his superior ascetic capacities. Through the whole of Lent he stood in a corner, in unbroken silence, without food except for a few herbs, without sleep, and without ever relaxing any of his limbs. Before Lent was over the brethren had had enough of this invidious display; they threatened revolt, and begged Pachomius to rid them of this 'bodiless' old man. Pachomius, who seems to have been rather slow in the uptake, at length recognized the visitor, and with all proper politeness he induced the formidable old gentleman to take his professionalism elsewhere.

Like all the best saints Macarius was on good terms with the beasts; he was kind even with the insect world, though it was not kind to him. Once, having slain a mosquito which bit him, he was so overcome with remorse that he retired, completely naked, to Scete, a place well known to this day for its voracious insects which can pierce even the skin of a pig, and gave himself up to the mosquitoes. They bit him so cruelly from head to foot that when he returned he could be recognized only by his voice.

Macarius had the usual homely common sense, the shrewd rough-edged tongue, that distinguished the best hermits. Truthfulness obliged him to acknowledge without reservation the excellence of some ladies in a neighbouring town whose reputation for unusual holiness he felt obliged to investigate. To his astonishment he found, not a pair of dour, ascetic virgins, but a couple of cheerful, prosperous married ladies living with their husbands in an ordinary domestic way, the two households, however, under one roof. The ladies told him that long ago they had thought of leaving their husbands and going away to become holy virgins, but that their husbands had refused them permission to depart. So they stayed at home and fulfilled their matrimonial obligations and other duties to the world. But they had taken a vow never to utter a wicked, unkind, worldly, or quarrelsome word, and never to fall out with each other, and thus they had continued in perfect amity and happiness for twelve years. This unusual spectacle of virtue and human kindness, combined with the practice of religion, drew from Macarius, despite his desert traditions and the implacable war waged by the hermits upon women, a remark which cannot have been uttered without cost by a Christian ascetic at any time: 'Marriage is nothing,' he said, 'virginity is nothing.' And he blessed the ladies and departed, finding absolutely nothing further to say.

Far up the Nile at Tabenna, Pachomius, the ex-soldier, gathered both monks and legends around him. Through the haze of mythology we can still discern the outlines of a mighty man, a brawny spirit endowed with a rough common sense. Perhaps his military training had bred in him a contempt for unorganized effort, however holy; he had a sound military faith in discipline, and a belief in striking, when action was called for, both swiftly and hard. He substituted discipline for extreme asceticism and permitted a reasonable use of food, believing that it was better to maintain the body in health than to wear it down with privation. Here the cowl first appears as part of the monastic dress; the hands were concealed under the frock and the cowl was worn at meal times in such a way that no man might see how much or how little his neighbour ate, so that there should be no vainglory in abstinence. He could handle rebellion, too, and deal unquestionable, if somewhat ruthless justice. He had also a truly military belief in the letter rather than the spirit of an instruction; if he gave an order it must be fulfilled exactly to the letter and no more, for to exceed was as grave an error as to fall short. Once in a time of dearth he dispatched a monk with a hundred denarii to purchase wheat for the monastery. Outside, in the world, the monk discovered that the dearth was universal, that all wheat was now under State control, and that none was to be had in the open market. He was obliged to apply to the governor of the province, who was under instructions to sell only at the government price and to hold up reserves for the greater dearth that would be felt by the following spring. The governor, however, was a Christian and saw an opportunity for his own spiritual advantage by selling the monk wheat to the value of two hundred denarii at less than the fixed price, one half to remain on credit on condition that the monks prayed for him. The eager brother accepted the bargain, loaded his wheat into a barge, and brought it in triumph to Tabenna, only to be sharply reprimanded by Pachomius, who would have none of the transaction, on the ground that the monk had gone beyond his instructions. He had bought twice the quantity of wheat that he had been instructed to buy, he had pledged the monks' credit for a sum which they would never be able to pay, and finally, added Pachomius, who perhaps knew something of Roman governors in remote places, if the barge had met with a mishap and sunk, and the wheat had been lost, the monks would all have been enslaved to the governor for debt. So the wheat was sold to the laity at the current price, the governor was paid cash in full, and the monks got the value of a hundred denarii and no more, while the monk who had been too sharp was never sent out to do business again.

Pachomius feared nobody, not even his cook. Once, returning to his monastery after a long absence (he had been beset by devils on the way), he was met by complaints from the younger monks that during his absence the food had not been up to the standard maintained when he was at home. There had been no vegetables cooked, no beans and no peas, in defiance of the rule that cooked vegetables were to be served on Saturdays and Sundays. So Pachomius went to the kitchen, and found the head cook not in his kitchen but sitting making mats as if he were a full-blown monk. The cook explained that the monks were so abstemious that food, when cooked, was not eaten; quantities had to be thrown away, so he had given up cooking and taken to mats, for one man in the kitchen was quite sufficient to chop raw vegetables and prepare all that the monks wanted for their meals. Pachomius took the five hundred mats the cook had made and burnt them all as a lesson that cooks should stick to their casseroles, that young men need some variety in their food, and that if the older monks desired to practise abstinence it was wrong to deprive them of their virtue by giving them nothing from which to abstain.

The neighbouring nunnery, conducted by Pachomius' sister and supported by his monks, also had to submit to his discipline, and was excommunicated for ten years for giving ear to a spiteful nun who had slandered a sister about an itinerant tailor who had accosted her to ask for work. As often happens in the pent-up atmosphere of a convent, feeling rose to fever-point; a wave of hysteria swept over the sisterhood. First the nun who had been slandered, and then her slanderer, committed suicide in the river. Pachomius had to be fetched to restore sanity, which he did by his usual resource of a fiercely drastic punishment.

Not quite so justifiable were Pachomius' rather severe dealings in the matter of a noble and productive fig-tree which grew in the monastery garden, the especial pride and joy of the gardener, a most exemplary man, who besides being an industrious and skilful horticulturist was a considerable ascetic. Very unfortunately Pachomius saw the devil of gluttony in the guise of a naughty boy sitting in the tree eating figs, and resorted to a crude method of depriving the devil of his fruit. Instead of chasing the boy away he ordered the gardener to cut down the tree. The excellent man, with a gardener's usual indifference to authority, and an equal indifference to devils where a good tree was concerned, committed the one act of disobedience of his whole life, and refused to cut down the tree. He was punished, for next morning the tree was withered, whether by Pachomius or by contact with the devil no one could say.

In contrast with Pachomius, orderly and exact, if occasionally drastic in his methods, is Schnoudi, the Coptic saint, a raging, weeping, furious and unsuccessful tyrant, founder of the White Monastery and its dependants near Palæopolis on the borders of the Libyan desert. Schnoudi's heritage was an unrestrained desert savagery, untempered by Roman sanity, by any saving touch of Hellenic tradition or culture. He was brought up near Tabenna, and took to religion at the age of nine. In his youth he lived for five years in a tomb, in which he left, when he emerged, all fleshly inclinations, and also all tolerance, mercy, and human kindness. He went to join an uncle, Bgoul, who ruled a handful of monks in the Libyan desert; and here, at his death, Schnoudi succeeded him. The monks multiplied under his fierce, but strangely attractive leadership, till there were two thousand in the White Monastery and its branches; and nunneries also sprang up around him. There was a most elaborate rule touching every detail of life, down to cleanliness in the kitchen. Obedience and submission Schnoudi would have at any price; there was a prison at the White Monastery, seldom without an occupant, and erring monks were flogged by Schnoudi's own hand. Once a culprit died under the lash, but that was reckoned only as additional proof of guilt, and Schnoudi's prestige was no whit affected by the mishap.

There was something of the atmosphere of a factory about the White Monastery with its enormous numbers, its mass-produced holiness, hard work and machine-like organization. It had a factory's peculiar troubles too; mass emotions and irresponsibility. If a monk were dismissed his fellows would strike, or go forth secretly at night to foregather with him in the desert or assist him. They malingered frequently,

and went to the infirmary as sham invalids for the sake of
the cosseting and the easy life that was to be had there; for
in the infirmary, it seems, the invalids were nourished upon
sherbet and cakes. Monks who were copyists by trade stole
the books they were copying, or their own copies, and sold
them; or those who did outside business for the monastery
cheated and peculated. There were even dandies who fancied
their attire and must always have a clean white frock.
Schnoudi was for ever exhorting them, raging, weeping and
storming at them, cursing them, and sometimes suddenly
petting and making much of them. Perhaps, if his temper
had been more even, his difficulties would have been less.

Schnoudi's nuns were no better than his monks: there were
eighteen hundred of them, requiring at least as much correction as their brethren. Once in a vision Schnoudi saw a number of virgins being chastised in hell, and an angel explained
to him that though they were virgins in body their tongues
were a two-edged sword. Schnoudi recounted the vision to
the nuns, without great effect, for they continued to sin in
every imaginable way, by refusing their tasks, by greediness,
the richer nuns failing to share with the poorer the sweets
and cakes sent by their relations in the world, and consuming
them in solitude in their cells. And sometimes, alas, they
were not even virgins in body. Schnoudi wept and stormed
at them, but more he could not do; his fingers must have
itched for his whip, but even Schnoudi could not flog a
nun.

At the nearest town, Panopolis, his neighbours were
Greeks, a charming, dilettante, cultured society, still worshipping the old Greek gods, collecting works of art, reading
poetry and seeing plays; their favourite was the *Birds*.
Perhaps they were the very circle in which Nonnus grew
up. They smiled upon their quaint neighbours of the White
Monastery, but Schnoudi did not smile on them. Among
his surviving works are fragments of a violent tirade against

them, in which he claims to have seen them, as he often did people whom he disliked, in a vision, in hell, and among them a certain wealthy Jew, a dilettante and collector, leader of the local artistic society. Words, however, did not upset the people of Panopolis, who, preferring Aristophanes perhaps, did not listen to Schnoudi or heed him, and Schnoudi was driven to deeds. With three companions he descended upon the Jew's house by night, snatched up all his *objets d'art*, and threw them into the Nile. In Schnoudi's story of the raid, it was carried out with the assistance of most miraculous happenings which often came to his aid upon his errands of holy justice. Once in a hand-to-hand fight with a pagan in the street, Schnoudi's opponent was suddenly and unexpectedly thrown into the river by an angel, or perhaps by a human partisan of Schnoudi. When the Emperor Arcadius ordered the destruction of the pagan temples and Bishop Theophilus burnt the Serapeum at Alexandria, Schnoudi saw his opportunity and descended upon the neighbouring pagan villages, setting them on fire and massacring the inhabitants without mercy.

He lived to be a hundred and eighteen, but his end was sad. To live to that age with any satisfaction must require gifts which were denied to Schnoudi. Discipline grew harder and harder to preserve, and no one loved him. He was reduced to calling down curses, to take effect posthumously, on the rebellious, and to threatening his own premature demise. At his age such a threat cannot have frightened anybody very much.

The female ascetics, counterparts of the desert fathers, are disappointing, at least in the accounts of them which earned a place in Rosweyde's *Lives*. They seem to have struck the wrong note in the minds of their biographers; they are pretty, waxen puppets, remote from reality, intended to entice the erring and the fair to the path of virtue and renunciation. In most cases their biographers lived a century or more after their deaths, and whatever of truth may have survived about them seems to have wilted and faded in the attenuated atmosphere of the novelette. Romance and sentiment predominate, and since our sources are the Fathers, who are never to be trusted when the fair sex is their theme, a principal preoccupation is the possibilities, in romance and *galanterie,* that have been missed in the lives of their fair and vulnerable heroines, or missed by the narrowest of squeaks, or indeed not missed at all.

There was Pelagia, the lovely Antioch actress of the mid-fifth century, who was called Margarita, because she was so covered in gold and pearls that her skin could not be seen. She was suddenly converted and enclosed for the remainder of her life in a cell without a door. Mary, called the Courtesan, was a lovely orphan whom an ascetic uncle, Abraham by name, enclosed in a doorless cell at an early age. Her window, however, betrayed her. Through it she was spied by an amorous monk, and through it she jumped to be united with him. Subsequently she was found by her uncle in a brothel, and reclaimed; and the scene of tearful reconciliation, contrition and forgiveness enacted between the two, seated upon the harlot's bed, is one of an attenuated pornography sicklied o'er, but not at all concealed, by a thoroughly mawkish sentimentality.

The story of Euphrasia seems to have no object but to demonstrate the spiritual and material advantages to be obtained by making handsome presents to ecclesiastics and their establishments; and that of Euphrosyne is a very commonplace member of that large family of romances which have for their theme the masquerading of a fair young female in masculine dress. Euphrosyne, the better to avoid matrimony and dedicate herself to God, donned a man's habit and entered a monastery. Her sex was not discovered, but the results were more distracting to the monks than if it had been; and the abbot found no cure for the devastation dealt by her good looks but to enclose her in a solitary cell, which she inhabited for thirty years. In all these stories is nothing but conventional, sentimental novelette-writing. We miss the homely human touches, the simple, rather acrid humour of the desert fathers, in which a kernel of rough and solid truth seems to have defeated the disfiguring touch of even the professional hagiographer.

⋆ IV ⋆

The ascetics and anchorites, like all well-disposed celebrities, had to meet to some extent the demands of their public and play the part expected of them. As Christian philosophers they had to fulfil the philosophic tradition, not only in their disregard of the world and its standards, but also in the production of those sayings and sharp answers which had been an accepted part of the philosopher's trade since Socrates, and indeed before him. The Greeks, with their love of words and natural gift of repartee, had always admired *bons mots* and treasured up the smart sayings of their great men and, as in that age of rhetoric the love of words grew to madness almost, epigrammatic sayings were the rage. In the desert, among the holy men the production of wisecracks was quite an industry, and the greater a saint's reputation the more he was expected, Diogenes-like, to turn out something sharp, even at the cost of scoring off a visitor. The visitors, for their part, like Socrates' victims and the amiable dupes that figure in modern advertisements, were often very kind, and purposely asked the sort of questions that would give the great man his chance. Saint Antony, as has been seen, did his best to meet public expectation in this kind; and indeed almost all the hermits had a sharp and ready tongue. Many of the sayings that have been preserved,[1] it must be confessed, have lost in intervening ages something of what may have been their

---

[1] *Verba Seniorum.* Rosweyde, Migne, vol. 75.

original lustre, or perhaps those who heard and wrote them down missed the point, or perhaps they never had one, for the devotion of enthusiasts will sometimes induce them to believe that anything a great man says is clever and worth preserving. And sometimes the remarks recorded seem needlessly severe, and even brutal; as when Macarius (which of the great men of that name is uncertain) denied a thirsty visitor a draught of water, bidding him go and sit in the shade, because, he said, many sailors and travellers at that moment were deprived of even that. Another monk, on the arrival of a visitor, kindled a fire and took lentils and put them in a pot of water to boil. When the pot boiled he took it from the fire and would not finish the cooking or have the lentils eaten; 'It is sufficient refreshment', he said, 'for holy men just to look at the fire.' He was more astute, if less polite, than the hermit who gently told some visitors whom he had entertained to supper that they were the sixth party for whom he had prepared and set out a meal that day; he confessed to having eaten the six meals himself too, out of politeness of course, for he was such a finished ascetic that he could both dispense with food altogether and take six meals a day, as occasion required.

It was a frequent custom of the younger monks, by way no doubt of flattering their elders, to ask them for a 'sentence', an improving observation upon which to meditate in solitude, and the elders, as usual, loved to puzzle and humiliate the young. One came to a certain Father Agathon and asked him for a 'sentence', but Agathon sent him off saying: 'Go back to thy cell, and sit in it, and thy cell shall teach thee everything.' Agathon himself had learned to hold his peace by carrying a pebble in his mouth for three years. Silence was as rare as solitude in the desert, and the wit of the elders was greatly exercised to achieve it. Macarius of Alexandria, in desperation one day, on coming out of church with his disciples and feeling that the flood of chatter was about to break forth again, said to them, 'Brethren, flee.' The thick-headed brethren asked, 'Father, whither shall we flee farther than this desert?' In reply Macarius put his hand over his mouth and said, 'Flee ye on this wise', and going into his cell he slammed the door. 'I have often repented of having spoken', he used sometimes to say, 'but never of holding my peace.'

A well-meaning old hermit, discussing the ways to virtue with his neighbour, Father Alonis, asked him how a man might hold his tongue so as never to speak falsehood. Father Alonis answered, 'If thou dost not lie, thou wilt commit many sins', and continued by instancing a simple hypothetical case in which a man, wanted for some crime, might take refuge with him, when strict truth would oblige him to give the man up, whereas Christian charity should shield the man and lie to the police.

A conceited, learned young man, visiting a community of working brethren on Mount Sinai, indulged in the intellectual snobbery of Mary Bennett and scoffed at the homely occupations of the monks, saying that he infinitely preferred a book. The abbot bade him go to his cell to read a book till nightfall, and at evening sent him no summons to supper. The young man waited hungry and embarrassed in his cell, and at length emerged to find supper over and to be told that he had no need to eat since he cared only for spiritual things.

And there is some solid sense in the advice of an elder to a young man who wished to cure himself of negligence. 'Root out a small plant, which is negligence,' he said, 'and a whole forest of faults will come into being.'

Some devils who tried, with some nonsensical business with a feather, to make a hermit break a vow never to laugh, got badly scored-off for their pains. The sagacious old gentleman burst out laughing, of course; but when the devils claimed the victory he retorted, most sophistically, that he was laughing not at their wit but at the futility of their attempt to make him laugh.

The character of monasteries, even in the early days, seems established in the remark of an elder to a young anchorite who boasted that he lived on such easy, friendly terms with the beasts. 'Yes,' replied the elder, 'but just you try living in a monastery'; and the best and briefest of all the wisecracks is the smart rebuke of an elder to all cantankerous monastics, 'It is better to bite food than one another.'

✶ V ✶

In face of all the undoubted social amenities of the desert, the comings and goings, the visits, the gossip, the hive-like animation of the larger centres of asceticism, it is easy to underestimate the rigour of the lives led even by the rank-and-file of the hermits. In the climate of the Nile valley and its adjoining wildernesses, kinder perhaps than most to privation and austerity, it may be easier than elsewhere to subsist with a minimum of shelter and next to no food. But the feats of asceticism achieved by persons of far less reputation than Antony, Ammon, or the Macarii, are horrifying. Food, drink, sleep, the pleasures of female society, in fact all the manifestations of a man's physical being, and indeed of his spiritual being too, in so far as they were instruments to enjoyment, were snares of the devil, seeking to lure him to commit the sins of the flesh.

The sin of the flesh, in the singular, is perhaps a more accurate term, for to the Christian mind of the early centuries there was but one sin that mattered, concupiscence, and all the other forms of physical indulgence, food, drink, and sleep, were not so much wrong in themselves as conducive to it, tending to weaken a man's resistance to the one great deadly sin. Fantastic were the measures to which the monks had recourse, to torture and slay their carnal selves. Retreat from the world, they argued, was the first requirement: for to escape from all worldly sights and suggestions must leave the mind free to pursue undisturbed

[64]

its contemplation of God. The idea sounds plausible enough, but makes a false assumption of the human mind as a blank sheet of paper to be written upon only by direct sensation or suggestion from without. Isolation is no guarantee that it will remain a blank; and when the hermits in their solitude found that their minds pursued the strangest trains of thought, and threw up the most extraordinary, and often the most deplorable, imaginings, they concluded that their isolation must be inadequate, and sought to increase the barriers against the outer world. A few of the more intelligent took refuge in the more sociable life of the lauras.

There were the extreme solitaries who voluntarily confined themselves in a walled-up tomb or cell with only a little window through which food was passed in by a kind servitor, and the occupant's handiwork passed out to be sold to gain his living, such as it was.[1] Only occasionally do we hear that saints, male or female, jumped through the window to a spiritual fall. More often the living tomb was endured for thirty, forty or fifty years, and the wonder is that the falls were so few; for in their enthusiasm people who thought they had a call would plunge immediately into the extremes of renunciation without preliminary training or probation such as the elaborate *Yoga* of the Hindus. They tried to run, to fly, without having learned to walk, and somehow, quite commonly, they succeeded. If there was not an actual fall, the outraged flesh took revenge, of course, in the temptations, the uncontrolled imaginings from which all the hermits excruciatingly suffered.[2]

John Cassian, to whom we owe so much of our knowledge of the desert monks, devoted a large part of his inquiry

[1] In the Middle Ages there was a regular office for the walling-in of anchorites; and valedictory ceremonies proper to the lugubrious occasion were performed.

[2] Saint Jerome describes the temptations he endured during his desert sojourn. When his face was pale with fasting and his body black with dirt his imaginings were purple in the extreme.

to the question of dealing with these troubles, for he had
before him the practical objective of establishing religious
communities in Gaul, and it was important for him to know
how to cope with all the contingencies of monastic life. His
list of principal sins has eight chief headings, reduced in
later times to the Seven Deadly Sins, familiar in mediæval
literature. There were *Covetousness, Anger, Dejection, Accidie,
Vainglory, Pride, Gluttony* and *Fornication*, on all of which
he closely examined the more elderly and experienced fathers
of the desert, and his *Conferences* embody the discourses in
which each old gentleman is supposed to have delivered his
sum of knowledge on these subjects. The conversations are
seldom short, for the desert-dwellers had much to say,
especially upon the two last-mentioned of the sins, which
in importance, and certainly in interest, overshadow all the
rest.

Covetousness, as a matter of fact, had not much scope, for
all worldly wealth was left behind on entering the holy life.
Indeed, the only precept of our Lord's teaching which the
monks seem to have understood very thoroughly was that
which bade the rich young man sell all he had and give to
the poor. The Christians of the early centuries certainly
followed this injunction with great thoroughness; and as
Christianity spread among the wealthier classes the poor of
the congregations were in danger of becoming seriously
demoralized by the large sums distributed among them when
the owner of a full-sized Roman fortune suddenly decided
to adopt the holy life.[1] But even the most ascetic monks
needed some modest supplies and must earn them by industry of a kind, and the ordinary mat- or basket-making monks

---

[1] Pinianus, a wealthy patrician who arrived at Hippo about 410 as
a refugee from Rome, and gave away his fortune in alms, so delighted
the Christian congregation that they clamoured, rioted almost, to have
him for their presbyter. When however Pinianus' fortune was exhausted they lost all interest in him and he escaped to Palestine.

who sold their work were regularly in contact with money. Occasionally some would be found with a nice little hoard of money tucked away in their cells, or they would separate themselves from a too rigid laura to live alone, or worse still with a woman, a spiritual comrade, to keep them company, to help with the housekeeping and with the task of preserving the money which had been unjustifiably amassed or retained. It is strange, but perhaps consoling, to find that even in the misogynist desert a woman could be regarded as conducive to successful domestic economy and thrift.

Dejection[1] and its more physical relative *Accidie*[2] were common enough, the natural reaction of the more vigorous temperaments under the strain of fasting and physical privation, and the colossal inertia of confined life in a laura or a cell. Accidie, boredom we might call it, or ennui, was especially disturbing about the sixth hour, at the close of what was in reality a very long morning, for the monks had a brief and broken night's rest, and at most had but one scanty meal a day, partaken towards evening. By midday their mental and physical exhaustion must have been extreme, and so acute the ensuing onslaughts of accidie that it was regarded by some of the elders as in fact the 'midday demon' of the ninety-first Psalm.[3] Its simpler forms were idleness and mere ordinary laziness, or an aching desire for activity and change. The sufferer cannot stay in his cell, he longs for everything at a distance, other monasteries and communities, and must be off to visit them. Or he would like to see his relatives, or it would be a real work of godliness to visit and assist some good woman devoted to the service of God, who has been abandoned and

---

[1] *Tristitia.*   [2] From late Latin *accidia*, Greek: ἀκήδεια.
[3] Septuagint: δαιμονίου μεσημβρινοῦ; Vulgate: *dæmonio meridiano*. The English Bible (both versions) renders this both inaccurately and dully as the 'destruction that wasteth at noonday'.

cast out by her own kinsfolk. John Cassian, at the outset of his stay in the desert, had an attack of accidie, and in fear of it ran to a worthy father, called Paul, for spiritual aid, only to be reprimanded for taking to flight; for to run from accidie is to gratify the demon, who, seeing the victim flee, is the more encouraged. 'Budge,' says the fiend most literally; 'budge not,' says the earnest athlete of God, and the fiend is dismayed. But more often the fiend seemed to give the more friendly counsel, and the monk took to flight.

Of *Pride* and its more active counterpart *Vainglory*[1] much is heard, for they were the very faults that lay in wait for the successful ascetic who might gain a public reputation. For an ascetic it is just as easy to be puffed up about his feats of mortification as for a worldling to be vain of his magnificence and his wealth.

Chastity, for its admitted difficulty, was especially prone to vainglory, which could prove its undoing. A professed virgin, who had lived in a cell for six years practised her chastity solely in a spirit of vainglory and pride and, her attention being taken up with self-approbation and contempt of others who were in a less holy state, left a loop-hole for the devil to creep in. She opened her window to the kind young man who had regularly performed for her the necessary task of selling her handiwork and bringing her food, and the very instrument of her chastity and her seclusion brought about her fall.

Often, when the monks heard of the proficiency in holiness of some brother or sister, they would set a trap to catch them and convict them of pride. A desert monk called Serapion saw in Rome a holy virgin, to whom he successfully demonstrated that she was guilty of pride. She had lived in a cell for twenty-five years, saying that she was dead. He succeeded in persuading her to quit her cell and go to church with him, on the ground that, as she was dead, there

[1] *Superbia* and *Kenodoxia*.

could be no difference between remaining in her cell and leaving it to go to church. Returning from church, he dared her to undress and walk naked through the streets of Rome, for a dead person must be perfectly indifferent to public opinion. The virgin refused to scandalize the public, whereupon Serapion convicted her of pride; for if she still cared about the opinion of the living her claim to be dead must be merely a vainglorious pretence. Such a claim, not infrequently made by the hermits, could be useful on occasion, as when a certain holy man who professed to be dead refused to help his brother to lift an ox that had fallen into some mire, on the ground that dead men do not haul oxen out of the mud.

Even small boys could fall into vainglory. Two of them, returning one day from a regular errand to take food to a remote hermitage, encountered an exceptionally large and alarming asp which behaved in the most friendly fashion, lying down before them as if charmed and displaying its dark green neck in the most delightful way. They picked it up and carried it triumphantly to the brethren, their employers, who praised their faith and valour. The abbot, however, 'with deeper insight', had both boys thoroughly beaten, to cure them of fancying they had ascendancy over the beasts.

The rest of the story is worth repeating. When the recluse who had caused all the trouble heard of the beating he was grieved, and sent word that no more food should be brought to him. After some days the abbot, fearing he might die of starvation, went forth to visit him and was surprised to see a basket of bread, newly baked and fragrant, hanging by his door. Both the hermit and the bishop agreed that it was a miracle, the hermit ascribing the miracle to the abbot's virtue, the abbot, as politely, to the hermit's saintliness. The bread, however, was eventually eaten, and found to have a flavour as delicious as its smell. When the news of the hot

[69]

sweet bread reached the monastery the brethren vied with each other in their haste to betake themselves to the solitudes, declaring themselves wretched and mistaken to have remained so long in the luxury and ease of a laura.

Now and again the sin of vainglory had fatal consequences, as when an old gentleman jumped down a well at the instance of Satan disguised as an angel, believing that his faith would save him from hurt. His faith, unfortunately, did not suffice. Another was advised by the same agency to kill his own son, following the example of Abraham, in the hope that his faith would be similarly rewarded. The intended victim, however, less optimistic as to the result, ran away in time and spoiled the experiment.

Gluttony of course was a deadly sin, a lasting temptation to the under-fed ascetic, and the greatest foe, the holy men thought, of chastity. So they fasted more and more, striving to use as little sustenance as possible, and finally to dispense with food altogether. Even bread was not quite above suspicion; as one of the famous elders pointed out, it was not wine but bread that caused the sin of Sodom. 'How did thy sister Sodom sin, except that she ate her bread in fullness and abundance?' So if a hermit must have bread, a pound a day was ample nourishment, and if he could get along on a solitary biscuit a day so much the better, like Dorotheus, who toiled in the hot sun building cells all day, on six ounces of bread. Some had only raw vegetables or herbs, bruised and soaked in water, or with a little oil. Some, like Antony, managed to live on what grain or vegetables they could grow themselves. The first hermits had lived on wild roots and desert herbs, frequently poisoning themselves, till one poor creature, who had been poisoned and was about to die of starvation rather than risk eating any more doubtful vegetation, was saved by a charming gazelle, which, with the superior intelligence of the dumb beasts, was able to tell him what herbs were safe to eat and what were deadly. For a luxury, or to entertain a visitor, there might be a few dates or figs. John Cassian was once entertained to a great feast at which each monk was allowed three dates and one fig. It was indicated to him that on no account must he help himself to more.[1]

There was a saint who subsisted on six dried figs a day, but unfortunately he became so puffed up with his proficiency that he was possessed of all the devils he was in the habit of casting out. There was Onophrius, who tortured his body for seventy years and was covered with hair, whom the angels fed, very scantily, on a little bread.[2] There was a holy man called Elpidius who became so emaciated that the sun shone through his bones, and another who fasted till worms crawled out of his teeth. There was an aged solitary in Scete who had lived alone in chastity in a cave for eight and thirty years on a diet of grass, while another, who had not so lived,[3] joined himself to a herd of buffaloes to expiate his beastly behaviour, and shared their pasture and their life till he was covered with hair and practically a buffalo himself.[4] Even rage, John Cassian thought, might be an assistance in fasting: it is much easier for a monk who is in a rage with another brother to fast for many days, whereas in an ordinary peaceable good temper he might find it impossible to get through even a single day without food.

Water-supply the hermits loved to make even more inconvenient than it naturally is in the desert. Washing was of course discarded altogether, as Roman, worldly, lascivious, and dangerous, and only very small quantities of water were drunk. It was rationed as if it were a dangerous

---

[1] The story is from Sulpicius Severus, in his *Dialogue*. Postumianus, who tells the tale, lowers his voice to spare a greedy friend, a Gaul, who was supposed to be among the listeners, the pain of hearing it.
[2] They carried him off, however, when he was dead.
[3] He had lapsed for six months with a lady.
[4] There was, later, in Mesopotamia a whole herd of grazing monks who wore no clothes and lived like the beasts of the field.

intoxicant, less out of abstemiousness than because water itself as a beverage was somewhat under suspicion as conducive to rank and lustful humours that may betray even the most tried and trained ascetic when he is asleep. So the monks loved to carry their drinking water for many miles. The Nile, or one of its branches at the Delta, was a usual source of supply; to many a dweller in the deserts it might be many miles away. Sometimes there would be nothing but a shallow brackish well, undrinkable for any but a confirmed ascetic. In Climax the precious fluid was eighteen miles away. Moses the Black, the reformed sheep-stealer, as a young monk used to mortify himself secretly by rising in the night to fetch the water for the brethren while they slept. All night he toiled over the long miles with the water-skins, and in the morning when the brethren woke half their daily toil was already done. His abbot, Isidore, who was a man of sense, forbade him to continue in this secret well-doing, very probably because there was not now enough work for the other brethren to do.

Sleep was despised and feared, though only the greater proficients could dispense with it in any great degree. It had its especial dangers, for with sleep come dreams, which no man can control. Abbot Arsenius said that two hours' sleep were enough for any monk; and some instead of sleeping would work all night at a handicraft. The series of nocturnal offices, linking the evening's holiness with that of the next day, was designed to keep off sleep and the devil. Only with daylight, in many communities, was the monk allowed to snatch a little rest, because the Prince of Darkness has less dominion in the light. The great ascetics, the record-holders, could perform mighty feats of sleeplessness. Antony, Ammon, Macarius, Simeon were all adepts in this exercise. Evagrius, a gentle, softly nurtured, cultured Greek, stood upright, sleepless, under the open sky in the desert for forty consecutive days and nights, and a Syrian monk Adolius,

who, as Saint Jerome says, 'walked in the path wherein are
no stumblings' (adding with characteristic Jeromian relish,
'wherein there are many who have not walked'), stood in
the open air all night upon the Mount of Olives in all
weathers. He acted as 'knocker-up' to the monks who lived
there in their swarms, by hitting with a hammer upon a board
at their doors to get them out to mass. Often, in the morning,
his clothes were so wet with rain or dew that they had to be
wrung out, as if from the wash-tub.

Anger, covetousness, vainglory, dejection, gluttony, pride,
all might torment the hermits, and involve them in punishment or rebuke, but they could be expiated and cured.
Chastity was the one inexorable, absolute qualification for
hermithood; to lapse from it was a final disaster which must
permanently vitiate a man's character and destroy his reputation, and its preservation cost the hermits the greater part of
their waking energy and thought. The subject, in all its
aspects, was never far from their minds and seldom out of
their conversation. Germanus, John Cassian's friend, who
figures in his *Conferences* as his companion in his researches
among the hermits, always required some explicit pronouncement upon it by the fathers whom they visited and,
if any of the worthy old gentlemen showed signs of neglecting this important theme, Germanus, with a truly Gallic
interest in it, would shepherd him back to it and make sure
that it received proper attention. From one aged father,
Chaeremon, they obtained full measure indeed, in a discourse upon chastity, both in its observance and in its breach,
so exhaustive that modern translators have felt obliged to
leave it discreetly veiled in the obscurity of the original
Latin. It is also extremely dull, and perhaps the purity of
the patristic mind is to be commended in that the Fathers,
touching as they so often do upon this awkward subject,
contrive nearly always to be extremely obscene, but are
scarcely ever, at the same time, amusing.

[73]

Day and night, by nearly every monk, the struggle with the sin of fornication was waged; it was called the 'war' and the 'battle' without further description, because everybody knew what battle and war were meant. Deprived of the ordinary businesses of secular life, the poor creatures were at the mercy of those temptations which lie in wait for vacant minds. Monkish occupations occupy the hand alone, leaving the mind very free to wander; and the freedom which was intended for holy contemplation was an invitation to the most appalling fancies. Saint Jerome makes no secret of his lurid imaginings during his desert life; and men who in ordinary life would have been reasonably decent in mind most of their time, and probably decorous in behaviour, were a prey to the obscenest thoughts, for the cure of which they were without any intellectual resource such as that of the ascetics of the old Egyptian temples, who, when lascivious fancies assailed them in the night, would sit up and do mathematics. If the hermits were prevented, by lack of opportunity, from falling, they committed fornication in their dreams, and fancied themselves, on waking, defiled by the involuntary acts of sleep. So they feared sleep, and suspected both food and drink, even innocuous liquids, as conducive to these deplorable nocturnal adventures.

Naturally, from time to time there were those who could not stand the strain. Some, very sensibly, returned to the world, and found comfort and a remedy in marriage. Some, in the act of flight, were snatched back by their zealous brethren, and for them the hideous nightmare of temptation must begin all over again. Some took a wife in their cells, to the scandal of their neighbours; and some merely fell, if they could find a participator anywhere for their indulgence, and the resources of the holy deserts in this respect were surprising. For them there were horrible penances, grass to eat instead of food, and the whips waiting on the palm trees in the Nitrian churchyard. To escape the struggle by the drastic but practical expedient of self-mutilation was regarded as a poor-spirited way out of the difficulty. For the carnal urge, in so far as it was a cause of spiritual wrestling, was regarded as a stimulus to the spirit. Without it the spirit would be feeble and lukewarm, as indeed, by common consent, were all eunuchs, who, being freed from such desire, could be pure without a struggle. The lives of the saints, it must be admitted, would have lost much of their excitement without this intense preoccupation; there would have been no object in all the fasting and solitude, no heroism, and very little left to pray for.

No hermit was so holy, no sojourn in the desert so long, as to exhaust the efforts of Satan by this means. The body might be weak with fasting, but the passions still glowed; they seem almost to have burned the fiercer as the body failed. A little innocent gluttony, one cannot but think, might have relieved the senses and perhaps diverted the fleshly cravings that seem to have run all to lust; but the hermits would have none of that, believing that food would only add fuel to the flame of these distracting ardours. Pakhon, one of the severest of recluses, lived for forty years in the desert, with never a sight of womankind, and yet, he almost boasted, was never free for one day from carnal temptations. The devil, determined to overthrow him, sent him a charming young dusky damsel, who nearly prevailed over him; but he slapped her in the nick of time, whereupon she vanished, leaving a vile odour upon his hand that was not dispelled for over two years.

Once, in despair at his own weakness, he lay all day at the entrance to a cave where some hyenas dwelt, hoping that the beasts, at their coming and going, would take pity on him and eat him. But they merely sniffed at him and passed him by unhurt. And when, driven to extremes by the disdain of the hyenas, he held an asp to the offending parts of his body, the perverse reptile, like the hyenas, refused to bite.

The drollest expedients were sometimes resorted to by the ingenious. One old soul, with a homely humour worthy of Æsop, cured himself by making a doll of clay, calling it his wife, and telling himself that now that he was a married man he must work extra hard to support her. Later, with praiseworthy thoroughness, he made a second doll, saying that his wife had now brought forth, and that he must work still harder to support both wife and child. In time the hard work necessary to maintain a family completely cured him; it is better to be a bachelor than to have to work so hard as a man must who has a wife and family to support.

If the thought of women tormented the hermits, the hermits certainly returned the compliment in full measure, and were extremely disagreeable to any woman whom they might encounter. When a noble Roman lady visited Arsenius, a renowned elder, merely out of a blameless curiosity to see a famous holy man, he refused to see her, on the ground that it was unsuitable for her to visit a man. She retorted, by messenger, that she had not come to see him because he was a man, since there were plenty of men in Rome and better ones too, but because he was a prophet. When eventually she was admitted to see him, and very civilly asked him to pray for her, he replied that he would pray God 'to blot her out of his heart'. The poor lady retired crestfallen, but was reassured by her host, Archbishop Theophilus of Alexandria; she must not attach too much importance to the sallies of a hermit, for all hermits are particularly spiteful about women. 'By means of women', he said, 'the Enemy doth battle with the holy men.'

An elder called Paul carried his fear of unchastity so far that, meeting a woman by accident on a public highway, he forgot his errand and fled home to his monastery cursing the unoffending creature. For this unprovoked rudeness, it is some consolation to hear, he was punished by a paralysis in all his limbs, rendering him so helpless that he was taken to a convent to be cared for, where he was tended by kind and pious virgins for every necessity of nature till the day of his death.

There was a Mesopotamian hermit called Jacob, or James, the Great, who very astutely took Theodoret, the historian, a competent literary man, with him to his retreat in the Mesopotamian desert to witness his austerities. There, Theodoret reports, he put a curse upon some innocent maidens washing clothes at a well, by drying up their well and turning their hair grey, because they failed to take any notice of him.

This morbid preoccupation with sex took one of its strangest forms in those monks who organized communities of virgins and loved to occupy themselves with the discipline and conduct of a female establishment. A monk called Elias, who had been wealthy in the world and is described as 'fond of virgins', founded a nunnery and lived in it himself, because the ladies at first quarrelled so much that they required his presence to compose their differences. He did not, however, escape temptation, which in time grew so insistent that he fled to the desert, vowing never to return lest he should be led away by the devil to injure his own virgins. An angel in a dream, however, by a simple operation relieved his affliction, and persuaded him to return to the convent, as without him there was no one to keep the peace, a commodity as difficult of achievement, it seems, in communities of virgins as among the nations of Europe. He returned to the convent, but, as his immunity to temptation had been effected only in a dream, he had the wisdom to live outside its walls, but near enough to keep the nuns in order. His successor Dorotheus lived, very strangely, in a cell inside the convent on the first floor, with a window overlooking an inner court, whence he could supervise all the nuns' doings and overhear and compose their quarrels. Palladius hastens to assure us that Dorotheus never descended to the virgins, nor did the virgins ever climb up to him, for no ladder was ever set against the wall.

Occasionally there are instances of a surprising reasonableness towards a peccadillo or a fall. An elderly monk, Moses by name, was taken ill in Scete, and, fancying that the brethren were growing weary of nursing him, decided, against their advice, for it seems they knew their Moses, to go to Egypt to be nursed. In Egypt he was overcome by the charms of his nurse, a pious virgin, who eventually bore him a child. When he returned to Scete with a baby on his shoulder there was a flutter among the brethren; he even entered the church, and with great humility, still carrying the innocent fruit of corruption, entreated the monks to pray for his forgiveness. The brethren themselves forgave him, and re-admitted him to their company: the fate of the infant and its apparently deserted mother is unknown.

The practices of the ascetics in the name of discipline went beyond the chastisement of the senses. The spirit must be martyred also, to ensure it against pride and false righteousness. The domestic affections, even, were reprehensible, and ascetics who fondly imagined that solicitude for the spiritual welfare of their relatives was a virtue were soon disillusioned. A young gentleman of Asia, who had been in the army and held the office of tribune in Egypt, was converted, and adopted a severe asceticism. He was then seized with a desire (which clearly proceeded from the devil) to bring the gospel to his wife and his little son, thinking it wrong to neglect the salvation of those he loved. So, 'overcome by this plausible appearance of false righteousness', he forsook his cell and, against the advice of his abbot and brethren, set out for home. He was scarcely out of their sight when demons seized upon him, and he was carried back to the monastery raving and possessed to be bound with chains for a lunatic, like Malvolio, and beaten. Another monk, who received a packet of letters from home, flung it into the fire unread, lest his heart be seduced by earthly affections. Even mothers and sisters might evoke unchaste imaginings and were avoided. A monk escorting his mother upon a journey, and obliged to carry her across a river, wrapped cloths round his arms and hands, for fear of immodest thoughts if he touched her. Another, when commanded to come out of his cell to greet his mother, blacked his face with soot, and stood outside his cell with downcast eyes, so that he should neither see her nor be recognized by her.

But, for mortification of what a man might be pardoned for regarding as his better feelings, the palm goes to Patermucius, who, in obedience to his superior, did not shrink from cruelty towards his own child. In modern times such conduct would have ended in a police court; but in that age it was accounted for holiness. Patermucius, and his son aged eight, obtained admission to a monastery by the usual method of lying prostrate before the door till their persistence convinced the inmates that their intentions were serious. On being admitted father and son were separated, lest affection for the child should hinder Patermucius' spiritual progress. Later, he was obliged to see the child dressed in rags, neglected and unkempt, and so dirty that he must disgust even a parental eye. He must also witness him being whipped; yet still, for Christ's sake and the virtue of obedience, he must not protect nor comfort him; and his heart stood firm and unyielding. Eventually the abbot bade Patermucius throw the boy into the river. Without hesitation Patermucius snatched up the child, ran to the river and flung him in; but to avert any possible fatality the abbot had thoughtfully stationed some monks at the water's edge who rescued the boy in time. Patermucius' obedience, constancy, and faith were rewarded by the reversion of the headship of the monastery when the abbot died.

Obedience was often exacted in the performances of cruelly arduous and quite useless tasks which savour somewhat of the impositions of the harsh stepmother of fairy-tale, except that no good fairy or angel ever appeared to perform the task for the victim, or to show him an ingenious short cut. The monks were ordered to heave enormous stones for no purpose, till they were at the brink of collapse, to water dry sticks from distant wells for years, and to destroy the precious fruits of their own laudable toil, such as copies of books or jars of oil. But most often the tortures of the ascetics were self-inflicted and thus robbed of the acuter part of their pain.

A remarkable feature of these extraordinary lives is the extremely ripe age alleged to have been attained by many of the hermits. Eating scarcely anything, forgoing sleep, drinking appalling water, inhabiting the most impossible huts and holes, in a state of unredeemed filth and with sanitary arrangements that had better not be imagined, they lived to enormous ages. Octogenarians and nonagenarians jostle one another in the desert annals. Perhaps the oldest were singled out by historians, but they are remarkably numerous, and if here and there they are blind, or feeble in body, their tongues at any rate seem to have retained undiminished energy. Antony, Paul, Ammon, Schnoudi, Macarius of Alexandria, and Cassian's old Father Chaeremon, who delivered that exhaustive and disconcerting discourse upon chastity, were all alleged to have passed a hundred, though Chaeremon was so feeble that he had to go upon all fours. Women too were included in the common longevity; old Mother Talis, superior of a community of virgins who were so devoted to her that they did not need, like many others of their compeers in holiness, to be locked up, survived eighty years of uninterrupted austerities, and must have been about a hundred when she died, while another lady sustained sixty years of continuous asceticism in her own house. From the lives of the hermits it must perforce be concluded that a diet of a pound of bread a day, a few dates, and some dirty water, a stifling and unwholesome cell, and a complete absence of ablution, are the surest means for prolonging, if not of enjoying, life upon this earth.

Such then were the hermits, such was this strange tribe of holy cactus-flowers, grotesque and prickly, but with a distinction all their own, which blossomed so suddenly and so profusely in the scarcely-watered wastes where other vegetations were loth indeed to grow. They clothed the deserts with glory and filled them with a bright, if strident, colour and light. But we must not let the phenomenon, however brilliant, dazzle us beyond the wish to inquire how so strange a thing arose.

The Christian's way to the desert was first found, no doubt, in time of persecution; but the movement found its greatest impetus when persecution was over, under freedom and toleration, in an impulse, puritan in its essentials, to quit a world which, now that it was Christian, was recognizable as Christian no more. There had been a time when Christianity had seemed to offer a way of life in contrast to materialism, to worldly pomp and power and the things that were Cæsar's; now Cæsar and the Church seemed to converge, where one was there was the other also, and the fugitive from either must escape from both. In the desert only was it possible to avoid both the clergy and the police.

An unalloyed puritanism actuated, probably, only the greater among the ascetics; the motives of the rest must have been very mixed. On the spiritual side the riots attendant upon religious controversy, and these were frequent in Alexandria, must have driven many a man forth, in disgust if not actually in fear; and the Emperor Julian's edicts, aimed principally at Catholics rather than Arians, drove conspicuous Catholics, as they did the great Athanasius, into the desert to hide.

Once the movement was under way, it gathered in the sufferers from many kinds of annoyance, runaway slaves, fugitives from the law, members of every social grade up to people of senatorial rank, who saw no other way to escape the toils of the suffocating judicial and fiscal system of the late empire. Diocletian, by a piece of legislative ingenuity less fortunate than appeared at first sight, had localized the collection of the taxes by placing it in the hands of the *decuriones*, local persons of senatorial rank, who thenceforward had the odious task of collecting from their friends, neighbours, and relatives, burdensome taxes for the needs of a remote, even foreign government, for wars and other purposes in which their personal interest was nil. Legislation became necessary to stop the escape of *decuriones* from their districts, and since their duties descended to their legitimate offspring, they must have wives of their own class, not only casual or lowly amours. Similar burdens fell upon the trade guilds or *collegia*, whose members must therefore be kept up; and thus the children of *collegiati* and freed-women were to be counted as *collegiati* too.[1] So a bondage, a paralysis, gripped society; there was no change of place or of occupation tolerated by the law, and the only safe remedy was a complete disappearance for which the desert alone could afford a reliable opportunity.

The hermits themselves, in so far as they were conscious of a motive, would have pointed unhesitatingly to the example of the Hebrew prophets as their inspiration; like the prophets they wandered 'in deserts, mountains, and caves, and in the holes of the earth'. It did not occur to them that the prophets

[1] See *Theodosian Code*, laws of 315, 397, 412. Also J. S. Reid in *Cambridge Modern History*, vol. i, ch. 2.

had a special mission, not to spurn civilization but to correct it, and that to them the wilderness was not a permanent residence but a temporary retreat where they could gather strength and inspiration with which to descend upon offending Israel or its rulers to warn them of the wrath to come; and when the victims showed signs of having had enough of correction, the desert remained a safe and handy refuge. In the New Testament the desert still keeps its character as a place of retirement and preparation, not a permanent abode. But in truth the hermits recked little of Scripture and troubled their heads, such as they were, but little about authority. Certainly for their strange courses there is no support in the Gospels. Our Lord advocated poverty and the abandonment of material standards, but severe asceticism, practised as an end in itself, was no part of his message. His own behaviour showed an indifference to the flesh, but he never told any one to murder it. For the extreme standard of chastity set up in the desert there is no countenance in his teaching; married people were among his closest friends, and he made a wedding famous for all time by a charming, not at all ascetic miracle. His kindness to women made no distinction between the married and the unmarried, and included some in a less respectable category, provided they showed those qualities of charity and faith which were the essentials of his teaching. He liked them to be sensible, intelligent, human beings: he rebuked Martha for being over-occupied with her domestic duties, while for the Syro-Phœnician woman he performed a special miracle because she pleased him with an apt, almost challenging, answer.[1] He forgave the woman taken in adultery, and told the Pharisees that harlots could more readily gain the kingdom of heaven than they. Even Paul, though ascetic in his teaching, advocated celibacy only for those who could stand it, and the Corinthians, he certainly thought, were safer married: 'it is

---

[1] Mark vii. 28, 29.

better to marry than to burn'.[1] To Timothy he somewhat surprisingly said 'In the latter times some shall depart from the faith, giving heed to seducing spirits and doctrines of devils . . . forbidding to marry, and commanding to abstain from meats.' The devils, thought the poor unlettered hermits, were entirely on the other side. To Timothy Paul also said that he should treat the elder women as mothers and the younger women as sisters. As we have seen, the desert saints could not treat even their own mothers as mothers, nor their sisters as sisters, while from a strange woman encountered on the high road they took to instant flight. What was safe for Timothy, however, was probably not so for the desert-dwellers with their long years of cruel privation, denied not only the pardonable pleasures of the senses but also the natural relationships of family life.

Outside the Bible there was a wealth of models for the hermits to follow; they could take their choice. In the pagan and the Jewish worlds asceticism had been practised in many forms. There were the Hindu fakirs, known to the Greeks since Alexander's time,[2] called by them the *gymnosophistæ*, the 'naked philosophers', and regarded as akin to the Cynics, whom they undoubtedly influenced. They were known to the Christian world through the descriptions of Pliny, Plutarch, and others,[3] and later through Porphyry,[4] the pupil of Plotinus, in his *De Abstinentia*. As early as the third century, long before the great florescence of the hermits in the fourth, Tertullian[5] had repudiated what seems to have been a current comparison of Christian and Brahmin, and was loth to believe that resemblance to the fakirs could be justified in our Lord's teaching.

---

[1] I Cor. vii. The whole subject is reviewed in a most scholarly and exhaustive way by the Wife of Bath. See Chaucer, *Prologue to the Wife of Bath's Tale.*   [2] Arrian, *Indica*, xii.

[3] Plutarch, *Alexander*. Quintus Curtius, viii, 9. Pliny, *Nat. Hist.*, vii, 2,

[4] *Circa* A.D. 230–300.   [5] Tertullian, *De Jejuniis.*

For the Egyptians and Alexandrians there was a visible example in their near neighbours, the recluses of the Egyptian temples, living secluded from the world under a permanent or temporary[1] vow, strictly disciplined as to food and drink and sexual relations. These may have given the Christian monk some of the details of his dress, the cowl, and perhaps the scapula, the sandals and the girdle of cord.[2] But the Egyptian ascetics differed from the Christians in that they washed, and by that ingratiating habit of sitting up and doing mathematics when troubled by unbridled thoughts in the watches of the night.

There were the Jewish Essenes too, described by Philo[3] and by Porphyry,[4] a sect of celibates living near the Dead Sea, conducting a communal life by means of agriculture, rejecting money, property, and women; for woman, Philo reminds us, is a selfish creature, 'terribly calculated to mislead a man by her continual tricks . . . and she is always studying deceitful speeches and all other kinds of hypocrisy: like an actress in the theatre, she allures her husband's eyes and ears, in order to cajole his masterful mind. And if there are children, she is puffed up with intolerable pride.' The Essenes puzzled the solemn biologically-minded Pliny because they managed to maintain their numbers without recourse to the common processes of procreation. In fact, they merely recruited new adult converts and adopted young children.

There were also the Therapeutæ of Alexandria, a contemplative sect of Alexandrian Jews living in cells grouped together to form a community, near Lake Meroë. Their way of life, as described by Philo, more than any other resembled that of the generality of Christian monks, those at least

[1] Many were only temporary recluses, undergoing a kind of 'retreat'.
[2] John Cassian, *Institutes.*
[3] *De Vita Contemplativa.*
[4] *De Abstinentia.*

who live under a rule. There were women in the community, but they dwelt apart, and encountered their brethren only on certain feast days, which occurred every seven weeks. Then there was feasting indeed and wine was drunk, but not, Philo assures us, after the manner of the Alexandrians at their parties, who seem to have been in the habit of drinking till they raged like mad dogs and bit one another's noses and fingers; and then, while the guests were in their cups but not yet quite helpless, the host would levy a subscription towards the next party, after which the guests might get as drunk as they liked. The Therapeutæ had hymns and liturgies much after the Christian fashion, but they had a right to terminate sermons by clapping three times in token that they had had enough.

So close was the general resemblance of the Therapeutæ to the Christian monks that they came to be regarded as the origin of all Christian monasticism. Eusebius, Jerome, and many others, including Sir Thomas Browne,[1] have decided that such virtuous and pious persons must have been Christians, not Jews, that they were in fact communities of the first Christian monks, founded by converts of Saint Mark, who had preached Christianity at Alexandria; and the Catholic Church has claimed as the first representatives of Christian monasticism these most orthodox and punctually observing Jews. So thoroughly were they annexed that eventually even Jewish scholars began to cast them off, repudiating the *De Vita Contemplativa* as not by Philo at all, but a Christian attempt of the third or fourth century to gain dignity for Christian monasticism by inventing for it a respectable Jewish ancestry. And in the nineteenth century a German Jewish scholar satisfied himself that the Therapeutæ were a fiction from first to last and had never existed at all.

There was yet another model which seems to have pro-

[1] *Dissertatio de Therapeutis.*

[86]

vided direct inspiration to the early monks, more especially to the hermit and the solitary. Nearer than the fakir, the Egyptian recluse, or even the Jewish contemplative, to the Greek-speaking, Greek-thinking Christian, especially the Alexandrian, were the Cynics, who flourished in Alexandria far into the Christian era. In outward seeming, in his poverty, rough manners and speech, the hermit was just a kind of Cynic. He did not wear the Cynic's cloak, nor carry his staff and bag, but in much else, his dirt, his contempt for comfort and equipment and for society with its vulgar materialistic standards, above all in his cultivation of a rather brusque repartee, he was the same.

It is the Cynic's shallow contempt for ordinary life, and his jocular snarl at it, which gives the Christian hermit a different character from the oriental ascetic, with his positive ideal of freeing the spirit from all earthly bonds for union with God. Some of the greater ascetics, Antony for instance, whose intellectual calibre was bigger than that of most, had some grasp of this positive side of the ascetic ideal, but most of the hermits were actuated by nothing more elevated than an active, personal contempt for the world and a desire to show themselves superior to it. And their repartee, such as it was, aped the smart, stinging slap-in-the-face which the Cynics loved, indeed were expected to give to the society they despised and its representatives, or indeed to any one whom they wished to score off. The adventures of Maximus the Cynic testify to the confusion of saint and Cynic in the popular mind.[1]

But it is possible to make too much of origins and to dwell upon influences too much. Neither flight from political dangers and burdens nor the example of their forerunners the Essenes, the Therapeutæ, the Brahmins, nor even of the Cynics, can account for quite the whole of the Christian ascetic movement or deprive it of a certain originality. Its

[1] See p. 306.

influence penetrated to all Christian countries, and is active still. Such vitality is never found in an abstract principle, however excellent, nor in the mass desires of mankind, however urgent. There must be a leader to give it living expression and a voice, and when he is found there will be great upheavals, the awakening of slumbering potentialities, a stirring of vast masses of humanity, by influence, by suggestion, by conscious imitation. Such a man was Antony, whom the anchorites knew for their father, greatest, though not the first, of his kind. He had the magic of a great personality: what he did others must do also, they must follow him, like the children after the Pied Piper, compelled by an irresistible tune. So the dry tinder of discontent and despair in these long-suffering populations which were finding the obligations of ordinary life too much for them caught fire, and the desert filled up with anchorites and monks till that very solitude which was their main objective became the hardest thing of all to find.

The deserts could not, of course, hide them for ever; the sharp eye of organized ecclesiasticism, which hates the solitary and his independence, was not slow to find them out, and the desert communities were ultimately caught into the ecclesiastical machine, as the civilized, respectable monastic movement, guided by Basil the Great, got under way.

Through the next two centuries the desert folk kept up their numbers, till in the seventh they had to encounter a desert movement more violent and more militant than their own. As a crowning act to the Monophysite controversy which had raged in Egypt the Egyptian Christians, aided by the monks of the desert, were able to cast off the Roman dominion, which had never sat easily upon them, by selling themselves to the Arab conquerors; and eventually, cut off from the rest of Christendom, isolated politically and diverging more and more in organization and ritual, they became the despised but independent and self-sufficing Coptic Church.

II
THE PILGRIM
Etheria

'And thryes hadde she been at Jerusalem;
She hadde passed many a strange streem;
At Rome she hadde been and at Boloigne,
In Galice at Saint Jame, and at Coloigne,
She coude muche of wandring by the weye.'

I

The globe-trotter, in the long course of his history, has never been much esteemed. As a spendthrift of money and time, a rubber-necked gaper seeking a change of skies rather than a probably much-needed change of heart, he has been the moralist's bane and the caricaturist's livelihood. Yet there is something to be said for him; if not a very exalted person himself, he has very respectable relations. He is a humble cousin of the explorer whom every one applauds, and though he may have no scientific purpose, and may be less adventurous than his noble kinsman, his incentive is surely the same. Curiosity inspires him, curiosity compels him from the comforts and security of home to endure strange climates, fatiguing journeys, food that may be unpleasing if not injurious, strange beds and even stranger bedfellows.

His curiosity is indeed quite unscientific, for it is romantic and sentimental, unhampered by any discrimination or taste. It should be all for places with natural peculiarities or which have been the scene of historic happenings, or of incidents of famous legend or story, for in his excited imagination history and mythology do not greatly differ. And such places must be new to him and far afield, for among his habitual surroundings they can make him no appeal. Like the explorer he must have in him some element of the hunter, he must be out to fill his bag, to let no reasonable quarry go. No famous place must be unvisited that is within the compass of his pocket or his strength. Such is the true globe-trotter, seeking no carnal satisfactions, but a heavenly kingdom of the mind, where dull contemporary life fades away, where ruins are built again, and fallen temples rise with glistening columns, with capital and entablature complete, while gods and heroes walk the earth they left no matter how long ago and buried peoples start again to a bustling and probably quite unauthentic life.

It is hard to say when or where the tourist began. In the ages before history, indeed in many quite historical ages, people seem to have been pretty constantly on the move, and archæologists and anthropologists habitually assume that everything and everybody in most countries came there from somewhere else, though frequently little enough trace of them is to be found in their supposed homes of origin. But the ancient migrant peoples most likely had some materialistic object in their wanderings, flight from danger, or a search for food, or metals, or wives. The tourist proper is a phenomenon of civilization, his flight is from safety, from the boredom of ease; and with the dawn of history and literature he is already fully fledged.

The Greek, all curiosity and energy as he was, soon discovered the pure joys of travel; early Greek history is full of people who travelled with no object but to view the countries and societies of other men, and to enlarge and improve their minds. Pythagoras, that compelling personality who so impressed himself upon succeeding generations that he became mythical almost, was remembered as much for his travels as for his antipathy to a harmless vegetable; and Solon, whose very greatness seems to shroud his perfectly real and historic personality in an Olympian mist, employed his exile from Athens in travel, as the most profitable expenditure of time unhappily divested, temporarily, of political activity. And at the beginning of both history and geography stands Hecatæus of Miletus,[1] who

---

[1] Author of γῆς περίοδος (*Compassing the Earth*). There was also the Scythian Anacharsis who travelled to Greece. (Herodotus, iv, 76.)

travelled into Egypt and perhaps north of the Greek world into Russia, forerunner and acknowledged literary ancestor of Herodotus himself, the latchet of whose shoes, however, he can hardly be accounted worthy to untie.

Herodotus, professed historian and proud of his high calling, has about him also something of the globe-trotter in his insatiable curiosity, his omnivorous interest in everything he encountered. But he must have been disconcerting to the guides, ready as they were at every point with their rigmarole designed for the common sight-seers who could usually be counted upon to swallow anything; for he listened politely to the tale of the priests at Memphis about the children whom Psammetichus shut away from all human intercourse in order to discover, by eavesdropping upon their mutual conversation, what language might prove to be the original speech of the human race, and then went off to Heliopolis and Thebes to find out whether the priests at these places would agree with the priests of Memphis in their versions of the story. Such a proceeding is not for the tourist proper; it is the beginning of more than one science, and it was a little hard on the Egyptian priests to have to face the comparative method in anthropolgy.

Countries with great ruins and romantic pasts will always attract tourists and, after Egypt, Greece herself became their goal. In the century succeeding the death of Alexander the volume of tourist traffic in Greece is attested by the appearance of the tourist's chief need, adequate guide-books to assist his journeys. Of these, some charming fragments are still extant, by Diodorus, Polemo and Heliodorus, descriptions of the famous monuments and sights of their country, clearly intended for the assistance of an intelligent travelling-public with an antiquarian turn of mind. And there is, unfortunately also in fragments, a flippant and not at all archæological guide-book by a charming and lively Anonymous, known by the awkward and unkind name of Pseudo-Dicæarchus[1] because some foolish scholar once made a mistake about his name. He describes a tour through Greece in which distances are carefully stated and the character of the inhabitants vividly recorded. Pseudo-Dicæarchus is as disinterested as Bædeker and far more candid, and his picture of Bœotia cannot have greatly increased the tourist-traffic of that country. Oropus, for instance, was a nest of fleecers, and the greed of the customs-house officials was unsurpassed elsewhere. In fact, as Zeno had said, a bad end to the Oropians. The people of Platæa suffered from their too glorious past; they had nothing to say for themselves except that their country had once been the scene of a famous battle. At Thebes the women were elegant and lovely, but public safety (perhaps for that reason) was in a poor state and murders were committed almost daily on most trifling pretexts. Tanagra had the prize as the least disagreeable town in Bœotia, for the inhabitants were industrious and had enough to live on, and so were without a motive for crime. For a comfortable livelihood, in the view of this guide-book writer, conduces to honesty; and perhaps the production of the pretty clay statuettes, which have lent their town undying fame, kept their minds and fingers out of mischief.

If tourism throve so well on the poor facilities for travel in Greek times, it found great stimulus in the easy communications of the Roman Empire. The roads and the comparative safety of the seas provided facilities which were comparable only to those of modern times; for, to those who were accustomed to think in terms of an empire rather than of smaller polities, distance and slow means of transport mattered less than convenience and security. People who were subjects of a government controlling an area as big as a continent, spread out around the Mediterranean and Ægean

[1] Pseudo-Dicæarchus, once thought to have been Aristotle's famous pupil of that name, is now called a 'geographer' of the second century B.C. See J. G. Frazer, *Pausanias*, Commentary, Introduction.

seas, thought nothing of a journey of several weeks, if it was carried out in safety to its destination. The importance of the Roman roads, emphasized often enough, cannot be exaggerated. Wherever they penetrated, along them civilization circulated, and places connected directly or indirectly by the great road-system were parted by no barrier but a question of time. We hear occasionally of discomforts, of bad inns, of floods, of brigands, but only as exceptions to the rule of successful, uneventful travel. There were stations manned by the military to supervise doubtful districts or sections of road; there were the milestones, a Roman invention, which, as Quintilian pointed out, greatly cheered the foot-slogger on his way, and incidentally have left to posterity volumes of information about the Roman road system. And there were the Itineraries, dating from the early emperors, initiated by Julius Cæsar himself, re-edited in the fourth century, which served the purpose of modern motorists' road-books, and gave the roads their names, told where they led, the distances between places, and the times required to traverse them.

To the cultured Roman, who regarded Greece as the source and origin of all he cherished most in history and in literature, the roads led inevitably to Greece, whose decaying cults and half-forgotten shrines found a new life in ministering to the educated tourist's sense of the past. Greece is full of the records of these devotees, and for them was produced what is still one of the most useful guide-books in the world, Pausanias' *Description of Greece*, that comprehensive, if somewhat undiscriminating storehouse of information about the extant buildings and works of art, the temples and religious cults, of Greece in Hadrian's time. With his careful measuring of distances, his detailed description of routes, his somewhat didactic tone, his preoccupation with the historic and the literary rather than with what was contemporary and new, Pausanias is Karl Bædeker's only serious rival. He omits many a detail which we should value now, but we must be grateful for what we possess, as the traveller of that time must have been grateful when he set out, his Pausanias in hand, to find his way about the Acropolis, about Athens or Sparta or Thebes, or even about the remote hills and valleys of Laconia and Arcadia, protected to some extent from local priests and guides, whose information was as expensive, probably, as it was fictitious.

At New Ilium, a Hellenistic settlement on the site of ancient Troy (not described by Pausanias), the Emperor Julian in the fourth century found a population of guides making what they could out of the tourist, with the aid of the remains of Priam's town; and anything the tourist asked for that happened to be missing they did not hesitate to supply. There was a hero-shrine, probably of some antiquity, where sacrifices were still burnt before a statue of Hector, and to balance Hector a statue of Achilles had been recently added; for students of Homer when they came to Troy would feel defrauded if they found no monument recalling the central figure of the Iliad.[1] It seems a pity that the guides stopped short of showing an authentic wooden horse.

As the centuries passed over the empire, safety and ease of communication gave opportunity to a new religion which spread, as everything else did, by the universal channels of the roads. There was a fresh impulse to movement, and a setting in motion of fresh waves of activity, that flow first from the centre to the circumference, and later react backward from the circumference to the centre. Some one has praised Saint Paul for his truly Roman outlook in realizing that the Christian religion should be conceived of, not as a small Jewish sect, but in terms of the whole Roman world, like Lenin's Bolshevism, which was to be universal, not confined to Russia only. The Roman organization lay like a huge system of electric cables, ready for the switching in of a

[1] Julian, Ep. XIX.

new current from a fresh source of power, and the new religion spread because its path was prepared before it. The
Christian was quick to realize his opportunities. Soon there
is a lively bustling from place to place upon religious business; monks, bishops and priests speed from point to point
to visit, embrace, bless, scold or squabble with one another.
The imperial posts were seriously congested, Ammianus
Marcellinus complained, by the scores of bishops hastening to
and from their innumerable synods by means of the public
post-carriages for which a free permit was often given. And
the tourists, active as ever, have themselves undergone a
change, not in their character, but in their goal. They are
pilgrims now, and a pious purpose casts a holy glamour over
their habitual journeyings. For their new objective and direction they too must have their guide-books and itineraries, to
lead them by the safest, most convenient routes from farthest
Gaul or Spain or Britain maybe, not to the famous shrines
or cities of Greece, but to the Holy Land; and if in passing
through classical lands they cast a pardonable, secular glance
at the popular time-honoured 'sights', the tomb of Euripides,
the birthplace of Alexander, or the tomb of Apollonius of
Tyana,[1] the pagan associations of these objects serve but to
mark the stages of another, but equally romantic progress
to the Holy Sepulchre, Golgotha and the Cross. And even
the pilgrims' inevitable turn for relic-hunting has a respectable precedent in the Emperor Augustus, who, when he
visited the tomb of Alexander, carried away with him a
portion of the great man's nose.

Pilgrim and tourist are one in their beginnings, even if
they differ in their end. Chaucer knew what sends the pilgrim
forth, 'to seken straunge strondes, to ferne halwes couthe
in sondry londes', not consciousness of sin and desire for
penance, but 'Aprille with his shoures soote, and Zephirus
eek with his swete breeth'; in fact, just spring in the blood,

[1] A kind of prophet much advertised by the Stoics.

and a desire for change of air. And the Fathers knew it too, and in their censorious, uncongenial way, so different from Chaucer's, fulminated against the endless stream of pilgrims in ever-increasing numbers pouring from Britain, from Gaul, from Africa and the Danube, from Persia and Mesopotamia to the Holy Places, and not content with these, as they became hackneyed and a common experience, ranging land and sea in search of famous monasteries or the abodes of renowned ascetics and hermits, in out-of-the-way and hardly-accessible spots. Jerome has his usual tirades against this restless modern habit, though he was not averse to the visits of certain pilgrims to his retreat in Bethlehem, holy and high-born ladies, for instance, especially widows; and Saint Chrysostom has his word, characteristically stinging, for what he calls a whole world in motion on pilgrimages to see Job's dunghill[1] and the martyrs' shrines. Gregory of Nyssa, a mild, literary, and rather peevish saint, observing that monks were beginning to make these pilgrimages part of their rule, remarks caustically that they are not anywhere recommended in Scripture. 'When the Lord invites the Blest to their inheritance he does not require a pilgrimage to Jerusalem among their good deeds, nor is a pilgrimage included, as a cause of blessing, in the Beatitudes.'[2] It is just as holy to pursue holiness at home; travel abroad leads to temptations, to dangerous encounters, and the inns of the imperial roads were full of encouragement to evil and to vice; while, as for Jerusalem, it was just an ordinary town, full of miscellaneous and not wholly creditable life, merchants, actors, buffoons, prostitutes and the like. And if God is especially present in Jerusalem, why does he allow it to be so wicked? If Gregory went there himself, he assures us, it was at the emperor's special request, and he had a free

---

[1] *Ad Populum Antiochenum*, v. 69.
[2] Ep. II: 'On Pilgrimages to Jerusalem'. Erasmus and Sir Thomas More and Henry VIII all doubted the value of pilgrimages.

pass on the imperial post-vehicles, in which he was sheltered from mixed and vulgar company and could sing hymns and psalms the whole way. The pilgrims, it must be confessed, did not much heed the Fathers. Inspired, invited almost, by Constantine's architectural and other attentions to the Holy Places, by the discovery of the Sepulchre and the Invention of the Cross, pilgrimages through the fourth century became more and more the rage, a new pleasure and excitement for the well-to-do, an escape from drudgery for the poor, who could now lodge upon their travels at the expense of Christian charity.

From everywhere they came. 'Every one of any importance in Gaul hastens hither,' wrote an inhabitant of the Holy Land at the close of the century, 'even the Briton sundered from our world.'[1] As the years go by the sites that have been recognized for the benefit of tourists, and that are pointed out to them, increase in number; the sacred relics multiply. From quite early in the century we have an elaborate itinerary by an unknown person called the 'Bordeaux Pilgrim', which gives, most meticulously, all the stopping- and changing-places from Bordeaux by land to Constantinople, and on to the Holy Land, and the mileage between each two points. A number of places in the Holy Land and in Jerusalem, shown to the Bordeaux pilgrim and recorded by him, are already additions to those which appear in Eusebius' *Life of Constantine*. The Bordeaux pilgrim intended his guide-book to be complete; there are semi-scriptural details, such as the Column of Flagellation and the House of Pilate, over and above the more famous authenticated spots; and in the ruins of Solomon's Temple he was shown a room where Solomon wrote the *Book of Wisdom*, and a cellar where he fought with devils. The blood of Zacharias was to be seen on the pavement where he fell, and the marks of the nails in the boots of the soldiers who slew him. The

[1] Paula and Eustochium to Marcella. Jerome, Ep. XLVI.

process gathers momentum with the years, and by the reign of Justinian holy spots and relics are thick upon the ground. The pilgrims Theodosius and Antoninus Martyr saw the Sponge and the Reed that were used at the Crucifixion, and the Cup of the Last Supper, which were unknown in the fourth century, and in the desert Antoninus saw the Pillar of Salt that had been Lot's wife, not licked away to nothing by the desert animals as had been rumoured, but still life-size and entire. Two centuries earlier, we are assured to her great regret by a most careful and veracious witness, there was no Pillar of Salt to be seen.[1]

Most disturbing to the more sensitive kind of Fathers was the propensity of women to get abroad upon these trips. If the Church, eager at all times for support both financial and social, found a new opportunity in the well-to-do, un-occupied women who were a feature of Roman society under the empire, it ought not to have been surprised if the women themselves found new opportunities in the life of religion. But in their perpetual anxiety for female virtue, that bright and perishable ornament which is so easily, and sometimes, alas, not even reluctantly, lost, the Fathers were aghast at what they imagined would be its fate when liberated from their duenna-like eyes. Travel and familiarity with the public inns must inevitably be fatal to this fragile flower; virginity, or if that does not remain to be lost, chastity, will be en-dangered. Gregory of Nyssa voices, with his usual pessimism, the general lack of confidence of the Fathers in the resistance to temptation which might be looked for in the fragile sex. If a weak woman, he urges, stops at a roadside inn, the integrity of her mind must surely suffer; and besides, 'she must have some one to lean on, some one to lift her on and off her horse. Modesty will be endangered.' And if she

---

[1] See p. 125. In the next century the Empress Eudocia got away with the chains of Peter, the arm of Stephen, and the first of the innumerable portraits of Our Lord attributed to Luke.

survived the inns, Jerusalem, as pictured by Gregory of Nyssa, awaited her, and she might escape the frying-pan only to fall into the fire.

But the women were not to be restrained: they took to the road like ducks to water. Saint Silvia of Aquitaine was almost a professional pilgrim, a conveyer of relics if not a trader in them. The great Melania, a woman of immense wealth and no responsibilities except those she chose to recognize, spent years wandering in the East upon visits to the monks and the Holy Places, and eventually settled on the Mount of Olives in some kind of holy partnership with Rufinus, where she drew Saint Jerome's vituperation, not for her manner of life, but for her chosen partner[1] therein, with whom Jerome had one of his most celebrated quarrels. Very likely she was herself a bone of contention between the two men, for the proper place for a rich and independent widow was at Bethlehem, surely, at Jerome's feet.

There was Fabiola, of the celebrated Roman family of the Fabii, who, having incurred Saint Jerome's wrath by optimistically marrying a second husband after putting away an unfaithful first, took to good works and founded a hospital for pilgrims at Ostia.[2] She soon tired of that, fine lady as she was, and set off for a long pilgrimage in the East. She travelled from city to city, so content with continual movement that, as Saint Jerome says, she had no home but her travelling trunk. She had not only an active body but a busy mind, and having settled at Bethlehem in the little community which had gathered round Jerome there, used to amuse herself by asking him questions as to the meaning of passages of Scripture, which he was sometimes hard put to it to answer. Once he was so utterly floored that he was obliged to retire and write a whole book on the *Forty-two Resting Places of the Israelites*, in order to reduce her to silence. Only a wild rumour of the approach of the Huns,

[1] See p. 201. [2] Jerome, Ep. LXXVII.

which flew abroad in Palestine and disturbed the religious coteries, drove her from these migratory pleasures back to the monotony of social life in Rome.

And there was the dreadful Paula, Jerome's celebrated and devoted friend, widow of the senator Toxotius, who toured the East and the Holy Places and finally settled with her surviving daughter Eustochium[1] at Bethlehem, under Jerome's spreading wing. Her extensive tours are recounted by Jerome in an obituary letter addressed to Eustochium at her death. She visited the hermits in Egypt and would have settled there in company with the young girls who were her companions, greatly to the hermits' delight, but for episcopal intervention. In the Holy Land she was indefatigable; weeping, praying, she plodded to every likely and unlikely spot that was shown to the pilgrims of her day, and some were far from likely: the house of Sarah where Isaac was born, the stone that was Jacob's pillow when he dreamed, the house of Cornelius and the rooms of his four prophesying daughters, and the place where the concubine was cut to pieces.[2] Here she paused a while for reflection, as well she might. She saw also demons shrieking and writhing before the tombs of the saints, and women suspended upside down whose clothes did not fall off. So wrought up was she with enthusiasm at these sights that she wrote to Marcella, who was still living in Rome upon the Aventine in the religious community of which Jerome had been the inspiration, urging her to come to the Holy Land to share these peregrinatory joys. 'Together we shall look upon the waters of Jordan purified for the washing of the Lord, we shall pass the folds of the shepherds, we shall pray together in the mausoleum of David. We shall see the prophet Amos standing upon his rocky peak blowing his shepherd's horn. We shall hasten, if not to the tents, to the monuments of Abraham, Isaac, and Jacob, and of their three distinguished wives....'

[1] Blesilla had died of her self-inflicted privations some years before.
[2] Judges, xix, xx.

II

The pilgrims have not recorded much of their general impressions and experiences of travel. Too often, like the Bordeaux pilgrim or Paula, they merely enumerate places; or like Palladius, Cassian, the authors of the *Historia Monachorum*, and Sulpicius Severus, they were too intent upon the lives of the monks, and confined their observation too much to them. Considering what ancient remains, other than sacred sites, must have been visible in the lands the pilgrims visited, one might be tempted to suspect that they never went to these places at all, but for a certain intimate knowledge they show of desert features and ways. Except for a reference of Palladius to 'granaries of the kings of Egypt' (the pyramids of Gizeh), there might have been in Egypt no pyramids, no temples, no sphinx, no remains at all. The Bordeaux pilgrim refers once to the Dead Sea as of such heavy water that it turns a swimmer over, so possibly he bathed in it; and Sulpicius Severus, at the beginning of his narrative, has a charming geographical digression. The ship that took him from Narbonne to Carthage had to anchor in a storm off the coast of Libya, and we have a brief account of an excursion into the interior, enough to make us wish for more. He saw a sandy waste and barren mountains, and a scanty, primitive population living on barley and on milk, completely ignorant of the use of money. But on the whole there is a complete absence of conscious interest in strange countries, their appearance, and their ways, and we might share, though for a different reason, the Fathers' poor opinion of the pilgrims had not one of their number, by sheer good luck, survived to tell a different tale.

Towards the close of the fourth century of our era, a lady of some wealth and importance set out from the western shores of Europe, from some place upon the Biscayan coast of France or Spain, on a pilgrimage to the Holy Land, which she described in a long, detailed letter written to friends or relatives whom she left behind at home, and whom she calls, in the manner of her day, ladies, reverend sisters, light of my eyes, your affection, and by other flattering titles. She was determined that those who could not accompany her should, as far as she could contrive it, miss no detail of her trip; and here at first hand, from the traveller herself, we have a picture neither of a rapscallion female vagabond hanging about inns, parting with her virtue to the first comer, nor of a weeping, hysterical devotee, but of a lady of vigorous character, dauntless energy, and good education, lively and polite, interested not only in the shrines and places of holy association, but in topography, in natural features, in landscape and scenery; in short, with an eye for the view.

We do not know who she was. She tells, intentionally, practically nothing of herself. It is usual to call her Etheria, but the name is no more than a clever guess. She is one of the handful of choice spirits of whose life there are no recorded details, but of whom we have a clearer picture than could ever be gained from the professional historian or biographer.

For centuries she was but a shadow, known only by allusions in the work of an obscure monastic person called Abbot Valerius,[1] who lived in the mountains of north-

---

[1] Migne. *Patr. Lat.*, vol. 87. Valerius' *flornit* was *c.* 650–75 under King Wamba who fought every one, including the Moors, and was finally deposed by Earwig, a persecutor of Jews.

western Spain in the seventh century. He was a bookish person, a book-collector and copyist, who contrived, under great difficulties among an unbridled people in a district both rude and remote, to achieve a solid amount of scholarly work. He possessed a copy of Etheria's letter, which he describes in some detail but does not reproduce, and not till the nineteenth century was the letter itself brought to light in a copy at Arezzo,[1] mutilated but in sufficient bulk to be recognizable beyond doubt as the letter described and extravagantly praised, indeed, by Abbot Valerius.

Valerius had a hard life; the Galician mountains in the seventh century seem, by his own account, to have been inhabited chiefly by brigands, and even his fellow ecclesiastics were thieves.[2] His books and the copies which he made were constantly being stolen, he was assaulted, beaten, even serenaded with howls at night, adventures which, it is impossible not to suspect, had some provocation for, like a good Father of the Church, Valerius had a strong character, plenty of courage, and a fine resource in invective. We owe him a part, if not a very big one, in that great, even principal, benefaction of the Church to mankind, namely, the protection which, through the Dark Ages, she was able to afford to the literary treasures of Christian antiquity, and to that sort of person who can find satisfaction and usefulness only in a library or a study.

The fragmentary Arezzo copy of the letter opens when its author has already reached Mount Sinai, having completed her journey from the West and wandered considerably elsewhere in the Near East. Valerius, with a complete copy before him, knew, though he does not explicitly tell, where Etheria came from, and her route thence to the Holy

---

[1] 1887.
[2] He had a personal enemy, the thief of his manuscripts, whom he calls a savage, slippery man, a babbler of imbecilities, a sham priest, a slowwitted dunderhead.

Land. Her name, unfortunately, is shrouded in the mists cast by the inaccuracies of later copyists of Valerius' work in the monasteries of Southern France and of Spain. Echeria, Eucheria, Euheria, even Egeria, are its variants, due no doubt to that unfortunate Visigothic vagueness about consonants which, coupled with a similar Moorish vagueness about vowels, has made the Spanish language what it is. Egeria, attractive name enough, is dismissed by scholars[1] as savouring too much of an allusion drawn from the pagan authors, a too intelligent correction by some erudite monk, who, with Valerius' account of her before him, felt the aptitude of the name. But the name must have sounded unfamiliar to the Visigothic and Gallo-Roman copyists, so much is clear from the confusion; very likely it was Etheria, for a Greek name would not be strange in a cultivated Roman-Spanish or even Gallic family of her time, and Etheria is but a Greek version of the Latin name which has been handed down through the centuries in France as Célestine.[2]

According to Valerius, Etheria came from the 'farthest western shores of Europe', 'from the extremest verge of the western Ocean', and 'from the farthest limit of this western shore'; in her letter she herself alludes to the Rhône as a familiar object.[3] Debate has raged around the meaning of these words. Some will have it that she was Galician, from a sisterhood in Valerius' own part of Spain, but, in spite of Spain's reputation for producing outstanding characters under the empire,[4] the Galician mountains seem an unlikely home, in the middle of the fourth century, for a lady of Etheria's culture and mental equipment. Provence and Aquitaine have also claimed her, as a member of some sister-

---

[1] Bludau, *Die Pilgerreise der Aetheria*.
[2] Duchesne, *Eccl. Hist.*, iii. 113.   [3] See p. 127.
[4] Seneca was Spanish, also Theodosius, and the pretender Maximus. Martial, Lucan, Quintilian, the Emperors Trajan and Hadrian were Romans bred in Spain.

hood in one or other of these highly Romanized provinces.
Her language was Latin, which she wrote with great effect,
though scholars complain that it is unclassical and slipshod;
but the same scholars cannot decide among themselves
whether such provincialisms as she uses savour of Provence,
Aquitaine, or of Spain.[1] She knew enough Greek to quote
and spell correctly Greek phrases and names.

Valerius calls her a professed virgin, but her letter tells
nothing of that, and if virginity was her profession she made
of it neither a burden nor a boast. He also calls her *Beatis-
sima*; in a library catalogue at Milan she is *Beata*, and by
the fourteenth century she had attained, in the monastic
library catalogue at Limoges, the dignity of abbess. In
modern libraries she has become a saint. Some have sought
to identify her with Saint Silvia of Aquitaine,[2] that grim
professional ascetic who boasted, in order to shame a fellow
pilgrim who was sick, that she never washed nor ever slept
in a bed, personal habits not suggested by anything in
Etheria's letter. Others have thought that she may have been
Galla Placidia,[3] Theodosius' remarkable daughter, who so
arranged her relationships, sentimental and other, as to be
the daughter, sister, and mother of emperors, and finally
Augusta, regent for her little son, practically empress herself.
Always the centre of a romance or political intrigue—for
she was one of the earliest exponents of the uses of romance
in politics,—Galla when in Gaul was first a captive, then a
queen; she had no time for idle intellectual pleasures, for
archæological curiosity like Etheria's about the desert en-
campments of the Israelites, or for maiden meditations upon
the measurements of a prophet's tomb.[4] And it must be
hoped that Etheria was not that lady mentioned with oppro-

[1] Karl Meister, *Rheinisches Museum*, 1909.
[2] Gamurrini, the finder of the letter at Arezzo.
[3] Köhler (*Bibliothèque des Chartes*, xlv, p. 141).
[4] In any case at the time this letter was written Galla Placidia must
have been a little girl.

brium by Saint Jerome as a pernicious gadabout, sister to a noted Priscillianist heretic of his time.

To seek to attach Etheria to any famous person is to deprive her of half her charm. Unlike most of the ladies known to fame, she is nobody's daughter, wife, sister, or mother. She depends on no famous personage, no male relative, to explain her. Nor does she explain herself. Her object in her letter is to give her friends at home as clear a picture as she can of the scenes through which she passed. She never dwells, subjectively, on herself, but she has that rare gift of being able to put on paper what she saw and what she felt, and of enabling her reader to see with her. And not Cicero in all his glory, nor the elaborate Pliny, ever succeeded in conveying a more vivid picture than Etheria contrived to do in her solitary and, alas, incomplete letter.

For Etheria's home, if it is not an injury to her bright errant spirit to try to locate that which she herself, with such manifest elation, had abandoned, we are driven by Valerius' repeated references to the Atlantic seaboard, inevitably, to Aquitaine. Of this delightful province in the later Roman age, with its southern sunshine and soft Atlantic airs, we have a wealth of information in the poems of Ausonius[1] and in the works of the Gallic Fathers. In Aquitaine, as always in provincial France, people were primarily devoted to agriculture and the vine; and their leisure was given to sport, to letters, and to religion. There was an occasional wave of religiosity, as in the Priscillianist movement of the latter part of the fourth century, which, however, had its principal manifestations in Spain; and there was an outbreak of asceticism following the example of Saint Martin of Tours. But Gallic society on the whole took its piety as a matter of course, and the gaunt figure of Saint Silvia is happily an exception to the general rule. Monasticism in those days,

[1] Ausonius was a professor of Bordeaux who became Gratian's tutor; eventually he retired and lived in the country near the Garonne.

as John Cassian, the great Gallic divine, once sadly observed, did not find a congenial home in Gaul. Perhaps life was too comfortable, perhaps the native devotion to the soil and to the things of the mind was too strong for asceticism to make a great appeal. The universities of Lyons and Bordeaux set a high intellectual standard among well-to-do people; life was sociable, literary, gossiping, rather dilettante, morally not too severe.

An appeal had to be made, on one occasion, all the way to Bethlehem to Saint Jerome, by an ascetically-minded Gaul who could get no support locally for his efforts to restrain his sister's free-and-easy mode of life. She had left her mother's house because she felt unequal to sharing it with her mother's lover, only to set up a separate establishment for herself elsewhere which, as it included an ecclesiastical gentleman-friend of her own, was no better than her mother's.[1] The Gallic ecclesiastics who were not ascetics took life cheerfully, indulged in a good deal of splendour, and were cherished and embroidered for by the devout ladies of their flock. But the ladies were not all light; they had a great and dignified place in that old Roman Gallic society, as they have had through every age of French history. Sulpicius Severus, in later life an ascetic and in holy orders, lost in youth a wife whom he adored, whose memory he honoured by retaining ever after a most unusual affection for his mother-in-law. Ausonius in his *Parentalia*, a truly French celebration of his family as a whole, including most of his relations-in-law, has left an imposing portrait-gallery of women—grandmothers, mothers, aunts, sisters and cousins; sensible, capable women, loved and respected by their families to whom they were devoted; and there was one quite remarkable lady, a spinster aunt, who rejected domestic blisses and entered the medical profession in which she acquitted herself with success.

[1] See Jerome, Ep. CXVII.

[109]

In general, among these western Gallic women, there is a more reasonable human atmosphere than among their contemporaries elsewhere. The pictures we get from Jerome, Chrysostom, and others, of Melania, of Paula, Blesilla, Eustochium, Læta, Asella, Marcella, and even of Olympias, the great Constantinople heiress whose religious extravagances had to be restrained by imperial tutelage,[1] are not edifying. Among the western women there is less hysteria, fewer tears, and more sense. Religion, when it captured the Gauls, seems generally to have left reason and common sense unshaken. Perhaps the burden of age-old convention on the Western women was less crushing than on the Eastern, and the opportunities of the new religion, in consequence, less exciting; perhaps their lives had always been less circumscribed. Western society in the fourth century seems to have been already essentially Western, in spite of its integral part in a universal commonwealth embracing the whole civilized world. The Western pilgrim approaching the East is a stranger from afar, viewing the manifestations of religion in those remote and famous lands, glamorous through distance and an almost legendary report, with an astonished and definitely foreign eye.

Abbot Valerius, in the fallen-away and degenerate Dark Ages, was quite overwhelmed by the heroism and energy displayed by Etheria in face of all the difficulties and perils of her way, and uses them as a stick with which to beat some idle, lazy monks whom he wished to scold. 'Let us contemplate the blessed Etheria,' he writes, 'let us admire the courage of a weak woman, braver than the men of her time. See how with resolute heart she sets out for the extreme limit of the world. With audacity that admits of no obstacle she travelled

[1] She was left a widow with an enormous fortune at about twenty years of age, and took to such extravagant alms-giving that Theodosius took charge of her fortune till she should marry again, or till she should be thirty. She defeated him by being so indifferent that he returned her fortune to her.

through mountains, deserts, provinces and cities. . . . Let us blush, brethren, before this faithful daughter of Abraham, who attained the strength of iron in her feeble body, in the hope of future glory. . . .'

As far as courage is concerned, Valerius over-rated his heroine; energy and endurance she certainly possessed, but her journey was neither so difficult nor so dangerous as he liked to imagine. He judged no doubt by the conditions of his own time, when Western Europe under the Visigoths, the Franks, and the Burgundians was a far rougher place than it had been in the fourth century; Egypt and Palestine were already in the hands of the followers of the Prophet, who were spreading rapidly along the African coast and had already landed in Spain. The pilgrims struggled on, but such an adventure as Etheria's would have been scarcely possible for a woman. It is quite clear from Etheria's own account that neither she herself, nor any one she encountered, saw anything bold or strange or difficult in her journey; it is taken by every one concerned as a matter of course. There are only the barest references to the means of travel, for such details she regarded as too commonplace to be recorded. Wherever she went there was accommodation for travellers, inns, and lodging provided by monastic settlements and the like. And behind them all is the solid, reassuring fabric of the Roman rule, with its roads, its discipline, its public safety. Twice only is there a hint of danger. In Mesopotamia Etheria reached the confines of the Roman sway, and was warned not to venture farther; beyond it there were barbarians, Persians, unknown dangers, in fact outer darkness, into which nobody in his senses would venture. And once, in the desert between the Isthmus of Suez and the Nile, she had an escort of soldiers for a couple of stages, after which the soldiers are dismissed as quite unnecessary.

Almost everywhere Etheria went she was on a beaten track; other pilgrims had been before her. There were the guides with their set piece to recite, and, as always, what the tourists asked for, in their touching faith in the verbal exactitude of the Scriptures, was infallibly shown. Here and there, in addition to the local guides, important ecclesiastics came forward to welcome her, an honour accorded also to Paula, a tribute, Jerome says, to high worldly position and holy repute.

Etheria did not, of course, perform her journey alone; she had attendants with her, or a party of fellow tourists. Usually she rode upon a horse or mule, except on rare occasions, as when, with formidable energy, she made the ascent of Mount Sinai on foot, a rough and precipitous climb of over seven thousand feet, seldom undertaken by tourists to this day, and recommended in modern guide-books as 'suitable for experienced climbers only'. The height and steepness of the ascent of Sinai impressed her, but she never dwells on the difficulties of the way, nor expresses any fears spiritual or physical.

She owns, on more than one occasion, to being extremely curious by nature; and indeed the reader is ungrateful who does not admit his debt to her habit of inquiry into everything she saw. It is curiosity which keeps her incessantly in motion, ever pushing her journey a little farther, making some extra détour, no matter how arduous, to see some famous monument or place. Repeatedly she assures us that she visited this place or that 'for devotion's sake', with an insistence that cannot but suggest that she felt the assurance was needed. There is no reason to doubt her piety, but she was at least as curious as she was pious, else her narrative had been a different, an infinitely duller tale. Once, having already completed two arduous and distant tours, she was inspired by conversations with other pilgrims to undertake, 'for devotion's sake', the toil of an expedition to see Job's tomb in Northern Palestine. She uses the word 'toil' and then corrects herself—'if indeed that may be called toil in which one sees the fulfilment of one's desire.'

III

E theria's narrative, in its present mutilated state, finds her already in the Sinai Peninsula engaged upon a systematic topographical study of the wanderings of the Israelites. According to Abbot Valerius she had already visited the holy deserts of Egypt and the celebrated hermits who lived there. She had 'done' the Nile, in fact, and its pilgrim sights, and when eventually she returns from Egypt through southern Palestine to Jerusalem, she expressly states that she is covering familiar ground which she has described to her readers before.

How she reached Egypt from Gaul is unknown. Like the Bordeaux pilgrim she must have passed through Constantinople; for when eventually she leaves the Holy Land she travels northward through Syria to Constantinople, revisiting, by her own account, the stations of her journey out, and like him, she may have come all the way by land. Valerius says she braved the stormy seas, but omits to say which seas and for what portion of the way. The sea was preferred by many; Gallic pilgrims bound for Egypt sometimes took ship from a Provençal port direct to Carthage[1] and then travelled coast-wise, under Roman jurisdiction, to Nitria and the Nile. Rutilius Namatianus, who was prefect of Rome about the year 414, came home even from Rome to Gaul by sea, because he preferred the sea to the rocky heights of Italy and to the plains submerged by

---

[1] John Cassian and Sulpicius Severus.

autumn floods.[1] The route of the Bordeaux Pilgrim over
the Cottian Alps, to Milan, then to Sirmium, and over the
great road that ran through Pannonia and Dacia to Constantinople, seems a long way, but it was a safe one, and
no doubt to be preferred by those to whom shipwreck and
pirates are not the only terrors of the sea.

And if Constantinople seems to us out of the way, not
quite on the most direct route from Southern Gaul to
Jerusalem, it would not seem so to the pilgrims. From the
fourth to the fourteenth century, and to many people later
still, Constantinople was the centre of the world, with Rome,
Alexandria, Jerusalem, and Babylon at the ends, as it were,
of radii.[2] People who had bad maps, or none at all, were
untroubled by misgivings as to distance, and they travelled
the more in consequence, covering distances which, to later
ages equipped with more accurate information and better
means of transport, seem impossible. To a person with time
to spare, and with hospitality given free at the hands of
Christian or other charity, the world was more accessible
than it is now, with approximately accurate maps which needlessly emphasize distance rather than propinquity, and with
expensive hotels. The Roman roads made a chain which
bound the ends of the earth together, and the amount of
travelling accomplished in Roman and in mediæval times
proves that peculiar notions of geography were no hindrance
to circulation.[3]

In Sinai, where we first discover our pilgrim, she is already
in the hands of the guides, the local monks and ecclesiastics
who, as in Egypt, lived in swarms upon and around the holy
mount. As a serious student of topography she carries with

[1] *De reditu suo*. A poem (fragmentary) describing his route.
[2] Constantine the Great (in a letter from Constantinople), refers
to Alexandria as in the 'East'.
[3] Representatives of the Fuggers in the sixteenth century once went
from Spain to Vienna *via* Danzig without a qualm.

her a copy of Exodus, to be referred to at each important
site, somewhat to the confusion of the ciceroni, who had
their own account to give of what they had to show. But
if deficient in Scripture they had their skill as showmen, and
the first glimpse of Sinai was properly led up to so as to
have its maximum effect. The pilgrims were led on foot
through the mountains to where the ground opens out and
forms 'an enormous valley, wide and exceedingly beautiful,
and across the valley appeared God's holy mountain, Sinai'.
The valley measures, Etheria informs us (unfortunately
not quite accurately),[1] 'as far as we could judge by sight, or
as we were informed, sixteen miles in length, and four wide,
and here the Israelites encamped while Moses was in the
Mount close by'. There were a number of Exodus sites to be
seen in the valley, and some prehistoric remains which the
guides called the 'Graves of Lust' mentioned in Exodus; for
all the peculiarities of the district, natural features or prehistoric remains, had been suitably christened to suit texts of
Scripture. The Graves of Lust, it will be remembered, were
the graves of those unfortunate Israelites whom the Lord
smote with a distressing plague because, with their usual unhappy propensity for doing the wrong thing when they least
intended it, they had presumed to eat the quails which literally blew in upon them in drifts two cubits high around the
camp, assuming, not unnaturally, that these were the fulfilment of a recent divine promise of a month's supply of
flesh food. Their mistake, as often, was only revealed to
them when it was too late.[2]

The valley had other *Sehenswürdigkeiten*: the spot where
the Golden Calf was made, the place where Moses tended
his father's flocks, and the Burning Bush out of which the
Lord spake to Moses, still green and burgeoning. The Bush

---

[1] The valley is actually about four miles long and two wide.
Bludau, *Die Pilgerreise der Aetheria.*

[2] Numbers xi. 34.

however, Etheria may not see immediately, it is reserved as
a *bonne bouche* when Sinai has been climbed and redescended.
'And as our route was first to ascend the Mount of God
which can be seen from here and is easier to ascend from
this direction, and then to descend to the head of the valley
where the Bush was, that being the best descent from God's
mountain, so we determined to see first all that we desired,
and then to descend so as to arrive at the Bush, and thence
to return by way of the same valley through the whole
length of it, in company with the various holy men who
showed us all the places in it mentioned in Scripture.'

The ascent of Sinai was formidable; it had to be accomplished on foot, and there were a number of lesser peaks
which had to be climbed first, involving many hours of
strenuous exertion. 'Now the whole mountain range looks
from without as if it were but one, but from within it is
found to be many mountains, and the whole range is called
the Mount of God. But the particular mountain on the summit of which, as it is written, God's majesty descended, is
the centre of all.' And God, very dramatically, has hidden
Sinai from those approaching it so that it cannot be seen
'till you reach its very base on the side by which you
ascend'.

The ascent could not be completed in a day. It was evening
when the party reached the foot of the Mount, and they
accepted the hospitality of the holy men of the place for
that night. Early next day, Sunday, the ascent was begun.
'These mountains are climbed only with extreme toil, for
you cannot go up gradually by degrees, by a winding track
snail-shell-wise, so to speak; you must climb straight up the
whole way, as up a wall, and you must come down each
mountain in turn until you reach the very foot of the middle
one, which is Sinai proper . . . the toil was great, for I had
to go on foot, the ascent being impossible to accomplish
in the saddle, and yet I did not feel any fatigue. For one

does not feel fatigue when one feels that one's desire is being fulfilled.' At the top of the mountain a priest came to meet her, who served the little church which crowned the summit, a 'hearty old man, a monk from early life and an ascetic', and a whole population of monks and holy men who lived by tending some gardens that lay about the foot of Sinai. Holy spots were, of course, thick upon the ground, the two caves where Moses received the first Tables of the Law, and then the second Tables after he had broken the first. But on the top of Sinai Etheria is no longer thinking of Moses or the Decalogue, but of the view. 'I must tell you, ladies, my reverend sisters, that from where we stood, around the walls of the church, that is from the top of the sacred mountain, those mountains which we climbed with difficulty, compared with the central one on which we stood, seemed to be quite little hills, although I had thought I had never seen any higher, except that this centre one enormously exceeded them.' Like many another traveller at a view-point, she was shown places which she could see and many others which she certainly could not: Egypt and Palestine, the Red Sea and the Mediterranean, and the 'boundless territories of the Saracens, all so far below us as to be past believing, but the holy men pointed out each one'.

From Sinai Etheria was taken to Horeb,[1] to the cave whither Elijah fled from Jezebel and where, after the wind, the earthquake and the fire, he heard the still small voice. There was a stone altar on which Elijah made an offering to God, and near by a large flat surface of rock, where Aaron with the seventy elders stood to receive the Law, and on the rock another rough stone altar. Now the day was wearing on, and the circuit leading to the Bush was not nearly completed, but there was still something to see in Sinai, the

[1] Antoninus Martyr, who visited Horeb in the sixth century, was made to shave his hair and beard and throw them away. Etheria was not, it seems, subjected to trials of this kind.

living hermits in their cells about the place who, to Etheria and her companions, were just as good as the vestiges of Moses and the dead Israelites and on no account to be missed. 'It was necessary that we should walk past and see all the holy places and the cells that were there.'

At length the Bush was reached, in a valley full of cells. It was of a species allied to the Glastonbury thorn, and so 'is still alive', Etheria assures her friends, 'to this day, and throws out shoots. There is also a very pleasant garden in front of the church, with excellent and abundant water', and here the party supped with the monks, with whom they stayed that night.

Next day there was a host of famous spots to be visited, for the resources of the local monks in this respect, it seems, were inexhaustible. There was a great stone, where the Israelites made the Golden Calf, a hill whence Moses descried them dancing before it, and a great rock where Moses, in his petulant fashion, flung down and broke the first copy of the Tables of the Law. There were some prehistoric remains, round stone enclosures, which Etheria was told were the dwelling-places of the Israelites, and a stream which Moses had made them drink. There was the place where the Golden Calf was burnt at Moses' bidding, and another where, by prayer, he stayed the flames which threatened to consume the camp. There were the places where the children of Israel lusted for meat, and where it rained manna and blew quails, and a spot of sinister significance at which Moses bade the Israelites run from gate to gate, for a purpose which Etheria refrains from stating. Readers of Exodus will remember that the reason why they ran was to massacre some three thousand of their erring brethren as a preliminary instalment of the atonement required for worshipping the Calf.

'Now it would be too much to write down everything separately, for no one would remember so many things, but

when your Affection[1] shall read the holy books of Moses
you will recognize far more exactly the things that happened
there.' Much more Etheria saw, and on leaving Sinai she
most politely records her gratitude 'to all those holy men
who condescended with ready heart to receive my littleness
in their cells, and to guide me through all these places'.

Up which of the awe-inspiring eminences of the Sinaitic
peninsula, 'one of the most mountainous deserts in the
world, full of gaunt peaks and dreary ridges',[2] our indefatigable pilgrim climbed, under the impression that it was
the spot where Moses received the Decalogue, cannot with
certainty be determined. To this day scholars have not done
debating as to which was in fact the scene of this august, if
regrettable, event. There are two candidates for the title,
Jebel Serbal and Jebel Musa, the former just under, the
second just over, seven thousand feet high, both amply provided with sacred spots associated with Bible stories, and up
one of these, no doubt, Etheria climbed. It is usual to
deny her Jebel Serbal, on the ground that she could not
have scaled the last precipitous inclines of the 'enormous
smooth dome of granite[3] surmounted by a cupola of like
nature' which forms its crest, and Jebel Musa seems to be
indicated by some of her descriptive detail. Her ascent, however, provides one of her rare allusions to the severity of an
undertaking. Moreover, in the latter part of the fourth century, the probable date of her pilgrimage, Jebel Serbal was
the generally accepted Holy Mount,[4] and remained the resort
of pilgrims and tourists till Justinian endorsed the rival
claims of Jebel Musa by erecting on its slopes a church to the
Virgin and a fortification to protect the monks of the mountain from the raids of Arab tribes. This sealed the fate of

[1] Etheria's correspondents, to whom the letter was addressed.
[2] Cook's *Handbook to Egypt*.
[3] Murray's *Handbook to Egypt*.
[4] W. M. Flinders Petrie, *Researches in Sinai*.

Jebel Serbal, whose monks, having been massacred and raided by the Arabs at intervals since the unhappy end of the forty[1] martyrs in 373, preferred the better shelter of Jebel Musa, taking with them, no doubt, the sacred sites and landmarks which they had been accustomed to venerate and point out on the other mountain, for nothing is easier to remove than rocks, stones, bushes, or caves, if these are objectives to tourists. Further support was given to Jebel Musa by Saint Catherine of Alexandria, said by some to be a daughter of Moses, whose body was deposited by angels on a neighbouring hill, and placed by the monks in Justinian's church in his fortified enclosure on the slopes of the mountain.

Etheria, at any rate, had no misgivings about her mountain; to her it was the authentic hallowed spot that had seen the promulgation of the Decalogue, just as, in company with Saint Stephen,[2] Antoninus Martyr, and every well-instructed nursery child, she believed without question that Pharaoh's host in pursuit of the Israelites was overwhelmed in the Red Sea, for she had no part in the theory of modern archæologists, who have drowned poor Pharaoh and his army ignominiously in a mere marsh or bog.[3]

The party then proceeded to Pharan, where they rested for two days. Setting out thence they came to the sea, at a place where the 'route leaves the mountains and begins to run continuously by the sea, and so close to the water that the waves wash the feet of the animals, and sometimes the

[1] Forty is the usual number for martyrs: many such groups are commemorated in the Near East.   [2] Acts vii. 36.

[3] In the Book of Exodus they were drowned in a Sea of Reeds, the Bitter Lakes perhaps, north of Suez, or the marshes where is now Lake Timsah, quite close in fact to the Wadi Tûmîlat, where the Israelites began their flight. See Petrie, *Researches in Sinai* and Naule, *The Route of Exodus* (Papers of the Palestine Exploration Fund). Major C. S. Jarvis (*Yesterday and today in Sinai*) has drowned the Egyptians in Lake Bardawil near the Mediterranean, and turned the Israelites out of Sinai.

track is through the desert, a hundred, sometimes more than
five hundred paces, from the water's edge. For there is no
road at all there, the whole is sandy desert.' And there is
something curious to tell about the people of the desert and
their ways, 'the inhabitants of Pharan, who are accustomed
to travel there with their camels, put signs here and there,
and follow these signs when they travel in the day-time, but
the camels mark the signs by night. In short, the inhabitants
of Pharan travel more safely and quickly by night in that
place, being accustomed to it, than other men can travel in
places where there is a clear road'.

Etheria's next objective is to complete her study of the
wanderings of the Israelites into Egypt, following them up
backwards, so to speak, to their source. So she passes from
Sinai along the Red Sea shore to Clysma (Suez), where she
rested for a few days, 'for we had done a lot of travelling
over the sandy desert tracks', and thence by four desert
stations to Rameses, where Egypt proper begins. At the
stations there are military posts with soldiers and officers, and
here Etheria takes a military escort between three stations,
the sole indication in her whole story that the question of
personal safety had ever to be considered. Had no reference
been made to the use of an escort we should have been
uncertain whether she always, or never, had one. But,
characteristically, she has given the one detail which can
illuminate a whole landscape, and we catch a glimpse of a
state of tranquillity in the desert which has rarely been
equalled down to our own day; the traveller was safe in
those trackless ways, provided they were under Roman sway.

In addition to the military escort the usual troop of monks
and clergy was still with her, to point out all the famous
places of the Exodus story. These good people were not
always very careful in their attribution of names to places.
The pilgrims, as a rule, would swallow anything; all they
wanted was a recital of familiar place-names, and they would

not notice if the guides pointed out the halting-places of
the Israelites in the wrong order or too far apart. But Etheria
did; she listened with astonishment to the muddled story
of the guides, whose account of the route of the Israelites
was like the rolling English road. 'For your Affection must
believe me, that, as far as I could make out, the children of
Israel wandered in such a way that as far as they went to
the right, just so far came they back again to the left, and
as far they went forward, just so much did they return backwards, and in this way they proceeded till they came to the
Red Sea', which, strictly speaking, they should never have
reached at all.

Rameses, where Etheria entered Egypt, once a flourishing
town, was now just open country, having been burnt, she
was told, by Pharaoh in his rage and disgust on finding that
the Israelites had slipped through his fingers at the last.
There was a large extent of ruins, 'lying just as they fell,
and one huge Theban stone carved with two enormous
figures',[1] christened Moses and Aaron by the bishop of the
next town, Arabia, who had come to meet her, a courteous,
pious old man, kind to pilgrims and very learned. There
was also a sycamore-tree, 'very old and therefore very small',
called the 'tree of truth', which had been planted by the
patriarchs, and, like many a sycamore-tree in Egypt, had
magical properties to cure disease. And here, as she was in
a settled, civilized country, Etheria sent back the soldiers
of her escort, who, 'according to Roman discipline', had protected her in the 'suspected places'.

The remainder of her route to the coast traversed the land
of Goshen,[2] at that time one of the richest and most fertile
parts of Egypt. She admires its opulence and charm, its vines

[1] Rameses II and the God Atmu. The stone is still extant. See
McClure and Feltoe, p. 18. Petrie, *Hyksos Cities*, pl. XXXII.
[2] The waters of Lake Menzaleh flowed in on it and partly covered
it in the sixth century.

of various kinds, some yielding wine, others balsam (*sic*), its orchards, its highly cultivated fields and pleasant gardens. 'Our whole route lay along the bank of the Nile through a continuous series of handsome farms, once the homesteads of the children of Israel. And what more is to be said? I believe I have never anywhere seen a more beautiful country than the land of Goshen. And travelling thus for two days through the land of Goshen we reached Tanis, where holy Moses was born.' Once more she seems a trifle uneasy lest the reader should suppose that this second visit to Goshen— 'for I had already known these places when I had been at Alexandria and the Thebaid'—was merely for pleasure's sake. Goshen was the starting-point of the Israelites' journey; 'that made it necessary for me to return to the land of Goshen'.

With Goshen the topography of Exodus is exhausted, and a return is made northwards, by a route described before, to Ælia Capitolina, which was Hadrian's name for Jerusalem, or rather for the town he built in the year 130 upon what must have been the heap of ruins to which Titus, in the year 70, reduced the Holy City.

⋆ IV ⋆

After these adventures Etheria remained for a time in Jerusalem; but soon she is setting out again, in company with a number of 'holy men from Jerusalem and certain brothers, that is monks', upon fresh excursions, first across Jordan to explore Biblical sites in the desert beyond. Here we have a further recital of places associated with the journeyings of the Israelites, and everywhere there are monks and priests to show the travellers round. There is the place where Moses wrote Deuteronomy, and the water which flowed from the rock which Moses struck, to be seen and tasted too, very beautiful and clear, and sweet to the taste. She ascends Mount Nebo, in the saddle this time, to see the place where Moses was shown the Promised Land; and here for once, and once only, she is confusing, because she is herself confused. In the little church on the top of the mountain, where to this day are ruins and prehistoric remains, was a little raised place 'of about the dimensions that tombs usually are'. She asks the local monks what this may be, and is told that 'Here Moses was laid by the angels, for, as it is written, "No man knoweth his sepulchre"[1]: at any rate, it is certain he was buried by the angels. For his tomb where he was laid is not shown at the present day, but as

---

[1] The Bible says, also, that he was buried 'in the valley in the land of Moab' in any case not on Mount Nebo (Deut. xxxiv. 6). Jude ix alludes to a fight between the archangel Michael and the devil for Moses' body.

our fathers who dwelt here showed it to us, so do we show it to you; for our fathers said that this tradition was passed to them by their ancestors.' This was a tale even more tangled than the zigzaggings of the Israelites, and Etheria makes no attempt to disentangle it. Despite Deuteronomy, Moses, like Hamlet and many another popular hero, had a grave where the guides chose to show it; and if the tourists possessed a superfluous knowledge of the Bible, well, they must make what they could of the guides' story.

While Etheria was within the church she was told of a beautiful view to be seen without, so she 'rejoiced greatly and immediately came out' to see the greater part of Palestine, the Jordan, Jericho beyond it, the lands of the Sodomites, of whose cities Segor alone remained standing to her day, and the cities of Sihon, king of the Amorites, and Og, the king of Bashan. There was also the place where an inscription told of the fate of Lot's wife, but Etheria is very distressed that (unlike Antoninus Martyr two centuries later) she cannot say she saw the Pillar of Salt; it had not been seen for some years, the local bishop told her, having been covered by the Dead Sea. 'Certainly, when we saw the place there was no pillar to be seen; I cannot', she regretfully adds, 'deceive you in this.'[1]

Her next journey is northwards to that famous focus of ancient and mediæval devotion, the tomb of Job. The excursion had been warmly recommended in Jerusalem, as well worth the toil, 'if indeed that can be called toil by which one sees the fulfilment of one's desire', and as usual the reader is assured that all her journeyings are for the sake of prayer, and that her companions also are travelling for no other motive. The Jordan valley, through which she passed, is 'very beautiful, abounding in vines and trees, and much excellent water is found there', and there are ancient grave-mounds, and foundations of the palace of that shadowy

---

[1] See p. 100.

personage, King Melchizedek, where she is told the local antiquaries still dig up fragments of silver and bronze objects. There is the place where Abraham returned in triumph to receive the congratulations of Melchizedek, and where the local kings, after the slaughter of Chedorlaomer, (an Arab chief perhaps, who had carried off Lot), vanquished the Luzims and the Emims and caused the kings of Sodom and Gomorrah to fall into the local slime pits. She visits a garden with a beautiful spring, where the Baptist baptized, with its proper complement of hermitages, and farther on there is the brook Cherith, a fine torrent discharging itself into the Jordan, and the monk who dwelt there told her ('for I am very inquisitive') that this was the spot where the raven fed Elijah twice a day with bread and meat, when he withheld the rainfall from Ahab as a punishment for provoking the Lord more than all the kings of Israel before him, by making a grove, and by other arrogant doings. Elijah unfortunately forgot that rainfall is needed to keep a desert torrent full, and that by choosing this method of punishing Ahab he would also punish himself, for the brook Cherith in time ran dry, and Elijah had to remove himself to the ministrations of the widow at Zarephath.

Etheria's narrative breaks off here, owing to the loss of a page from the manuscript. Abbot Valerius tells us that she climbed Mount Hermon and Mount Elias; and where the story is resumed Etheria is already at the tomb of Job, listening to the story of its discovery, a hackneyed tale, familiar in the history of a hundred relics, how in response to a vision some monks dug in a cave and found a stone sarcophagus with Job's name engraved upon the lid.[1] No mention is made of the celebrated dunghill, or perhaps Etheria refrained from mentioning an object so unrefined.

Etheria had now, by her own confession, spent upwards

[1] Its modern representative is a monument of Rameses II with hieroglyphics and a relief of Osiris.

of three years in the East, and felt that her return might soon
be looked for. 'Having seen all the Holy Places,' she writes,
'I had a mind to return to my country.' But not the whole
of her mind apparently, for in the next sentence she is plan-
ning an expedition into Mesopotamia, which, by her con-
veniently vague notions of geography, requires only a very
slight détour from her homeward route northward through
Antioch to Constantinople. For there are very holy hermits in Mesopotamia, of a 'holiness that can scarcely be described', and the shrine of Saint Thomas at Edessa, where is a
letter of our Lord written to King Abgar[1] preserved for the
faithful to see. 'Your Affection must believe me that there is
no Christian who, having come to visit the holy places at Jerusalem, does not extend his journey thither, for the sake of
prayer.' So she sets out from Antioch, and after some days
reaches Hierapolis, where, 'as the city is exceedingly beautiful
and rich and abundant in everything', it was 'necessary' for
her to make a short stay. Fifteen miles more, and she is at
the Euphrates, 'of which it has been aptly written that it is
the mighty river Euphrates'; it is enormous, almost terrible,
for it 'flows down with a current like the river Rhône, only
the Euphrates is bigger'.

Etheria crossed the Euphrates, remarking with awe that
it can be crossed in big ships only, and eventually reached
Edessa, where she admired the fine church of Saint Thomas,
'in the modern style, where his body lies complete',[2] and
was received with gladness by the bishop, 'a monk and con-
fessor', who proved a willing guide and showman. He led
her first to the palace of King Abgar, our Lord's correspondent, with its marble statues of Abgar and his son, 'with a
sheen as if they were made of pearl' and 'wise and noble
expressions on their faces', good portraits, it has been suggested, in the Roman style of the first century; and the palace
was full of fountains containing fish 'such as I never saw

[1] Eusebius, Hist. I. 8.　　　　[2] See p. 106.

before, so huge, so bright, and of such an excellent flavour'. These fountains of miraculous origin were the sole water-supply of the town; they flowed from the palace in a 'great silver river'.

Once upon a time, it seems, the Persians attacked King Abgar, intending to besiege his town. But Abgar went forth armed with our Lord's letter and prayed, and darkness descended on the Persians, who could see to advance no farther and were obliged to beleaguer the town at a distance of three miles. They then cut off the water-supply, which at that time came from without the town, hoping to force the garrison to surrender; but up gushed the spring in the town, and the water the Persians had diverted dried up at once, and was no more seen, so that it was the Persians, and not the Edessans, who were like to die of thirst. And ever after, enemies were always dealt with by reading our Lord's letter aloud to them at the gate, when they instantly fled away. There was a fine tomb-monument of Abgar and his family, 'very beautiful, but rather old-fashioned'. Finally the bishop gives her copies of our Lord's letter to Abgar and Abgar's to our Lord to take home with her. 'For although I have copies at home, yet it seemed to me nicer to receive them from him, lest perhaps the copies which had reached us might be incomplete, and indeed that which was given to me here is fuller. So if our Lord bids it, and I return home, you too shall read them, ladies, my own souls.'

Still our pilgrim has not begun to retrace her steps. 'It was necessary for me to go still farther to Charræ [Haran] . . . where holy Abraham dwelt.' Again there is a polite bishop, delighted to do the honours, who showed her the church of Saint Elpidius, on the spot where Abraham's house was, 'built on the same foundations and of the same stone', and Rebecca's well; and as it happened to be the festival of Elpidius himself the monks from all Mesopotamia were collected there to pay their *devoirs* to the saint. The folk of this region were for the most part still heathen; it was puzzling, too, to find that the heathen venerated a shrine of Abraham's uncles Nahor and Bethuel, and the good bishop is asked how Abraham's uncles came there, since the Bible says nothing on the subject. The bishop, who had a different sort of mind from Etheria's and was not interested in testing monumental remains by Scriptural evidence, could only say that since their memorials were there the uncles must have come there too. There were questions which quiet old gentlemen in remote places could not be expected to answer.

Six miles farther yet Etheria travelled, to see Rachel's well, and a cottage where Laban's farm had been. By little stages, a few more miles and yet a few more, to add one famous locality after another to her collection, she has drawn gradually farther and farther eastwards. But the point has at last been reached where her advance must stop. Always to the true globe-trotter there is something more, just a very little farther on, which, after the distances already covered, it seems a pity to miss. Etheria has crossed the Euphrates, all Asia lies beyond. Ur of the Chaldees seems to beckon her; perhaps it is not so very far, and she asks the bishop whether that too might not be visited. But the bishop is firm; it is ten stations farther on, and more important than the distance, the whole district is now in the hands of the Persians, and no Roman may enter it. So she is obliged to content herself with a few more Bible sites around Charræ, with visits to the truly marvellous ascetic monks of the neighbouring desert, and with listening to the stories and anecdotes which every one was ready to tell her; 'but I would not have your Affection believe that the monks ever told me any stories other than those from the Scriptures of God or the lives of the greater monks'.

The last part of the journey from Antioch to Constantinople is not described, having been dealt with before. There is still one more détour to Seleucia in Isauria, to see the

I   [129]

shrine of Saint Thecla, the Apostle's friend.[1] Here Etheria has
the unexpected pleasure of finding a very dear friend, who
is now the superior of a large group of female ascetics dwelling in cells around the shrine; in fact 'there is nothing in that
place but the numberless cells of men and women, and there
is a fortification round the church to protect it' and to act
as a refuge for the ascetics from the Isaurians, a people who
have left behind them a reputation for unmitigated violence
and brigandage[2] at this time. After a few days with her friend
Etheria reaches Constantinople without further digression,
and makes there a systematic tour of all the shrines and
churches, to give thanks for having had not only the will
but the power to perform her journey. She dispatches her
letter to her friends, 'ladies, light of my eyes', and just as
we expect her to indicate a speedy return and are mildly
wondering that she should trouble to dispatch a letter that
may reach her home very little sooner than herself, we discover, not perhaps with much surprise, that she is not going
home at all. She is off again, back to Asia Minor which she
has just quitted, to visit the shrine of Saint John the Divine
at Ephesus. And so the letter closes, giving her dear friends
no hope at all of her return; for even the trip to Ephesus
may not be her last. 'And if, after this, I am still in the body,
and if I am able to visit any more places, I will tell your
Affection all about them either in person, if God deigns to
permit me, or in any other event by letter. And I pray you,
ladies, light of my eyes, to be so good as to remember me,
whether I am in or out of the body.'

Whether Etheria ever returned to her home in the West
we do not know, nor whether this letter was her last. It is
difficult to picture her ultimate destiny; she seems unsuited
either to the grim heroics of a wayside martyrdom, or to a

[1] See p. 294.
[2] In Asia Minor at this time people accepted invitations 'the
Isaurians permitting'.

quiet old age amid the trivialities and tattle of a nunnery. Perhaps she remained at Constantinople, an ornament of the fashionable catholic society of the capital. Here was an arena worthy of her gifts; and if she were at the court, and had not a husband already, Theodosius would certainly have married her off to a prefect or a tribune. But it is better not to know; it is better to see the last of our traveller setting out upon yet another trip, full of anticipations, a creature sublimated, liberated from the ordinary routine of human life. Out of the body she can walk the earth for ever, the eternal globe-trotter, insatiably curious, to whom nothing is toil that brings the satisfaction of her desire. She has acquired, a little casually, the title of saint. She should be solemnly canonized with all due formality and pomp, the pilgrim's tutelary, the tourist's patron saint.

Etheria was not only an enterprising traveller, and a
lively letter-writer; she had solid industry and could
perform an exacting task. Some one, an ecclesiastic,
perhaps, or the ladies to whom she addressed her letter, must
have asked for a careful record of the ritual and observances
of the ecclesiastical year at Jerusalem, and a detailed and
exhaustive report is appended to her letter. It is no tourist's
haphazard sketch, no superficial jotting; the facts seem to
have been painstakingly observed, and are set down with
an appearance of meticulous accuracy in a brief and business-
like style, very different from that of her letter. The result
is a document precious to antiquarians, if a trifle dull to the
common reader, a storehouse of curious information about
the Holy City, which was the spiritual, or rather, perhaps,
the romantic centre of Christendom in that phase of transition from the Roman to the mediæval age. The picture is a
strange one; the long recital of fasts, feasts, masses, and processions, of scenes of religious hysteria, is neither attractive nor reassuring; and the only redeeming feature is the
brisk and rather dry detachment exhibited by the pilgrim
herself in her record.

At the time of her visit four centuries almost had elapsed
since the Crucifixion, which was as remote from herself and
her contemporaries as the Smithfield fires from our own day.
In the intervening centuries, more especially since the edict

of Toleration, Jerusalem had become a great religious metropolis, a pilgrim centre like Lourdes or Compostella, only
in a state of perpetual eruption, not confined to a season
or single annual celebration. The pilgrims seem to have had
a way of settling down for years at a time, to enjoy the
religious amenities, though heaven knows how they obtained
their resources; and there was the parasitic population which
collects in pilgrim centres to prey upon the pilgrims, for a
flood of wealth must have been poured with them into Jerusalem, and we know what Saint Gregory of Nyssa thought of
the place. And since the events of the New Testament a vast
edifice of procedure, a complicated machinery of ritual has
been evolved; there is a ceremonial for every hallowed spot,
for each season of the holy year, for every day and every
hour of the day.[1] Magnificent churches have sprung up
everywhere; Etheria, envied by every modern antiquarian
and student of architecture, saw Constantine's great churches;[2]
the Anastasis, or Church of the Holy Sepulchre, and the
Church of the Holy Cross on the traditional site of Golgotha,
both dedicated in 336. She saw Constantine's Martyrium
close to Golgotha, his Baptistry, his great Church at Bethlehem, and a number of other buildings erected at his instigation. She saw the old cathedral church on Mount Zion, already almost an object of antiquarian interest in her day,
which was used only on certain special occasions, and all the
earlier Christian glories of Jerusalem which vanished utterly
at the Persian conquest or were disguised beyond recognition

[1] The history of Jerusalem from Hadrian to Constantine is obscure;
there must have been considerable Christian activity, for the old
church on Mount Zion must have been older than the time of
Constantine, and the elaborate procedure described by Etheria could
scarcely have grown up entirely between 313 and her time.

[2] These, with most of Justininian's buildings were destroyed
by the Persians in 614. Only a tiny fragment of Constantine's Church
of the Anastasis can be seen in a Coptic hospice, and in the hospice of
the Russian Palestine Society, near the Church of the Holy Sepulchre.

by the transforming hand of the caliphs.[1] The crowds of
monks, pilgrims, and tourists troop all day, and sometimes
far into the night, from one great shrine to another; there is a
perpetual migration to and fro. At cock-crow daily the doors
of the Church of the Holy Sepulchre are flung open to the
throng already pressing against the doors, and the long day
of prayer and psalm and procession begins. The bishop comes
and goes, there is reading, praying, singing. The crowd bends
over the bishop's hand and is blessed, not once, but many
times in the day. There is sext and nones, and at vespers the
place is a blaze of candles and tapers, and after vespers there
is a procession to the Church of the Holy Cross, which has
a 'vast number of great glass chandeliers' (of which we would
have welcomed a detailed description); and the long day ends
with more lights and much processing, headed by the bishop,
and much blessing both before and behind the Cross, 'and
the whole does not end till darkness has set in'. So much
for a plain weekday. On Sundays the crowd, which is larger
yet, fears that all will not be admitted, and so the people
assemble long before cock-crow outside the doors of the
Anastasis, and there are hymns and antiphons to pass the
time. At cock-crow the church, ablaze with lights, is thrown
open, there is an elaborate office with censers to fill the place
with odours; the Gospel is read, and the wrought-up crowd
falls to moaning and groaning 'with so many tears that the
hardest heart might be moved to weep also, for the things
that our Lord suffered'. The faithful are blessed and the
weaker brethren may go home and get a little sleep, but at
daybreak the proceedings, more arduous even than on a
weekday, are resumed at the church at Golgotha, where, as it
is Sunday, there are sermons and 'of all the priests who take
their seats, as many preach as desire to do so, and after them

---

[1] The letter as it stands contains no separate descriptions of these
buildings: any such description of them would be in the lost earlier
portion of the letter.

the bishop preaches'. The sermon is a customary feature of Sunday everywhere, but only in Jerusalem was a congregation expected to listen to more than one.[1] The number of the sermons greatly delays the dismissal, Etheria adds, and no wonder, but even when that service is over the indefatigable monks and people can still continue the round of ritual in other churches till vespers in the afternoon.

For the festival of the Epiphany, which at that time in the Eastern Churches was equivalent to Christmas,[2] the start is from Bethlehem, six miles away, in the small hours; Jerusalem is reached 'at the hour when one man begins to be able to discern another,' and a long programme occupies the day till vespers; and for eight days the feast is kept up with 'joy and festal array', with elaboration of ritual additional to the daily use, at different churches and in different places for each day. The 'festal array' draws from Etheria an almost unique outburst, for which the antiquarian is grateful. In all the churches in Jerusalem and Bethlehem 'you see nothing but gold and silk and jewels. If you look at the veils they are entirely of silk, with stripes of gold; if you look at the curtains, they are the same. The sacred vessels of every kind are of gold set with jewels, on that day. It is impossible to reckon the number or the weight of the lamps, the candlesticks, the chandeliers, and the various vessels. What shall I say of the ornamentation of that edifice,[3] which Constantine, at the instance of his mother, adorned with gold, mosaic, and costly marbles, as much as the resources of his kingdom permitted.?'

Lent has extended itself over eight weeks, for, as no one fasts on Saturday or Sunday, eight weeks are needed to bring

[1] Etheria was not quite accurate here. A plurality of sermons on occasion was not uncommon.

[2] Chrysostom in 386 remarks that the celebration of the festival of the Nativity in the Churches of Syria was a novelty.

[3] Constantine's Church of the Nativity at Bethlehem: see Eusebius, *Vita Constantini*, iii, 43.

up the total of fast-days to forty, with one extra day, the
Saturday of Holy Week, the most rigid fast of all, and such
an orgy of ritual that it can be regarded as the climax of the
Easter festival. The first two days of each week in Lent make
but little addition to the ordinary weekday round. On Wednesday and Thursday there are additional sermons and continuous observances till vespers at the Anastasis, whither the
bishop is escorted in procession with hymns. On Fridays the
proceedings, which begin before cock-crow, continue through
the day and night till dawn on Saturday, when strict obser-
vers who have fasted throughout the week may take their
first meal since the previous Sunday.

Through Holy Week the number and intensity of the
rituals increases. There is a great gathering before dawn at
Bethany to commemorate the raising of Lazarus, when the
crowd is so great that it covers all the fields. All day and
every day the ceremonial grows, lasting into the night. The
crowd surges from church to church, to the Mount of Olives
and Gethsemane, commemorating the events of our Lord's
Passion at each traditional site, singing hymns and working itself up into a state of frenzy as its physical exhaustion
increases. Eventually, when on Wednesday the passage
about the Betrayal is read at night in the Anastasis before
the cave of the Sepulchre, 'there is such a moaning and
groaning of all the people that no one can help being moved
to tears'.

A few hours of sleep are allowed that night to ordinary
people, but none to the monks, and at cock-crow on Thursday another long day begins, rendered more arduous than
its predecessors by the inexhaustible resources of the com-
posers of ritual. Mass is celebrated twice, and the fantastic
and harrowing day ends with a tiny respite for supper at
home, and a warning by the bishop that 'great toil awaits
them, to-day, in this very night'. No one sleeps; night hath
better sweets to prove. It begins at the Mount of Olives,

where hymns are sung from the first hour of the night to
the fifth, and thence processions climb up to the place of the
Ascension, and then pass to Gethsemane, to Golgotha and
the Cross, for prayers and hymns; but progress is slow, for
the people are weak with vigils and fasting, and yet for all
their exhaustion they can make such a moaning and groaning
as may be heard as far off as the city. There is a short dismissal, but the people will not go till they have been up to
Zion to pray, and to the Column of Flagellation. At the
second hour they all assemble again at Golgotha for the great
ceremony lasting six hours or more when, before the bishop
on his throne, the sacred wood of the Cross in a silver-gilt
casket is displayed to the people. The bishop holds it in his
two hands while the crowd file past, and bow and kiss the
Cross, and touch it with their foreheads and eyes ; and there
is a guard of deacons to keep watch upon the doings of the
people, because somebody once bit off a piece of the Cross
and carried it home.[1] Solomon's ring is shown, and the old
Horn of Anointing is kissed. For hours the crowd moves
slowly by, and afterwards stands for three hours in the great
court outside, an impenetrable mass of people, indifferent
alike to rain or heat, while the passages of Scripture relating
to the Passion are read, and there is tremendous wailing and
mourning for the things our Lord suffered. Evening then
descends with the complete series of offices usual on week-
days yet to be accomplished, and still a great crowd, all but
the weakest and the aged, keeps vigil through the night at
the Church of the Holy Sepulchre.

But Good Friday, as in some Catholic countries to-day,
is the beginning of the end; after it the tension slackens, the
religious exaltation is spent. Possibly the resources even of
the inventors of ritual are depleted. On Saturday there is

[1] The Rood, however, was never diminished by any depredations
of this kind; it always grew again, Sulpicius Severus tells us, and
remained permanently the same size.

actually an omission in the daily observance, and after vigils and a mass at the Church of the Anastasis to celebrate the Resurrection, 'everything is done quickly on account of the people, that they may not be detained any longer'.

Easter Sunday has its offices and processions but is merely the first Sunday of Easter week and is an anti-climax; there is no more emotion to be had out of anybody, and Easter week is a falling-off. But there are many more occasions in the holy year; there is Whitsuntide, and the dizzy wheel of vigils, commemorations, and festal celebrations, with accompaniment of processions, hymns, fastings, prayers, and readings, revolves tirelessly throughout the year. With a dauntless, almost ruthless patience, Etheria plods stoutly through them all, determined that her correspondent who commissioned this report shall be faithfully served. And when she has finished the sacred calendar there are still baptisms, dedications, and other individual occasions, to cope with.

Her account as we have it now is incomplete; it ends abruptly at the fourth day of Dedications, which are to last eight days; and how many more of these festivals, lasting a week and upwards, go to make up this truly wonderful year we can scarcely endure to guess. But there can be no doubt that Etheria accounted for them all faithfully, in as much detail as she could contrive, to the bitter end.

For himself, the modern reader, for whom Etheria did not write, cannot but sigh with relief at the premature conclusion of the tale. He is a little drowsy with the endless repetition of readings and sermons and prayers, of psalms and hymns. He is stifled with the emotion-laden atmosphere, with the smoke of the candles and censers, with the swarms of bishops, sometimes fifty at a time, with the crowds of people, townsfolk, pilgrims, monks, who regarded cleanliness, we must remember, as very far from godliness. Weary with the ceaseless migration from shrine to shrine, short of sleep and food, he is the more amazed that what he finds fatiguing, even nauseating, to read of in a few brief pages, was the principal occupation, eagerly and passionately pursued, of thousands of people, many of them, probably, persons of considerable culture, who seemed to have or to wish for nothing better to do.

Etheria can be acquitted of any part in the emotional wallowings; she pities without sharing them. Messrs. Spencer and Gillen, those insatiable collectors of human phenomena, recording the curious habits of Australian aborigines, are not more detached from their human material than she. Her own feelings are most often stirred by things of beauty. As in the country or in the mountains it was the view that excited her, so in Jerusalem it is the magnificent churches with their marbles and their gilding, their gold and jewels, their silks and great glass chandeliers. A hundred Fathers might write of Jerusalem, indeed a good many did, without thinking to tell us what anything looked like, or of what the furnishings were made. There is so little in all patristic literature to suggest that there was a world to look at and people in it with eyes to see. Not only are we ourselves Etheria's debtors, but the Fathers also, whose world she has partially rescued from the shadows of morbid emotion which they have cast upon it.

III
THE HERETIC
Pelagius

'*Miserable man! A Toad is a bag of Poyson, and a Spider is a blister of poyson, and yet a Toad and a Spider cannot poyson themselves. Man hath a dram of Poyson, originall Sin, in an invisible corner, we know not where, and he cannot choose but poyson himself and all his actions with that.*'
—JOHN DONNE.

'*Every theory is against free will, and all experience for it.*'
—DR. JOHNSON.

⋆ I ⋆

Very insufficient attention has been given of late to
the first British author, the heretic Pelagius. Perhaps the things of which he wrote have lost the
importance they once had, and the language he wrote in,
unfortunately, is now numbered among the dead, for he was
obliged to write in Latin, neither the languages, nor indeed
the nations of Europe as we know them to-day, having yet
been invented. But in his lifetime he was famous as few
writers have ever been; he was read from end to end of the
civilized world, and for centuries after his death his name
had only to be mentioned to evoke the most tremendous
contention and fuss. In everything we know of him he was
most typically British, and he was found by his continental
contemporaries, those of them who did not like him, just
as subtle and hypocritical, as provokingly phlegmatic and
obstinate, as the British have always seemed in foreign eyes.

Pelagius owes his fame, and owed his condemnation as a
heretic, to his defence of free will: he was its first public
defender in the Christian world, as against fatalism and strict
causality and their theological embodiment, the doctrine of
original sin, with all its implications. To a modern mind, to
assert that the will is free seems a harmless, if also a thankless
enterprise; but for theologians free will has the most appalling possibilities, incompatible with the doctrine of almost
any Church, and Pelagius chose to propound it at a moment
when the theological atmosphere was so inflammable that the

[143]

smallest spark was dangerous. The explosion was terrific, and when the smoke and the fumes rolled away Christian thought was found to have been rent, irreparably, in twain.

Pelagius did not invent free will. For some reason unknown to us it had suddenly begun to occupy men's minds in his time; several people wrote books upon some aspect of it, and Pelagius himself was said by his contemporaries to have had his ideas at second-hand from Theodore of Mopsuestia, a bishop in Cilicia, a bold independent thinker of the sort that flourished in the remoter Asiatic bishoprics at the close of the fourth century. Theodore, however, adventurous as he certainly was, and originator of a later more important heresy,[1] did not initiate the controversy about free will; and Pelagius' debt to him was probably no more than he owed to other ethical speculators of that generation, who inside the pale of Christianity were still attracted by the ethical teaching of the Stoics, moral responsibility and the perfectibility of man.

Free will had never recommended itself to the Greeks. Early Greek thought was fatalistic, mechanistic; and even Socrates, with his novel conception of conscience, could not free himself from the idea of necessity; to him good was inseparable from knowledge and imposed itself upon the will, thus limiting its freedom. Aristotle conceived of the freedom of the will but gave it a bad tendency, a leaning to evil. The Stoics saved freedom by asserting not only the moral liberty but also the ultimate perfectibility of human nature; and Pelagius, whose idea of liberty meant liberty for good, was recognized to have been influenced by the Stoics.

In Christian thought the counterpart of necessity was sin, viewed as a congenital weakness in the soul, an infection of nature, inherited from Adam at the Fall, and involving the entire human race in death. 'As by one man sin entered into

---

[1] The Nestorian.

the world, and death by sin: and so death passed upon all men, in that all have sinned.'[1] This startling, even shattering, condemnation of a whole species through the sin of one, was first pronounced by Saint Paul, for though the older Hebrew literature is full of a consciousness of sin, the closely-knit sequence of the Fall, sin, and death is nowhere else explicitly defined,[2] and not very much notice was taken of this fateful passage in Romans till Alexandrian philosophy with its fascinating speculations about the origin of evil, and the Gnostics and Manichæans with their tempting explanations, forced Christians too to face the subject, and compelled them to make up their minds. Then all sorts of questions were asked, definitions were manufactured, the phrase 'original sin' came into use, and dogma about it was evolved and imposed. Till Pelagius' time, however, there was some freedom of discussion on the subject, and much latitude of thought. Tertullian and Origen, Clement of Alexandria and many of the earlier Greek Fathers, were extremely vague about the sin of Adam, its nature, his own condition before, and that of humanity after it. Chrysostom defended the freedom of the will, and none of the above-named authors would have passed the tests which were ultimately imposed.

When, therefore, Pelagius wrote a series of commentaries, as good Fathers of the Church were expected to do in those days, on the Epistles of Saint Paul, and, against the fateful passage of Romans about the inheritance of sin from Adam and consequent death of the human race, quite casually subjoined that those who objected to the hereditary transmission of sin did not agree with it, that Adam injured posterity by his bad example only and not by heredity, there was no reason why he, or any one else, should expect the tempest which those words were to evoke.

[1] Romans v. 12.
[2] Some sections of Hebrew literature prefer Cain as the parent of human iniquity, and some Eve.

Inherited sin, original sin as it came to be called, is at first sight a gloomy and discouraging idea, but for those who knew how to use it there was a brighter side. As Christianity, in the first century of its freedom, captured the well-to-do classes of the empire, the sin of Adam and the Fall were a very comfortable excuse for those who found the precepts of their new Master somewhat difficult to apply exactly; and baptism and the Atonement[1] were a very useful resource for escaping, by an ingenious pair of miracles, any awkward consequences of moral error. Moral responsibility had in fact been transferred elsewhere. So the wealthy society of the empire, which, like most rich societies, was greedy, selfish, pleasure-loving, lazy and idle, had no need, in adopting Christianity, to face the discomfort of abandoning its customary mode of life in order to follow the stern ascetic precepts of Clement of Alexandria and Tertullian, or to conform to the unattractive bleakness of the early Christian notion of how the faithful ought to live.

Pelagius, simple-minded moralist as he was, asserted boldly, perhaps a little too boldly, that humanity had sole responsibility for its own actions, and liberty of choice between right and wrong; that sin is a failure of the will which, with effort, can be avoided, and is neither incurable nor inevitable. In his simplicity he seems to have hoped that by learning to regard sin in this new and practical light humanity might be induced to commit rather less of it. Over and over again he hammered at this simple and homely precept, that a man, if he chose, could live without sin, not intending thereby an impossible standard of stainless perfection or any extremity of sainthood; merely that by a very

[1] This is no place to discuss in full the doctrine of the Atonement. The idea in its complete development is scholastic and mediæval (Anselm), the word is of the Reformation. A world of literature has been written on the subject. The word is used here, for convenience to cover δικαιοσύνη, καταλλαγή, σωτηρία: i.e. the effects for man of the Crucifixion: justification, reconciliation, salvation.

little effort a life of respectability and rectitude was not beyond the reach of the ordinary man.

The idea was an uncomfortable one, and inherently dull, tending to no exercise of wit, to no philosophical discussion; for it was ethical, and ethics, whether theoretic or practical, do not enliven conversation in society. Ethics, in fact, at that time, in the Christian world at any rate, were somewhat in eclipse. Their natural and excusable unpopularity had been intensified by the competition of far more interesting themes, carrying, so to speak, full religious value. The need, in that first age of her liberty, for defining her beliefs had led the Church into the mazes of controversy, and as Christianity spread among the cultured classes, trained as they were in the schools to dialectic, rhetoric, and the joys of sophistical argument and analysis, mere homespun ethics were fading out of sight and out of mind. By the end of the fourth century, after several decades of ecclesiastical liberty and prosperity, interrupted only by the spasmodic discouragements of Julian's reign, Christian society had become on the whole very much like other societies; while it had all the advantages of being able to plead an inevitable, inherited tendency to sin in order to excuse its irregularities.

Pelagius lived a long time in Rome, at the turn of the fourth and fifth centuries, and had a large circle of friends, many of them among the wealthiest families, where his precepts no doubt were needed. The wealth of the great senatorial families was enormous; they could lose their palaces[1] and estates in Italy and Rome, when the Goths sacked them, and retire to other vast properties in Sicily and Africa and remain nearly as rich and quite as silly as before their troubles began. Saint Jerome and Ammianus Marcellinus, two writers of different creeds but very similar in their censoriousness, have left us vivid pictures, with the puritan's

---

[1] The palace of Pinianus and Melania the younger covered most of the site now occupied by gardens inside the Lateran Gate. See pp. 66, 217.

exaggeration perhaps, of the gay life of Rome at that time. The young girls minced about the streets in transparent dresses, swaying their hips like dancers or mannequins, the young men wore embroidered shoes, the steps of the palaces were powdered with gold dust, and pious widows went abroad carried by eunuchs in litters, wearing dresses with scenes from the life and death of Christ embroidered upon them in gold thread. And there were the secret love-affairs, the corrupt duennas, the back-stairs priests, curled and scented, following the old pagan track of the sycophant and parasite to the tables and boudoirs of the great houses, flattering the wealthy widow, haunting the promising death-bed, for the pickings to be gathered in the name of holy charity and alms.[1] And there were little rites and ceremonies of an older date, that good conservative Romans, with their natural gift for acquiring new religions without abandoning previous ones, could not give up even when they were Christians. Little lamps were still lit nightly at the doors under pretext of lighting the entrance; and ladies unblest with children might still sit in secret on an emblem consecrated for the remedy of that sad state by a long line of respectable but not at all prudish ancestors. To these people Christianity brought the novelty of fresh religious observances and activities, but not necessarily a change in their habits and amusements. To a person from Britain, a remote and very rural province, the Roman nobles and their ways must have seemed very voluptuous, very Italian, very strange; he must have thought that the sin of Adam and the consequent escape from individual responsibility were making life altogether too easy for them.

There were many well-meaning, excellent persons to whom the teaching of Pelagius made a profound appeal. But, as often, simplicity was mocked, deluded by a false

[1] There is a law of 370 against bequests to the clergy; *Codex Theodosianus*, XVI.

light: theologically it was all wrong. An eminent Roman Catholic,[1] who has on the whole been lenient to Pelagius, contemptuously calls his teaching 'conventional popular morality devoid of religious quality', admitting, not very wisely perhaps, a contrast between the two. And indeed, if a man by his own exertions, by the light of his own better nature, is to save himself, what becomes of religion in an ecclesiastical sense, of the Church as the sole dispenser of grace and the means of salvation? And where is there room for the doctrine of the Atonement, necessitated by original sin and the Fall?

Indeed, there is no room for them at all, and Pelagius, caring all for ethics and nothing at all for theology, never saw the implications of his own beliefs. He seems never to have thought of testing their consistency with the doctrinal system to which he was bound. That unity which, in the first century of her liberty, the Church was bound to seek, meant not only the resolving of all controversies but complete spiritual control of the individual, the surrender of his conscience and his soul to her authority and discipline, in return for which she gave him salvation, which she alone could dispense by means of grace; and the teaching of Pelagius that a man's better nature could achieve his salvation struck at the foundations on which Church authority was to be built.

In the conflict which ensued the balance was so even, the appeal of the point of view of Pelagius to large numbers of the better sort of men and women was so strong, that it was by accident only that he did not prevail. Had he succeeded, morality in religion would have had ascendancy over theology, and the history of Christendom would have worn a different, if also a duller, face. Europe might have been a scene of mild and reasonable Gospel piety, and its church, if one can imagine Europe in any age without the Church of

[1] L. Duchesne, *Early History of the Church.*

[149]

Rome, would have been of a broad or low Anglican type. There would have been less drama, less tragedy and comedy, less purple and scarlet, perhaps less blood and fewer fires.

The accident that prevented all this was Saint Augustine. It happened that at the moment when Pelagius began to capture men's minds and to rouse their dormant conscience, Augustine, emerging triumphant from the Donatist struggle which had raged in Africa, was beginning to acquire a reputation as a leader in the Latin Church. His own personal experience had led him to two very clear convictions, both hostile to moral responsibility and free will. The sudden termination of a somewhat disordered early life by a violent spiritual call naturally disposed him to conceive of sin as something inescapable, and of salvation as obtainable only by grace, through the intermediary of the Church, unrelated to any personal effort or merit; and in the struggle with the Donatists he had learned to set the need for unity and discipline in the Church above all things. His views, on each important point, were therefore diametrically opposed to those of Pelagius. The clash between them was quite unlike the old sophistical word-battles, such as that between Catholics and Arians, between Homoousians and their almost homonymous competitors the Homoiousians. These had been attempts to define the nature of God; the difference between Pelagius and Augustine was upon a more interesting and intimate matter, the nature of man; and the impact was tremendous.

Augustine had not always been so passionately hostile to free will. In earlier days, before he encountered Pelagius, he had been able to discuss it without acrimony, had in fact written a book *On the Freedom of the Will*,[1] which, though its approach to the subject was rather different from the subsequent controversy, did not altogether fit in with his later attitude. A certain freedom in the will was admitted, but

[1] See p. 172.

with an evil tendency, derived perhaps from Manichæan influences in Augustine's early life.

In the ensuing conflict Pelagius never took the offensive;
he had neither inclination nor talent for polemics. When the
storm broke he seems to have been rather puzzled as to what
it was all about, and why he had occasioned so much rage.
He had no dialectical training, and could not be swept into
the usual battle of words. He stuck to his point, reiterating
it with a pertinacity that amounted to obstinacy, and certainly
to monotony, and with an imperturbability that drove
Augustine's fiery African temperament to polemical par-
oxysms. Gathering momentum as his ideas developed,
Augustine hurled himself against Pelagius with all the
rhetorical and forensic thunder at his command, with all
the force and speed of his voluble pen, and all the organization he could improvise. He was the first among churchmen
to see that the fabric of the Church depended on the three
cardinal points, the Fall, the Atonement, and the necessity
for grace, and that to attack them was to threaten her
security: as for the converse of this position, that to defend
them is to attack human nature, he had no misgivings—preferred, indeed, that it should be attacked.

To many of their contemporaries Augustine's ideas were
as novel as those of Pelagius; he was met in many highly
respectable quarters with doubts and questionings. Even
Chrysostom had said that grace does not affect man's freedom of choice. There were numbers of great churchmen
who saw no particular danger in the teaching of Pelagius;
and two great Popes, Damasus and Innocent I, who knew
Pelagius personally, thought him a most estimable person.

Pelagius was defeated, but Augustine's victory, if it
sufficed for his time, was not complete; he did not succeed
in making the Church accept the whole of his system. He
began with original sin and its medicine, grace, the Pauline
doctrine of grace, not too explicitly defined, but familiar to

everybody; but as the struggle developed he arrived at what
was subsequently called the Augustinian theory of grace,
something arbitrarily bestowed or withheld independently
of a man's moral quality or merit. This led him further to
something which the early Church and many of the later
Churches, including that of Rome, have never been induced
to accept, Predestination or Election, a piece of nightmare
fatalism, logically defensible but intolerable, in its truly
hideous implications, to ordinary human sensibilities. 'The
Church has followed Augustine as to the necessity for grace
and the original lapse, but . . . it has been necessary to
abandon more than one detail of his line of argument and
even of his teaching',[1] writes an eminent Roman Catholic
historian; and certainly, by keeping such parts of his system
as were useful and rejecting the rest, the Church, with her
astute and competent eclecticism, found an instrument very
apt for her purposes.

Augustine and Pelagius had a further, very awkward
difference, as to what they meant by sin and grace, and used
the words, each of them, with perfectly different meanings.
Indeed, regarding sin they never even found out that they
meant two quite different things. To Augustine sin came
to mean only concupiscence, and in his anti-Pelagian
polemics there is little other meaning to be attached to the
word. Sins of the flesh, and the disorders of conduct into
which they lead a man, had plagued him through the
whole of his early life until his conversion. When the shock
of that ultimate revulsion overwhelmed him he was seized
with an agonized disgust from which even marriage and
conjugal love were not excluded. To him original sin
became the sin of the flesh (in the singular), the act by
which every human being must start his journey into life;
and though the legal sanction and ecclesiastical sacrament
of marriage might diminish the guilt of that act as far as the

[1] Duchesne, *Early History of the Church*.

parents were concerned, it must pass unabated upon their offspring, upon every little boy and girl born into this world alive. It was, in the words of the Articles of the Church of England in one of their more Augustinian moments, an infection of nature, a fault or corruption in every man, deserving God's wrath and damnation; and no individual could by any efforts of his own extricate himself from it. Only by grace preventing, that is to say by a mysterious force from above, could the stain be neutralized and the individual be admitted to the path which may lead eventually to salvation. This idea of sin[1] was very well adapted to Augustine's own personal experience, in which there were objections to having to postulate sole individual responsibility. He must be credited here with some exaggeration of his own moral obliquity; for, setting apart one or two incidents which disturb a modern conscience more than they did his,[2] there was probably very little in his early career that was not common among the generality of well-to-do young gentlemen in African or other society of his time. But, in the light of his conversion, grace seemed the only means to salvation in which he could permit himself to believe.

Pelagius' idea of sin was far wider; it included concupiscence of course, but embraced all the common, everyday faults and misdeeds, lying, cheating, swearing, jealousy, unkindness, greed, and hate, which, after all, do far more to soil the face of human life in general than sexual errors,

---

[1] Augustine's equation of sin and concupiscence may also have been influenced by his early contact with Manichæanism, in which this is the principal significance of sin.

[2] When Augustine finally decided to marry he cast off, without making any provision for her, a lady who had been devoted to him for many years. Then, finding that his intended bride, the choice of his mother, the sainted Monica, was so young that she would not be marriageable for a couple of years, he took another mistress to fill the gap.

however deplorable. He saw these as separate evil actions, avoidable lapses, failures of will or self-control, for which the individual alone is responsible, not derived from Adam or any one else. He had, perhaps by race, the good fortune to possess a more temperate nature than the fiery African, and we know that he thought the difficulties attendant upon the practice of chastity greatly exaggerated; nor did he share the current view that it could compensate and cover a multitude of other sins.[1]

Of the misunderstanding about grace Augustine at any rate was perfectly aware, and devoted a large part of his attack on Pelagius to demonstrating that Pelagius' idea of it was wrong. What precisely the Church meant by grace then, and even later, is not very easy to detect. Till Augustine's time there was considerable vagueness about it, even a lack of interest, an inclination to leave Saint Paul's references to it, with all their difficulties, unquestioned for the present. Pelagius himself, as he spared no pains to explain, meant by grace neither more nor less than the freedom of the will, and the knowledge of good and evil by which a man can discriminate between right and wrong. Beyond this his imagination, inferior perhaps to Augustine's, could not go; and from his plain ethical standpoint he could neither be shaken nor frightened away.

Pelagius had another opponent, very different from Augustine. Saint Jerome was brought into the struggle, not independently but as a supporter and ally of Augustine, for a quite separate set of reasons all his own, none of them either theological or involving any principle. On their plain merits the views of Pelagius might have appealed to him, and he might even have been hard put to it himself to pass an examination on the subject of grace by Saint Augustine, had such a grotesque contingency ever arisen. He was a scholarly ascetic, by this time of a considerable age, im-

[1] Letter to Demetrias. See p. 197.

mersed in his literary labours and half obscured by the incense of admirers in his retreat at Bethlehem, whither he had escaped from the interruptions of Rome and from the cackling tongues of its scandalmongers. He was drawn into the dispute by the circumstances of three of the most important quarrels of his highly quarrelsome life, with two of which[1] it was possible to connect Pelagius; and the third, with Augustine himself, having recently been patched up, gave Augustine just the opportunity he needed for gaining Jerome's support in token of reconciliation. Alone, Jerome would not have been of much service, for the old lion of Bethlehem, his jealousy and his tempers, were too well known to influence any one very much; and he was too distinguished and too independent to be anybody's cat's-paw, or even lion's-paw. But he was a useful base for attacking Pelagius, who at a later stage resided at Jerusalem, and great caution and circumspection were needed in initiating the attack, for at first Pelagius was not generally suspected; he was so well thought of that outside Africa it was undesirable to attack him by name. Augustine and Jerome, the real aggressors, tried at first to conceal their identity behind certain agents whom they had chosen to play the active parts.

Their choice of intermediaries was not very fortunate. Orosius, a fussy little Spanish monk,[2] and a couple of deposed Gallic bishops, who had been guilty of intriguing with the usurper Constantine in Gaul, made such a mess of their parts as accusers that they obtained the acquittal of Pelagius in two synods, held at their own instigation, in which they were expected to get him condemned and excommunicated. Augustine then saw that the conclusion of the affair rested with himself alone, and he spared no pains to that end. A torrent of anti-Pelagian works was loosed from his pen; synods, principally in Africa, popes, and finally the

[1] See p. 201 et seq.
[2] Author of a History of the World against the Pagans.

emperor, were mobilized, and eventually Pelagianism was condemned and denounced by an imperial decree.

So Pelagianism became a heresy, but it could not die. As Bede says regretfully, two centuries later, 'Augustine and many other orthodox Fathers of the Church have uttered many thousand Catholic sentences against it, nor yet availed to correct it.' It possessed an essential spark of vitality derived from the illogical but irrepressible faith of the human heart in its own intuitive knowledge of good, and of the human intellect in freedom; it also expressed, perhaps, a truly British contempt for authority.

II

When Pelagius is first heard of he was living in Rome, in the years before its capture by Alaric.[1] Every one calls him a monk, an indefinite title at that time; for properly organized monasteries did not yet exist in Italy,[2] and to be a monk was to live withdrawn from wordly concerns under a quite independent self-imposed discipline. Actually Pelagius was never ordained; he was frequently referred to with contempt by subsequent writers, themselves in holy orders, as a mere layman. Of his early life we have scarcely any information; his own books tell us nothing direct. We can only guess from certain characteristics in his behaviour and his books what his early training and education may have been.

His nationality was certainly British. Every one calls him Brito, and Britannus,[3] and there is no reason to attach these very respectable titles to any one but a British person at that time.[4] Within the British Isles there have been rival claims to Pelagius. The Welsh have decided that his real name was

[1] A.D. 410.

[2] There were communities in Egypt and Syria and they were beginning to exist in Gaul. But the majority of the monks lived separately under a self-imposed rule, if any.

[3] Augustine, Orosius, Prosper of Aquitaine, Gennadius, Marius Mercator.

[4] Brittany was called Armorica at that date, and is dismissed as a claimant by Garnier, the Benedictine editor of Pelagius' work, who probably did not wish to saddle that good Catholic country with a heretic.

Morgan,[1] Græcized for ecclesiastical purposes into Pelagius, for both names are connected with the sea; and Welsh tradition has made him abbot over two thousand monks at Bangor and given him a Cambridge education, many centuries before there were colleges at Cambridge and some generations before there can have been any large organized community of monks at Bangor, though there may have been scattered groups of monks in Wales as elsewhere. If Pelagius was born in Wales he must have left it when he was very young, for at that time it could hardly have provided him with the learning and literary training, the Latin and Greek, which he undoubtedly possessed; and if Pelagius was remembered in Wales, his memory, with other remains and traditions of the early British Church, must have taken refuge there during the Saxon invasions.

Saint Jerome, unsparing of insult, calls him 'the dog of Albion', adding that he was more useful with his heels than his teeth,[2] 'that Irishman from a tribe living in the neighbourhood of Britain', and 'an utter blockhead, stuffed up with Irish porridge'.[3] The word used by Jerome is *Scotus*, but we must remember that in his time the Scotch were still in Northern Ireland, not yet, except for casual raids, having crossed the North Channel to the country which they subsequently occupied and christened, and that, whether we call the porridge Irish or Scotch, Jerome certainly meant an

---

[1] Bishop Ussher is partly responsible for preserving this theory in his *Ecclesiastical Antiquities of Britain*. It appears also in the Welsh version of the Thirty-Nine Articles. See Williams, *Christianity in Early Britain*, ch. xiii.

[2] 'Canem *Albinum*', an expression open to debate, has been transformed by scholarship into *Alpinum*, which seems to have no point at all; British dogs were famous in Roman times.

[3] Jerome: Prologue to *Commentary on Jeremiah*, i and iii. 'Scotorum pultibus prægravatus.' Souter casts an 'if' upon the attribution of these epithets to Pelagius. Certainly Rufinus could not be intended, and otherwise it is difficult to see at whom, in the *Commentary on Jeremiah*, these epithets could be aimed.

inhabitant of Ulster. What these Ulstermen, or Scotch, or their Irish (subsequently Scotch) porridge had done to Jerome to provoke abuse, we have not been told. He was offensive about the Irish long before he knew Pelagius, and whether Pelagius was really Irish, or merely vaguely British, Jerome, when he used the word *Scotus*, meant it as an insult. Jerome cherished some curious notions of the Irish and their habits, of the Attacotti especially, a northern Irish tribe who settled later in the Lowlands of Scotland. The British, he believed, had wives and children in common (though he admits that in this they were no worse than the people in Plato's *Republic*); and he had been told in Gaul by some one living in Britain that the Attacotti were cannibals, that they ate their dead fathers as an act of reverence, and also ate portions cut from living men and women.[1] Jerome's authority, whoever he was, must have read Strabo's *Geography*, a book already at that time nearly four hundred years old, in which these distressing allegations are brought against the Irish in general. The community of wives may have been borrowed by Strabo from Cæsar, who applies it to Britain, as a kind of polyandry; wives, he says, were shared among brothers, or between fathers and sons. But Cæsar's information, derived from his spy, an Atrebate of Southern Britain, included under a veneer of scientific solemnity some fantastic tales such as that the British would not eat chickens, geese, or hares, so perhaps the Atrebate was a trifle irresponsible. Four hundred years divide Cæsar and Strabo from Jerome; and Theodosius found the Attacotti capable of such admirable discipline that he used a cohort of them for garrison work abroad. Even Saint Chrysostom, who had also read Strabo, including the piece about the cannibals, admitted that such practices among the British were done with long ago, having given place to holy Christian fasting from sustenance of any kind. In the four centuries since Cæsar's landing, Britain,

[1] Jerome, Ep. ix, *Contra Jovin*: ii, 7.

[159]

having little else to do, had become very civilized, whatever strange practices may have lingered upon her Scotch and Irish fringes.

Pelagius may very well have been Irish, and Jerome perfectly accurate, if also rude. There were Christians in Ireland before Saint Patrick went there, as Jerome knew,[1] and the Irish themselves regarded their Church as of great antiquity and cherished a tradition that an Irishman had been present at the Crucifixion and brought home to Ireland the religion to which he was converted at that great event. Though there is no contemporary record of the story, it is not impossible, for the Irish no doubt enlisted in the Roman forces like everybody else, and might be posted for service in the East. We shall see that Pelagius was affectionately remembered in Ireland through many centuries, and that, after the Roman evacuation of Britain, Ireland became a principal repository of Pelagian literature.

If Pelagius were indeed an Irishman, others, it has been suggested, beside Jerome would have enjoyed being opprobrious by calling him *Scotus* or even *Hibernus*, or a barbarian, at any rate; instead, they are unanimous in calling him British, apparently without intended insult. To save his Irish nationality for those who prefer it, the suggestion has been made that he came of one of those Irish tribes who settled in southwestern Britain early in the fourth century,[2] and adopted the Roman-British civilization.[3] Thus Pelagius could be both Irish and British, brought up in the refinements of Roman-British culture and in the teaching of the Church. He would know Latin, and perhaps Greek, and would be within reach of continental currents of thought.

But it is useless at any time, from the fourth century to our own, to argue about the precise nationality of any British

[1] Ep. CXXXIII to Ctesiphon.
[2] Saint Patrick belonged to one of these.
[3] J. B. Bury, *Origin of Pelagius* in *Life of Saint Patrick.*

person. Then, as now, the Irish, Welsh, and Scotch were just as likely to be found in any other part of the British Isles as in their own; and the term British serves well enough, apart from individual local susceptibilities, to cover them all. From whatever corner of these islands Pelagius came, he had all the qualities and characteristics which we are accustomed to call British to-day; indeed, it is difficult, at times, not to call him English in the sense in which that name is often used to cover our composite, far from pure-bred race. To talk of an Englishman in England before the Saxon invasion is not really an anachronism. In France, long before the Franks crossed the Rhine, there were Frenchmen, complete with the qualities that are most recognizably French, in Aquitaine, Auvergne and Provence, in the world of Ausonius, of Sidonius Apollinaris, and the Roman-Gallic churchmen. When the Franks arrived upon the soil of France, in the hands of the Gallic bishops equipped with Roman culture, they were turned into excellent Frenchmen. National character, whatever ethnologists may say, seems profoundly influenced by local conditions, sunshine and rainfall, altitude, soil and subsoil, hard or soft water; for a man's food is the product of all these. Certainly the Saxons, Angles, Jutes and the rest of them were not English when they left the continent; something altered them when they had settled here, not perhaps the Roman-British civilization, of which they made something of a mess, but the climate, the landscape, the moist and balmy airs, and no doubt the food, the roast fat mutton whose emollient savour hangs, and must always have hung, about the majority of British dwellings. Something very English was certainly here before them, if only Pelagius, a most representative Englishman, innocent though he must have been of any drop of Teutonic blood.[1]

[1] He has also been claimed by East Anglians, and their descendants, the New Englanders: but Pelagius' spiritual progeny are innumerable, and no doubt were to be found on the *Mayflower*.

Whatever his geographical origin, Pelagius must have come of a well-to-do family, for he had had an excellent education, and there is nothing barbarous or uncouth about his mental equipment or his style. Orosius[1] says that he was of a too humble origin to have had any education, but this must be nonsense unless we are to believe that Pelagius had almost supernatural powers of acquisition in later life. He wrote a beautiful Latin, straightforward, concise and clear, unmarred by any provincialisms or debased forms, and un-encumbered by those florid rhetorical ornaments that were the passion of his age. Jerome found the excellence of his Latin somewhat galling; it was worthy, he said, of one born on a better soil. Greek Pelagius knew also, for as we shall find later at his trials in Palestine, in which the proceedings were conducted in Greek, it was accounted to him as an advantage by his accusers, who were Latins, that he under-stood Greek while they did not. He knew the Latin poets well and some of them, perhaps, by heart. There are echoes, in his books, of Virgil and Horace, of Juvenal and Ovid, used, not as formal quotations, but as people now use tags of the Bible and Shakespeare as accepted means of expres-sion, too familiar to need quotation-marks or explanation. He knew Lucretius too, but disapproved, as would be ex-pected, of his scientific notions, for the strict causality of Lucretius could hardly appeal to an advocate of free will. Twice in his Commentary on Saint Paul's Epistles he quotes Lucretius, derisively, to endorse the Apostle's contempt of philosophers.[2]

Christian literature Pelagius read of course; he quotes the Bible freely, in the old Latin version,[3] which must have reached Britain before his time and continued in use till

[1] *Apologeticus.*
[2] Lucretius, i, 149 and 205, 'Rem nullam e nihilo gigni divinitus unquam', and 'nil igitur fieri e nilo posse fatendum est'.
[3] The predecessor of Jerome's Vulgate.

Augustine of Canterbury modernized and continentalized the British Church in the sixth century. He had read Chrysostom and Origen and knew the work of his contemporaries, Augustine of Hippo, Jerome, and Theodore of Mopsuestia who was regarded as the originator of his heresies.

Pelagius' Latin style, as direct and plain as Cæsar's, provides a hint, if only a negative one, of the place of his education. We can only say for certain that he was not reared in one of the great schools of rhetoric, which had such a baleful effect upon the Christian literature of his time. Somewhere he had learned to write Latin without the florid ornament, the tedious repetition, that mar the work of nearly all the Fathers. The Fathers were not entirely to blame for this; their literary style was inevitably acquired in the pagan schools in which they had no choice but to receive their education. Latin literature had died, at last, of a surfeit of words, and the strange thing was that Christian literature flourished and grew fat upon them, finding in them a vitalizing sustenance through infancy, youth, and, indeed, maturity. The Fathers were dazzled by words, lost in them, and their writings are a grim testimony to what rhetoric did to the Church in its early ages. The tradition has never been broken. Always Christian divines go back to patristic literature for their pattern and their inspiration; its sound, like the echoes in an empty cowrie shell, booms for ever in their ears. Ambrose, Augustine, Gregory, Jerome, Basil, Chrysostom, themselves the ripest fruit of the rhetorical age, formed the minds and the style of the Latin divines and doctors; and the pulpits of the Roman Catholic and the Reformed Churches alike are the direct descendants of the professorial chairs of rhetoric at Athens, Antioch and Alexandria, Milan, Lyons and Bordeaux, and other universities of that last age of the ancient world.

If Pelagius stands, almost alone, outside the tradition, we

must conclude that he was educated in Britain, where the Latin classics were read and admired, and where perhaps taste was not yet perverted by rhetoric. Tacitus says that among the alluring vices which Agricola cunningly taught the British in order to weaken them, they began to aspire to rhetoric; but perhaps they only aspired and the rhetorical tradition did not sink very deep. The Roman-British civilization had a considerable knowledge of classical Latin letters, and Latin was at least understood by nearly everybody. Martial, in the first century, boasted that he was read in Britain, and Latin poetry must have been well known through many classes of society, for even bricklayers knew their Virgil.[1] A Greek teacher, Demetrius of Tarsus, found employment in Britain about the year 80, and Juvenal records a project for installing a professor of literature in remote Thule. Great readers the British certainly were, as Jerome told Fabiola,[2] one of his most devoted female admirers; and a little later Fastidius, a British bishop,[3] wrote to a pious British widow that it is the duty of a virtuous lady when not engaged in good works to be found always with a book in her hand.

Pelagius, like Plato, hated rhetoric. In his commentary he goes out of his way to gibe at the rhetoricians. To '*I will destroy the wisdom of the wise*' Pelagius annotates 'he rebukes philosophy and the rhetorical art'. Pelagius might have fared better had he despised rhetoric less, for in the storm of words that broke upon him his adversaries could

---

[1] A brick was found at Silchester (now in the Reading Museum) with a tag from Virgil scratched upon it: '*conticuere omnes*'.

[2] Ep. IX.

[3] Suspected by moderns of Pelagian tendencies for advocating, rather more definitely than he should, mankind's capacity for moral improvement. For the bookishness of the British see Probert, *Laws of Cambria*. The Welsh triads, which go back to British traditions, expect heads of families to be provided with a book, a tutor, and a harp. See Williams, *Early Christianity in Britain*, ch. xii.

not believe in his inability to play a game that every one was supposed to know, and ascribed his deficiency to guile.

It has been suggested[1] that Pelagius left Britain owing to a quarrel with his parents. For this there is internal support in his writings, in some rather unfilial observations. *'Children, obey your parents,'* he annotates 'obedience is good, but only if rational; to *'Parents, provoke not your children to wrath'*,[2] he subjoins 'lest by beating them to excess or unreasonably, you teach them to be ill-tempered'. And *'Honour thy father and thy mother,'*[3] he qualifies with 'that is to say, if they are good parents'. He has, however, something kind to say on occasion about parental affection, and it may be needless to read into these remarks anything more than a feeling that parental authority in the Roman world was excessive, and sometimes abused.

According to several accounts, all of them from the pens of his enemies, Pelagius was gentle and silent until roused, a big massive man, with broad shoulders, a red face, black hair and beard, and a thick neck. Orosius, himself an excitable, fussy person, who was made to look rather foolish, and probably to feel very small, at the first trial at Jerusalem, half in admiration, half in fury, calls him a huge towering Goliath[4] with a great fat face, adding at the same time that he was handsomely dressed, and his general appearance stately. He insists repeatedly on Pelagius' massive figure and great height. Elsewhere he tells us that Pelagius was no ascetic, that he went to banquets, took baths, and that he tolerated remarriage to the eighth time (like the Wife of Bath), and accepted the repentance of fornicators. Jerome also calls him huge and corpulent, as indeed the remark about

[1] Professor A. Souter, in the *Expositor*, 1915, *Pelagius' Doctrine in relation to his Early Life*.
[2] Eph. v. 14.
[3] Eph. vi. 2.
[4] Apolog., ch. 27 and elsewhere: Goliath is a frequent epithet.

the porridge implies, but Pelagius is not alone among churchmen in the possession of a portly figure. Ecclesiastics are not uncommonly rotund, and one of the most eminent and admirable churchmen that ever lived, Saint Thomas Aquinas, had a piece of his refectory table cut out to accommodate the majesty of his person.

So Pelagius was no great advocate of asceticism. Like Saint Basil[1] he disliked extremes of asceticism and mistrusted the results of hysterical, and perhaps unsuccessful, mortification. 'The body should be tamed, not broken,' he wrote to Demetrias, a young lady about to become a nun;[2] and he adds a warning against the common fate of those who have attempted too much asceticism and have sunk beneath the burden of what they could not perform. It is remarkable that Basil and Pelagius, two original and extremely independent minds who probably had never heard of one another, should upon this subject have held identical views in contradiction to those of nearly all their contemporaries.

Pelagius was retiring and reticent. He preferred writing to speaking, Jerome says, adding that this was because he was sly and preferred to teach his heresies in private and to employ others to speak for him in public in order that they, and not he, might incur the blame for his heretical teaching. Jerome also says that when he was obliged to speak before an audience Pelagius was diffident and hesitating, and made out that he was readier to learn than to teach. Like many Englishmen Pelagius did not show to advantage in public, and had no gift for speaking. If silent, however, according to Augustine he was also keen and swift in mind. He could, on occasion, make a sharp, even rude retort: when he was asked at the synod at Jerusalem whether he really held the

---

[1] Basil evolved his system of community rule, the forerunner of the monastic system of the Greek Church, as a remedy for the wild and disorderly lives of the ascetics. See pp. 276–7.
[2] Letter to Demetrias.

opinions which Augustine had condemned, he ignored the question and snapped back, 'What is Augustine to me?'—a pardonable but injudicious retort. But he was already a man harassed and persecuted, with his tormentors yapping round him, and in the forefront[1] the snarling, frantic little Orosius, who was enough to exasperate anybody, quoting Augustine to back himself up and give himself an importance which he could not otherwise claim. On another occasion, at Lydda in the second synod, Pelagius made an admirable, if brusque, answer to a particularly silly question. A quotation from a book he had not written, torn from its context, was brought up against him and he was asked to condemn it. 'People who say such things I condemn as fools, not as heretics,' he said, 'for there is no doctrine in the matter.' Normally he was very tranquil, very calm, very polite, and very exasperating to his excited persecutors.

Of his character only the best is recorded, and that by our sole sources, his enemies. He was pious and chaste, Augustine says, a good and praiseworthy man, who had made great progress in spiritual life; and if a man is to be persecuted and denounced it is surely inconvenient to be able to find nothing to his personal discredit. The gossips of Rome would certainly have made the most, as they did in the case of Jerome, of anything derogatory that could be discovered about him; but nothing was ever recorded against his private morals or way of life, and his personal excellence was a strong influence in support of his teaching.

[1] Orosius contrived to make even the patient John of Jerusalem rude to him.

III

Pelagius lived a long time in Rome, how long we cannot exactly estimate. He must have been there before 384, for he was a friend of Pope Damasus who died that year, and he left Rome about 409 in the general exodus before the Goths, by that time at least a middle-aged man. He was therefore in the capital of the empire through some of the wildest and most eventful years it had ever seen; and the studious and contemplative life he seems to have led is an indication of the extent to which Rome had become a political backwater since Valentinian I made Milan his capital in 365. There is nothing in the writings of Pelagius or his Roman contemporaries, whether pagan or Christian, to indicate the storms that were being lived through, or that were impending. That curiously petty world in the old capital, where a forgotten senate still met and consuls still gave fabulously costly games, was as remote from the tragedy of the tottering empire as the society depicted in Jane Austen's novels from the Napoleonic wars. After their victory at Hadrianople in 378 the Goths should have been hard to overlook, and from the accession of Theodosius to the sack of Rome there was every kind of excursion and alarum. Emperors were murdered, usurpers of remarkable pertinacity arose, and with great difficulty were made to fall. The Gothic menace steadily grew, and at the death of Theodosius only Stilicho was left to uphold the empire, not only against the Goths but against treachery and intrigue; and by 408 Stilicho, too, was murdered.

In those years strange transformations had crept over the Church. The Priscillianists, a rather unexplained sect of ascetics in Spain and Gaul, had been repressed and persecuted. Their leader, Priscillian,[1] had been executed in 385 by the order of Maximus the usurper of Britain and Gaul, the first Roman ruler to shed blood in order to enforce orthodoxy; and in the east Theodosius had issued edict after edict to repress heresies, in the hope of obtaining unanimity among the Christians. Probably neither Theodosius nor Maximus ever thought that they were establishing a precedent which was to have an endless chain of consequences, a dire effect upon the world. Their object was immediate unity and an abatement of the clamours of jarring ecclesiastics, which should not have place in a world threatened by grave external dangers. But when the empire was a thing of the past and the Goths forgotten, the principle they had established was to remain. Disputes which hitherto had been sustained in perfect liberty of verbal argument had entered the jurisdiction of the civil legislature. The step was a momentous one, and the Church, at first, was a little aghast at the weapon that had been brought into action, and was not in a hurry to employ it, perceiving perhaps that it might recoil upon her own head and draw blood where least intended.

None of the protagonists in the Pelagian controversy seem to have been involved in these political developments, or at all concerned about them at the time, though the interference of the emperors in ecclesiastical matters proved much to the point for Augustine's purposes in later years.

[1] Priscillian was a Spaniard. His sect had some curious practices, such as fasting on Sundays, and secret meetings; and there were the usual rumours about their relations with women. They produced something like a schism in Spain, and their principal opponent, Ithacius, bishop of Ossonova, fled to Gaul and raised the Gallic bishops against them, with the exception of Saint Martin of Tours.

In 381, a couple of years before Gratian's murder, Saint Jerome came to Rome, having left his first Syrian retreat through an unpleasantness with the other monks there. He was a kind of secretary to Pope Damasus, who loved learning and commissioned several of his greatest works, including the new Latin version of the Bible,[1] which was to be based on a collation of the Greek and Hebrew texts. His learned labours were sweetened by friendships with the great ladies, among whom were several widows who could dispose of their own fortunes, which were enormous, and their own way of life. There was Albina who conducted a kind of ascetic female community in her palace on the Aventine, and her daughter Marcella, both of them widows of rank, Fabiola of the Fabii, Asella, Lea, and Jerome's most intimate friend Paula, widow of the senator Toxotius who could trace descent from both Æneas and Agamemnon, and her daughters Blesilla and Eustochium. There was great activity in letter writing, for it was a time when people wrote immense elaborate letters, treatises almost, to near neighbours who lived perhaps round the next corner. Jerome's intimacy with these ladies, combined with offensiveness to the rest of Rome, for he loved to scold and to lecture, made him unpopular; the usual things were said about his relations with his widows,[2] especially with Paula, whom he called the mother-in-law of God because her daughter Blesilla, a young widow, had taken a vow of chastity, and was thus, in the language of the Church, a bride of Christ. Paula, a great Christian scholar has said, was the ideal sheep who would put up with anything in the way of a shepherd's holy liberties,[3] There were also disputes, by word as well as with the pen, so exacerbated that Jerome and his opponents spat in one another's faces. When Damasus died in Decem-

[1] The Vulgate.
[2] Jerome, Ep. XLV.
[3] Duchesne, *Early History of the Christian Church*, vol. ii, p. 382.

ber 384 Jerome seems to have had expectations that he would succeed to the papal throne, but he was too unpopular. Siricius, a deacon of Liberius, the previous Pope, was very speedily elected by popular acclamation, with the object no doubt of avoiding a repetition of the schism which had disgraced the accession of Damasus, and Jerome felt that there was no room for him in Rome any more. He was finally hunted from the capital by the spiteful tongues of society, unbridled now by the death of Damasus, and roused to fury by the death of Paula's daughter Blesilla who succumbed to the rigours of the ascetic discipline to which Jerome had encouraged her, within a few months of her retirement from the world. Jerome, with a temper permanently spoiled, returned to the freedom of the Eastern deserts, and eventually to Bethlehem; not alone, for Paula and her surviving daughter Eustochium soon followed him, to be principal ornaments of the admiring community which entrenched itself around him there.

Jerome and Pelagius may not have met during those years in Rome, but they must at least have heard of one another. Pelagius knew of Jerome's work, and Jerome, as Damasus' secretary or friend, must have known something of Pelagius, and that Damasus regarded him with favour.

Between the years 380 and 385 young Augustine of Hippo was also in Rome. He was not yet a Christian, being still under the influence of the Manichæans who had captured his youthful fancy at home in Africa; and as a reflective, intellectually serious person, if not of very strict personal habits, he was repelled by the religious manifestations, both pagan and Christian, in the capital, and turned his back on temples and churches alike. Law and rhetoric, in which he had been trained, were his interests; he opened a small school, but got into difficulties because he found the students most assiduous till the day came when the fees were due, when the class decamped to sit at the feet of another teacher till pay-day should arrive in that class-room also. Not moving in Christian circles, Augustine probably did not meet Pelagius, and finding Rome disappointing in every way, he availed himself of the recommendation of the great senator Symmachus, one of the remaining pagan magnates in Rome, to a readership in rhetoric which happened to fall vacant at Milan. There a destiny very different from that of a provincial professor awaited him, and he was baptized by the great Ambrose in 387.

A year or two later he was in Rome again, for about a year, after the death of his mother Monica, whom he had intended to accompany back to Africa; and in Rome he must have encountered some discussion about free will, for about this time he wrote his book on the *Freedom of the Will*,[1] the very subject on which he was to fall out with Pelagius later; but there is still no indication of any meeting between the two men. The book seems to have no bearing upon Pelagius, or upon the later controversy. Pelagius at this stage, like Augustine, was an obscure person; his views were probably scarcely developed, or unknown beyond an intimate circle. But the book shows that free will was an open subject that could be discussed without a storm. It is a good book, one of Augustine's more philosophical and less rhetorical works; it is also by no means a favourite and is little read, partly, perhaps, for the awkwardness of its title, and partly owing to the greater popularity of his more emotional writings. In it Augustine takes the freedom of the will for granted, assumes that it has an evil tendency, and discusses it in relation to the nature of God. Why does God, who knows all, permit evil, and allow to man the freedom to err? The answer is unsatisfactory. Divine foreknowledge does not imply control; evil actions are foreseen by God, but not prevented, and so Divine prescience does not limit the freedom of the will. In this dual conception of the universe are

[1] *De Libero Arbitrio.*

lingerings of Augustine's old Manichæanism; but he does
not really care about the answer, for he is not interested in
freedom. 'Even God himself is not free'; being incapable of
evil, he too is subject to necessity.

In 388 Augustine was back in Africa, and there set out
upon that swift, almost headlong personal development from
an ardent, loquacious, but obscure convert to the vigilant,
implacable champion of Catholic unity, the tireless, ruthless
defender of ecclesiastical authority. Circumstances awaited
him in Africa which, though they must have been in evidence
in his unconverted days, struck him now with something
like a shock. The Donatist schism had divided Africa for
more than half a century. It was a purely African affair, un-
interesting in its origins to the rest of the world; for it
involved neither dogma nor principle, and had neither
spiritual nor intellectual significance of any kind. It had
begun, at Carthage, in a sordid squabble about the election
of a bishop, and over some buried treasure, the alleged property of the Church. Cæcilian, the bishop whose election
was in dispute, rashly reprimanded Lucilla, a wealthy lady of
his congregation, for the rather unpleasing extravagances
of her devotions, which included kissing the lips of the corpse
of a dead martyr. There was some give-and-take about live
bishops and dead martyrs, and Lucilla set herself to lead the
revolt against Cæcilian. She and her friends elected a bishop
of their own, who was succeeded by Donatus, after whom
the schism was named. The dispute seemed to gather to
itself all the petty rivalries of Africa; politics came into it,
and some class-feeling. Down-trodden and oppressed people
of every sort, of whom there were plenty in Africa, joined
the Donatists; and a party, for it was a party rather than a
sect, called the Circumcellions, consisting of runaway slaves,
dispossessed peasants, renegade monks, and ecclesiastics who
had been disgraced or deprived by ecclesiastical discipline,
went about righting wrongs by clubbing, seeking martyr-

dom and murdering those who denied it to them. There were also Rabelaisian practical jokes, raids and incendiarism and riots, comparable in character, though not in scale, to the Peasants' War which followed upon Luther's defiance of the Papacy. Towards the close of the fourth century the African Church was seriously divided and it was the Donatists, the schismatics, who could claim the larger party. To this scene of disorder Augustine returned from Italy with his conversion fresh upon him; and the disgust it inspired in him must excuse to some extent his subsequent harsh intolerance of any divisions within the Church. He was no doubt right in deciding that this sordid manifestation of indiscipline and contention must be terminated; and if he was to take sides he was right to take that of the orthodox Church party against the Donatists, for whom there is really nothing to be said. But the struggle had upon him, and, through his influence, upon the Church in after ages, disastrous effects. At first, with the Donatists in the majority, he advocated tolerance and persuasion, but as the contest progressed he was turned into an embittered, implacable advocate of persecution for all who would not submit to the authority of the Church. Contention seemed to evoke in him that dark frenzy, that black fire which, in the Africans of that time, seemed ready always to blaze forth when the atmosphere favoured it. In his horror of the Donatists he learned to regard all heresy as of equal vileness; to rate submission to ecclesiastical authority before all else, above individual conscience and above morals. He once said that virginity among Donatists was no better than fornication, and that the debauches of the faithful were better than the fasts of the heretics.

The scenes which eventually attended the defeat of the Donatists achieved a hideousness and savagery out of all proportion to the schism, sordid and petty as it really was. In 414 Honorius deprived the Donatists of all civil rights and banished their clergy, and further repressive edicts followed. Deprived of everything in this world they decided to try the next, in which they could hardly fare worse. They took to wholesale suicide, threw themselves over cliffs, and rushed about demanding martyrdom from their persecutors and, indeed, receiving it. Augustine, to a friend's remonstrances, replied that these ghastly spectacles did not move him, for it was better that a few should perish who were in any case condemned to eternal fire than that all should be damned for want of coercion.[1] It is the idea of coercion here that is new. The civil authority had interfered in religious matters, on occasion, for the sake of peace and unity, with decrees against classes of persons; but that a churchman should advocate that the faith should be kept pure, that it should be defended, by cruelty, was new. It is to this side of Augustine that churchmen looked back in after ages to reassure themselves in moments of natural hesitation when they piled high the faggots and heated the irons red for the greater glory of God.

Most unfortunate was it for Pelagius that the innocuous commonplaces of his moral teaching should have been brought before Augustine at the height of his struggle with the Donatists. The two movements were worlds apart; no mood provoked by the wild but uninspired Donatists could possibly be relevant in estimating the value of what Pelagius was trying to say. To Augustine Pelagius was but one more manifestation of the plague of heresy, breaking out just as it seemed to be in a fair way to extinction. It is difficult, at this distance of time, to forgive Augustine, and it was impossible at the time for Pelagius and many others to understand the rancour and vindictiveness which inspired Augustine's attack.

[1] Ep. CCIV.

[175]

*   IV   *

Pelagius' early works, all on religious subjects, seem
to have been innocuous on the whole, if also rather
insignificant. They established his reputation as a
worthy, learned man, but, except for a few sentences preserved by Augustine for purposes of denunciation, they have
failed to survive. He wrote a very orthodox book[1] about
the Trinity, for the Catholics and Arians had but recently
had another bout with one another in the persons of the
great Ambrose and the Empress Justina at Milan, and it was
still undesirable for respectable churchmen to leave their
opinions on the subject in any kind of doubt. He wrote a
treatise addressed to Saint Paulinus of Nola,[2] the great Gallic
ascetic and scholar, who was a friend of nearly every one
of importance in the Church at that time; it contained, by
Augustine's later account, a good deal that it should not,
about the faculty for good in man's nature, and his power to
act, by his own initiative, aright. 'And the grace of God',
says Augustine, many years later in one of his anti-Pelagian
works, 'he restricted to mean the gift to man of that faculty,
mentioning grace only to avoid the reproach of having
ignored it altogether.' There was also a work called the
Testimonium, intended as a kind of literary tribute to the

[1] About 386. The book is lost, as also a treatise addressed to a bishop
unknown, named Constantine.
[2] Paulinus, though he took no active part in the controversy,
always favoured the Pelagians. The book has not survived.

[176]

memory of Saint Cyprian, the great Carthaginian bishop
and martyr of the Decian persecutions. All these books were
full of good moral admonitions with which no one could
quarrel, and the last is mentioned by Gennadius of Marseilles[1]
in his biographical dictionary as an excellent work necessary
for devout persons to read. Pelagius, however, found opportunity to say that man's will is free, that he can live, if he
chooses, without sin, words which passed unchallenged for
years till the controversy was launched. By that time, for the
book did not somehow seem sufficiently compromising,
words had been added to the text by his opponents, and its
meaning altered for use in the accusations brought against
him at the synods in Palestine; but he was able to demonstrate the alterations to be forgeries.[2]

Meanwhile these books were widely circulated and read,
and brought Pelagius nothing but admiration and respect.
There are signs, though the report is of later date, that there
was some early friction between Pelagius and Augustine
before they were in direct personal contact. Some one brought
Pelagius a copy of the *Confessions*, as a new work by a rising
author, and read it to him aloud. When the reader reached
the famous 'Da quod jubes, et jube quod vis', Augustine's
cry from the heart, which disclaims all personal freedom and
responsibility, casting all on God, the very antithesis of
Pelagius' guiding principle, Pelagius is said to have interrupted the reading with a protest. 'He could not bear it, and
almost quarrelled with his reader.' Whatever the source of
the story, it is consistent with Pelagius' ideas, and Augustine
used it later to prove that there had always been conflict
between Pelagius and himself.[3]

Had Pelagius' literary efforts ended with the *Testimonium*

[1] A literary editor and biographer, who was accused by the Benedictine editors of Pelagius of Pelagian leanings, principally on account
of this remark.
[2] See pp. 214, 240.
[3] See *De Dono Perseverantiæ*, ch. xx.

much trouble might have been avoided. But some malicious prank of fate drove him to the one step which was certain to destroy a person of his cast of mind; he chose to write a commentary on the Epistles of Saint Paul. There are many books of Scripture on which Pelagius might have commented and no one been the worse, if not much the better, for he lacked inspiration as a commentator; but deficient as he was in philosophic background, and incapable of mysticism, he was the last person to make anything of Paul. There were positive dangers too, pitfalls into which he fell. Half a dozen sentences in his *Commentary on the Epistle to the Romans* loosed the Pelagian controversy on the world.

The commentaries are full of well-meant industry. They are also rather pedestrian, even lame; Pelagius hobbles painfully and not very helpfully after the mystical and rhetorical flights of the apostle, not really knowing what they are all about; he does not really try to elucidate, and echoes even the apostle's contradictions without a qualm. In an *Argument* on the debated question of the authorship of the Epistles, Pelagius makes fun of an opinion, current at the time, that Paul did not write the Epistle to the Hebrews because it does not bear his name,[1] on the ground that the absence of a signature might just as well be taken to mean that this Epistle is not by any one at all. Paul, Pelagius concludes, wrote the Epistle anonymously because he very naturally feared that his persecutions of Jewish Christians in the days before his conversion might make him unpopular as an author among Jewish Christian readers. On the other hand, Paul's Jewish origin, which Pelagius emphasizes repeatedly, led him, Pelagius argues, to display his highest flights of oratory in addressing his own people.

[1] The authorship of Hebrews was disputed in the early centuries and again by Erasmus and Luther. Modern opinion favours a composite authorship.

Following the *Argument* is a *Prologue*, in the form of a dialogue between Jews and Gentiles as to which shall stand higher in the estimation of God, somewhat in the manner of a rivalry of the beasts in Æsop (for instance the frog and the ox), fortunately without a final disaster to either party. The Jews contend that they are the Chosen People, and recite God's benefactions to them in the Old Testament, while the Gentiles retort that despite their divine patronage they crucified the Saviour in addition to their other, earlier misdemeanours in spurning the heaven-sent manna and dancing before idols. In the end Paul himself intervenes to show both sides that they have erred equally, but that all alike shall have forgiveness and be saved.

The commentary, as Marius Mercator[1] contemptuously remarks, confined itself to annotating individual words and phrases; it gave no general estimate of the apostle's teaching. But even a piecemeal handling could not avoid subjects that might be dangerous for Pelagius, such as the comparative merits of faith and works for salvation. Pelagius, the moralist, was inevitably in favour of works and opposed to his author's predilection for faith, and from thence it is but a short step to many controversial points. Danger might still have been avoided had not Pelagius intrepidly tackled the Fall, and the hereditary transmission of sin. The words upon which the charge of heresy rested are in his remarks upon the fifth chapter of Romans. Here Paul makes the remarkable pronouncement that the fall of Adam brought hereditary sin upon the human race, and a wholesale condemnation, except in so far as by the operation of grace and the Atonement many shall be saved. 'Wherefore as by one man sin came into the world, and death by sin, and so death passed upon all men, for that all have sinned. For until the Law sin was in the world, but sin is not imputed where there is no

[1] A supporter of Augustine, who took up the attack on Pelagius in its later stages. See p. 231.

law. Nevertheless death reigned from Adam to Moses, even over them that had not sinned after the similitude of Adam's transgression. . . . But not as the offence, so also was the free gift. For if through the offence of one many be dead, much more the grace of God . . . hath abounded unto many. . . . For as by one man's disobedience many were made sinners, so by the obedience of one shall many be made righteous. Moreover, the law entered that the offence might abound. But where sin abounded grace did much more abound. . . .' This is not the clearest possible statement; but it links together sin and death, on the one hand, as received by inheritance from Adam, and connects the Atonement with them in such a way that any attempt to dispute them must inevitably tend to belittle the Atonement.

Upon this passage Pelagius' remarks were, in the light of future controversy, equivocal; Adam's transgression injured the human race by *example* only, by a kind of symbolism comparable to the salvation of the entire race by Christ. And to the apostle's reiteration of the death sentence upon sinners (by which, whatever Saint Paul meant, Pelagius and his contemporaries[1] meant the physical death of the body), Pelagius is at pains to vindicate the characters of the good old men of Bible times, yet are recorded to have died. He admits that there is some uncertainty in Scripture about the deaths of Abraham, Isaac, and Jacob; and most of the patriarchs were conspicuous for living to enormous ages. It must on no account be assumed, however, because these personages suffered some kind of bodily death, that they were not good men or that no just men lived before the New Law, only most probably they were few in number and among the crowds of sinners it was difficult to pick them out. Later, Pelagius was taken to task for saying that there had been good and just men before the invention of grace, and

[1] See Chrysostom and other commentators on Romans.

Augustine, in a work written many years later, is obliged to extricate Abraham, Moses and the prophets from the awkward predicament in which he had himself placed them, by suggesting that grace had some hidden, retrospective force by which, here and there, a particularly excellent patriarch was saved. But at the time when Pelagius wrote his commentary there was no reason for him to suspect unsoundness in this opinion, which indeed was blameless until Augustine's theory of grace had reached its full development.

Pelagius might be childish on such a question as the justification of patriarchs; but upon righteousness, which touched him more closely, his comments are neither childish nor vague. To the words, 'for if by the sin of one many be dead, much more hath the grace of God ... abounded unto many', Pelagius subjoins: 'Righteousness availed more to restore life than sin to kill.' It was enough, perhaps, to have used the word *righteousness* here instead of *grace*, though as yet his orthodoxy might not have been questioned, but he did not stop there. His next remarks quote the opinions of others, and are not directly sponsored by himself. 'Those who dispute the transmission by heredity of original sin, assert that if the sin of Adam was capable of injuring those who have not actually committed sin, then the righteousness of Christ must avail for those who are not believers, for the apostle constantly avers that the righteousness of one avails more for salvation than the iniquity of the other for damnation. They also say, that if baptism washes away that ancient guilt, those who are born of two baptized persons should be free from sin, for they could scarcely transmit to their offspring what they themselves did not possess. For the flesh, not the spirit, is inherited, and therefore the flesh is in the inheritance of sin, and alone merits guilt. For they say that it is unjust that a soul born to-day, not of the flesh of Adam, should bear that ancient stain, the guilt of another and they refuse to admit that God, who forgives a man his own sins, should impute to him those of another.'

Pelagius here has left the comparatively safe domain of ethics for the quicksands of theology: for to deny that God could be so unjust as to impute sin to infants is to imply that infants, being sinless, do not require baptism. For if the purpose of baptism is to remove hereditary sin, then if there is no such sin to be removed what indeed can be the need for baptism? One of the gravest charges that was brought against Pelagius subsequently was that he was an enemy of baptism, that he believed that infants, being innocent of any sin, original or other, are in no need of regeneration. Pelagius, a blameless, inexperienced celibate, believed no doubt that infants are free of any sin, but in the matter of baptism, though apparently inconsistent, he was in practice perfectly orthodox, and whatever purpose he thought it served in infancy, he had no doubt that infants should receive it.

Pelagius' reference of these opinions to others who are not named, brought him later a charge of slyness; he was accused of sheltering himself behind others whose names he had not the courage to mention. But to judge people's actions in the light of subsequent occurrences which could not have influenced them is a common historical fallacy, and it must be remembered that when Pelagius wrote these words there was as yet no Pelagian controversy, he had not yet been attacked, the dogma of original sin had not yet been imposed, there was considerable vagueness about grace, and free will was an open subject. He could therefore scarcely have wished to take cover from polemics which had not yet been initiated. Infant baptism was in process only of becoming the general practice of the Church,[1] and even had Pelagius intended to question it he would not at that stage

[1] Its universal adoption was partly due to Augustine's subsequent efforts in the controversy.

have had any cause for apprehension. It seems a little unfair also that his opponents, having on one occasion accused him of shielding his ideas behind the authority of others, should on another deride him, as they did, for not having even invented his own heresies. Certainly some of the doctrines subsequently ascribed to him and condemned could be deduced from his teaching about free will, but he never formulated any theological doctrine, nor argued about theology. What he believed he openly maintained both in speaking and in writing; theology he left to the theologians, and accepted unquestioningly, if also a trifle inconsistently, what the Church taught.

The commentaries when first published were, like his other books, widely read and admired and, at Rome at any rate, were not thought heretical. They travelled over western Europe, were copied again and again through the centuries, and though occasionally the dangerous passages were omitted, and gradually the ill-starred name of Pelagius was suppressed or altered to something more respectable, they proved, as we shall see, to have surprising powers of survival, and by an especially ironic turn of fortune were included eventually among Saint Jerome's works.[1]

Pelagius published one more book in these years, probably subsequent to the commentaries, on *Human Nature*, in which he did not return to the thorny question of baptism, but continued his development of his favourite, oft-reiterated theme, that man has within him all power for good, and has no right to excuse his misdemeanours by an infirmity and corruption of his nature inherited from Adam. We have only Augustine's quotations, chosen for purposes of refutation, to tell us about this book:[2] it seems to have defined sin as an isolated action of the will, not as a permanent, inherited, pathological condition as Augustine conceived of it. Pelagius

[1] See p. 243.
[2] Augustine's *De Natura et Gratia*, written in 415.

altogether exaggerated, Augustine thought, man's tendency
to plead in his defence the infirmity of his nature;[1] why, even
the pagans had noticed it ages ago, and he quotes against
Pelagius Sallust's 'Falso queritur de natura sua gens humana'[2]
in which, however, Sallust is entirely on Pelagius' side. And
if, Augustine continues, human nature is sufficient for its
own salvation, then Christ would have died in vain, but
Christ did not die in vain, and therefore, he concludes, completing the circle, man cannot be sinless, cannot save
himself.

[1] *De Natura et Gratia*, ch. i.
[2] *Jugurtha*.

★ V ★

In 408 or 409, certainly before the second siege of Rome, Pelagius, like many Romans, left the doomed city, accompanied by his friend and disciple, Celestius, an important and fateful figure in the Pelagian controversy, and came to Syracuse. Little is known of their stay there, except by its consequences. Syracuse was full of Roman refugees, who had estates there and could pass their time not too tediously, when they had done praying in the catacombs, attending the games in the magnificent amphitheatre, or listening to plays and rhetorical contests in the theatre. Pelagius made a considerable impression upon the refugees, and was for the first time recognized, perhaps owing to the influence of the more active and aggressive Celestius, as a teacher with a message of his own to deliver. Sicily, when he left it, retained a group of his supporters and ultimately became a refuge for Pelagians when they were persecuted elsewhere.

In Sicily Celestius first became known, no doubt to his great personal satisfaction, as the chief disciple, or spokesman, of his master. He was a typical Italian, energetic, voluble and showy, a lawyer by education, trained at the Roman bar, with a ready tongue, accustomed, indeed addicted, to argument. Marius Mercator says that he was a eunuch from birth, and also that he possessed an almost incredible loquacity. He had in fact all the aptitude for controversy which Pelagius conspicuously lacked. There could be no

[185]

greater contrast than that between these two men, the quiet unobtrusive Pelagius, and the aggressive advocate who could not be restrained from argument and from speculations that could very well have been let alone. He forced the whole question into the light, focussed attention on Pelagius, and, incidentally, upon himself, and deliberately fostered controversy.

In 410, or a little later, Pelagius and Celestius left Syracuse and arrived at Hippo, where Augustine was now bishop, a step which has been regarded by some, with polemical perversity, as a characteristic twist of Pelagius' serpentine nature, an attempt to hoodwink Augustine and to utilize his proximity, and perhaps his friendship, to cover heretical activities in Africa. But neither a simple man nor a subtle one could expect to use the champion of orthodoxy in Africa, at that moment involved with the Donatists, as a cloak for heretical propaganda. And there were many considerations that might bring refugees to Africa; it was farther from the Goths than Sicily, and Pelagius himself tells that he was anxious for a meeting with Augustine, just as Augustine, as he admitted in later correspondence, was anxious for a meeting with him.

Augustine, however, was not at home to the visitors; he was at Carthage, still very busy with the Donatists, whose case was to be tried before a Roman official sent over to Africa for the purpose. And when Pelagius and Celestius followed Augustine thither, whether by chance, or by deliberate design on Augustine's part, they failed to effect a satisfactory meeting. Augustine felt, perhaps, that he had neither leisure nor preparation at that moment for the questions which must eventually be faced; he saw Pelagius once or twice, but there was no discussion, and Pelagius, feeling, no doubt, that he had had rather a cool reception in Africa, went on to Palestine, where he had friends.[1] There was an

[1] *De Gest. Pal.*, xxvi to xxix.

exchange of letters between the two men. Pelagius wrote a brief, polite, almost affectionate greeting to the great African, with the flowery and quite meaningless compliments customary in letters at that time. Augustine's reply is equally laudatory, vapid and polite, but with a sting in its tail, a postscript which should have made Pelagius uneasy. He wishes Pelagius not only physical blessings, but those which pertain to spiritual health, and reminds him that any righteousness referred to in his complimentary allusions to himself was due not to his own will, but to God's grace. He adds, however, that he had no wish to deny the freedom of the will, a remark in which Pelagius very naturally found support for his own teaching.

Three years later, when these letters were cited at the trials in Palestine, Augustine was to be not a little embarrassed to dispose of his own early toleration of free will, and he was driven in self-defence to reiterate what he called Pelagius' denials of grace elsewhere. So far there was no visible conflict; if a better reception was to be looked for in Palestine, relations between Pelagius and Hippo were at any rate polite, and differences of opinion were no worse than could be referred to quite civilly in the postscript of an elegant letter.

At the invitation of Bishop John, an old friend apparently, Pelagius settled at Jerusalem, where he seems to have been welcomed in ecclesiastical circles, and might have expected some comfort and peace but for two awkward circumstances with which he had not reckoned.

In the first place, Bethlehem and its testy occupant Jerome, were near at hand, and secondly, he had left Celestius behind him at Carthage. Perhaps Celestius had chafed under the control of his peaceable, unprovocative master, and now welcomed the opportunity, which he used to the full, of assuming the part of protagonist in a controversy, and of drawing attention to himself.

With a simplicity rivalling his master's, and a boldness amounting to impertinence which was all his own, Celestius applied to Aurelius bishop of Carthage, for ordination. Aurelius was a close, enthusiastic friend and ally of Augustine, and he decided to make Celestius' application an opportunity to examine the rumours of strange doctrine which gathered round the two refugees from Rome. Trouble henceforth was inevitable. The African ecclesiastics were hysterical about Church authority, and quite indifferent to ethical theory; for, the Donatist controversy apart, enormous efforts had always been needed to keep discipline and unity in the African Church, and synod after synod had tried to tidy up the general disorder. There had been petty schisms in many dioceses, and free-and-easy habits about ordinations and baptisms. Holy rejoicings at festivals sometimes ended in complete intoxication; and beside the delinquencies of remote Mauretanian and Numidian clerics and congregations, paganism still flourished; there were holy trees and wells and rustic altars to the local deities in country places.

It is not surprising that the Africans were suspicious in regard to anything new; and it is significant that their inquiry had no direct reference to free will, but confined itself to original sin, and to the consequences to ecclesiastical discipline rather than to conduct and morals, of denying it. A charge of unorthodoxy was brought against Celestius by a deacon, Paulinus, a friend of Augustine, who had been secretary to the great Ambrose at Milan till his death, a typical hanger-on of great men, useful for those meaner tasks which great men like to have done for them. The charge was under six headings:

    I. That Adam was created mortal, and would have died whether he sinned or no.

    II. That Adam's sin injured no one but himself.

    III. That infants are born sinless, as was Adam before the Fall.

[188]

IV. That infants dying unbaptized have immortal life.
V. That the human race does not die for the sin of Adam nor rise again for the resurrection of Christ.
VI. That the Old Law (of Moses), no less than the Gospel, admits men to the Kingdom of Heaven.

These propositions are important, for they came to be regarded as the cardinal points of the Pelagian position, constituting the heresy. It must be remembered that they were never at any time formulated by Pelagius or Celestius; they were framed by Paulinus and his backers at Carthage, and were fastened upon Pelagius before he could know anything about them. Only the third and sixth points can be derived from his teaching. The remainder are remoter deductions of a theological kind; and Pelagius, being incapable of theology, repudiated them at the synods in Palestine.

Celestius was examined at Carthage and was by no means easy to dispose of; for, as an advocate experienced in handling witnesses, he knew how to conduct his case, and Paulinus, his accuser, had occasionally to be extricated by Aurelius as judge from the entanglements into which Celestius manœuvred him. The points stressed were the hereditary transmission of sin, which Celestius, on the authority of several good Catholic Fathers,[1] admitted that he doubted, and the question of the innocence or guilt of unbaptized infants. After several sittings the Council of Carthage excommunicated Celestius and produced a confutation of the six points, which was very useful later in the anti-Pelagian campaign. Celestius then very coolly removed himself from Carthage to Ephesus, which was quite outside African jurisdiction, and there applied for ordination all over again, and got it.

Pelagianism was now launched upon the world. The attempt at repression had given the simple precepts of Pelagius a definition and an importance which on their own

[1] Amongst them Rufinus of Aquileia. See p. 201–3.

merits they would never have achieved. Busy African minds were set speculating, and tongues wagging, upon sin, upon baptism, upon the nature of infants, and other subjects beloved of controversialists. The possibilities of error over all these points were enormous, and Augustine, who had taken no direct part in the Council, felt the time had come for him to enter the lists. The years between 411 and 415 saw the beginning of the torrential output of his anti-Pelagian works. So far Pelagius is treated with great circumspection, he is a 'good and praiseworthy man'; his doctrine only is questioned. First came some sermons, in which baptism and the state of infants at birth were dealt with, very necessarily, for there was a tendency to regard infants as so innocent as not to require baptism, and baptism as so efficacious that it was being deferred to as late a time of life as possible, to death-beds even, in order that it might remove the sins of a lifetime, and the soul enter the next world unencumbered with any guilt.

To these doctrinal vagaries Augustine replies that infant baptism is a rule of the Church, (which was far from true,[1]) that infants must have sin upon them, else they would not need to be baptized, that as infants cannot have committed deliberate sin their sin must be original, thus making baptism the evidence for original sin, putting the cart before the horse, and standing theology on its head.

The sermons were not enough. Estimable people kept writing to Augustine to ask what the trouble was all about. Denunciations and the usual methods of heretic-hunting, as applied to the Donatists, were clearly out of place with intelligent inquirers, many of them friends of Augustine whose minds would have to be satisfied. There was Marcel-

---

[1] The practice was not universal till later in the century. Adult baptism had actually been taught by Tertullian. Gregory of Nazianzus preferred three years old, and there were other theories as to suitable age. Infant baptism was largely due to Augustine's own influence.

linus, the 'tribune and notary', the perfect Roman official, a
Christian rather than a churchman, who had been sent to
Africa by Honorius in 411 to adjudicate between Catholics
and Donatists. He scared both sides by taking an oath in
the name of the Trinity, the Incarnation, and the Emperor,
that he would judge the case impartially according to the
evidence; and he reinstated the banished Donatist clerics
before the hearing, so as to exclude all prejudice at the start.
He was so polite that, when the two parties refused to sit
down in one another's presence, he sent away his own chair
also and remained standing throughout the hearing. He gave
the verdict, as indeed was inevitable, in favour of the Catholics and unity, and condemned Donatists who continued to
resist to the penalty of the law. But he did not intend the
Catholics to take the law into their own hands as they did,
and when he found his ears full of the din of fresh controversy, as the commotion about original sin and infant
baptism increased (for controversialists, like nature, abhor
a vacuum), he must have felt that there was no satisfying the
Africans, and he wrote to Augustine for a formula with
which to meet this fresh outburst of speculation.

He was liberally treated: in reply, he got the three long
books on the *Wages and Forgiveness of Sin*[1] in which the
guilt of infants is again deduced from the rite of baptism, and
Pelagius' idea of sin is again contradicted. And when these
did not satisfy him, for Marcellinus liked to have his mind
clear about everything, Augustine wrote his great book on
the *Spirit and the Letter*,[2] to the famous text, 'the letter
killeth, but the spirit giveth life', the least vindictive, the
most poetic and imaginative of all Augustine's anti-Pelagian
works, for which his admirers should be grateful to Marcellinus in that he elicited it. Here grace is defined as a heavenly
power, indwelling in the soul, part of the Divine Love;

[1] *De Peccatorum Meritis et Remissione.*
[2] *De Spiritu et Littera.*

the will is called free, but when it is good it is from God, and is indistinguishable from grace. The will to evil alone is strictly free.

Here indeed is something positive, mystical certainly, and not perhaps for the understanding of the many, but capable of providing inspiration to people with a turn for mysticism. The language is beautiful, and there is scarcely any of the usual tedious chop-logic. Had this been the only, or even the last book written by Augustine against the Pelagians, he might, despite his views on persecution, have deserved all the admiration accorded him through the ages by those who confine their Augustinian researches to the *Confessions* and the *City of God*. But even here, though the theme of the book is Divine Love, that love, like grace, is limited, and arbitrarily bestowed; it is granted to many, but also denied to many, who must eventually be left to outer darkness, to the wrath of God. Augustine was perfectly logical; he did not shirk the consequences of his own thesis, and condemned everything outside the operation of grace, that is to say, good works, unbaptized infants, blameless, if unbaptized, adult lives, and the Pelagians of course, to eternal fire.

In a letter[1] to two bishops Augustine dealt with a series of propositions of Celestius, that a man can, if he likes, avoid sin; and in a book on *Faith and Works*[2] (written perhaps while he was at the same time busy upon *The City of God*) he had to refute an error very naturally developed by ingenious minds from his own recent teaching, (the very same that Pelagius had set himself originally to combat), that faith and grace were so efficacious that good works were quite unnecessary and could be dispensed with altogether; indeed that a thoroughly bad life could, with their aid, be safely indulged in. And in the same year, 413,[3] Augustine had to

[1] *De Perfectione.*   [2] *De Fide et Operibus.*
[3] Marcellinus was executed that year for supposed complicity in the revolt of Heraclian.

compose for his friend Aurelius an explicit statement on the
thorny question of infants and baptism in the shape of a
sermon in which the unbaptized infants, heavily laden with
original sin, received their final dismissal from any share in
salvation, and their disastrous fate was made a cardinal
point against Celestius and the Pelagians who would not
accept it.

Inquiries were continuous. There were two young men,
Timasius and James, professed friends of Pelagius, either
merely treacherous or very stupid, who sent Augustine a
book by Pelagius to be explained.[1] The book, of course,
defended the power for good in human nature, and depre-
cated the usual habit of excusing error by alleging a
natural weakness and corruption. Augustine in his reply,
On Nature and Grace[2] quotes the work freely. It gave him,
he admits, some trouble, through its very 'plausibility'.
Again he covers the familiar ground, original sin, the inherited taint, the helplessness of man and the uselessness of
works, and proves that Pelagius' advocacy of free will is
really a denial of the Atonement, that it 'makes the Cross of
none effect'. And his thought approaches its full completion
in the doctrine of Predestination, the only logical conclusion
to his idea of grace.

There is much of Augustine's elaborate and voluble exe-
gesis in these works that evokes a smile in a modern reader.
For instance, on the question of death, if Adam had not
sinned he would not have died, he would have suffered
another, purer change; he would have been immune also
from old age and decay, like the shoes of the Israelites which,
Deuteronomy tells us, in all the forty years' wanderings in
the wilderness 'waxed not old'.[3] But he sinned, and so death
came upon all men, and the reputed translations of Enoch
and Elijah, who lived after him and inherited the conse-

---

[1] The *Testimonium* or *De Natura*.   [2] *De Natura et Gratia*.
[3] Deut. xxix. 5. *De Pecc. Mer. et Remissione*, I. 3.

quences of the Fall, do not imply that they attained complete immortality, merely they were preserved in Paradise without food, or by some kind of miraculous sustenance like the cake and the cruse of water that nourished Elijah.

The long lives of some of the patriarchs were also a difficulty, for, as descendants of Adam, and hereditary sinners, they were not strictly entitled to live so long. The puzzle haunted Augustine for years. Methuselah, for instance, where was Methuselah during the Flood?[1] He was not in the Ark, and by his great age, recorded in the Old Testament, he must have been still living when the Flood was over. There were, however, commentators who had decided that he died before the Flood; and, in any case, in such abstruse questions ignorance may be compatible with sound Christian doctrine, and error may not necessarily be heresy.

In a further work, on the *Perfection of Man*, Augustine refutes various propositions of Celestius about the ability of man to avoid sin, and gradually approaches that limitation of sin to concupiscence, the sin of the flesh, which was to be the basis of his controversy with the Pelagians.[2]

It is a limited idea of sin, too limited to be good for human morals, and we have to remind ourselves that it was the result of personal experience, of Augustine's morbid horror of his own past, the remorseful shudder of the rake turned puritan, which people who have never been rakes themselves cannot hope to understand.

The condition of infants and their prospects of salvation were, very properly, a focus of interest, for numbers of religious people owned them and were loth to consign their innocents to eternal punishment,[3] in the event of their being

---

[1] *De Pecc. Orig.*, xxiii.

[2] Anyone who wishes to explore further Augustine's views on these subjects should read his *De Marito et Concupiscentia* and *De Peccato Originali*, where these matters are dealt with exhaustively.

[3] Augustine was once induced to suggest that the punishment would be only a very mild one.

carried off by some infant ailment before they could receive baptism. Had not Christ himself shown especial tenderness to children? Perhaps, some of his friends suggested, children of baptized parents did not inherit any sin at all, for if baptism successfully washed away the parents' sin, how could they transmit 'to their children what they themselves did not possess'? It was the question asked by Pelagius himself, and at first sight it is not easy to answer. But Augustine was explicit. No, the infants are none the less guilty, for in spite of the baptism of the parents, in bringing the child into the world they have committed the carnal act, and the child inherits, not the effects of baptism, but the guilt of carnal sin.

There are other proofs, Augustine finds, of the guilt of infants, for instance their small size and helplessness, which testify to their inferiority, to the presence in them of a kind of blight. Had they been born free of sin they would not be small and feeble as are all Eve's children, ignorant and practically imbecile; they would have been adult, sensible, and competent from birth, capable of feeding and thinking for themselves, like the better sort of beasts.[1]

And finally, with a culminating dialectic somersault, the damnation of infants is a proof that they have sin; for damned they surely are if they die unbaptized, why otherwise should they be baptized? 'Damned they could not be if they really have no guilt'; and since they have committed no active individual sin and yet are damned, they must therefore have original sin. 'When these people [the Pelagians] are asked whether unbaptized infants are damned, they are perplexed and silent.[2] Who would then be so bold as to affirm

---

[1] *De Pecc. Mer. et Remissione*, i, 37–8; i, 20.
[2] The baptismal service of the Church of England, while very cheerful as to the fate of baptized infants, is as silent as the Pelagians on the subject of those dying unbaptized, possibly less from perplexity than tact.

that, without the regeneration of which the apostle speaks, infants could attain to eternal life? And they [the Pelagians] are terrified at the hard saying, and complain that it would be injustice if God allowed unbaptized infants to perish.' It cannot, adds Augustine in a characteristic peroration, be injustice, because there is no injustice in God.

★ VI ★

It is unknown how soon or how frequently Augustine's polemics reached Pelagius at Jerusalem. There may have been a considerable delay in their transmission, for Pelagius showed a complete indifference to opinion at Carthage and Hippo, and pursued his normal course quite unperturbed by the stir and controversy he had left behind him in Africa. In 413, with almost provocative unconcern, regardless even of the condemnation of Celestius in 411, news of which must by that time have reached him, Pelagius published a fresh exposition of his favourite thesis, human perfectibility and the freedom of the will, in the form of a letter to a young lady called Demetrias, who was about to take the veil. Like many letters of those days, it was a substantial pamphlet, many thousand words in length, setting forth the whole duty of the professed virgin, with a preface energetically vindicating the nature of man, his innate moral strength, and the perfect liberty of the will.

Demetrias was no obscure young person; her renunciation was an event of no mean importance in the Christian world. She was of the family of the Anicii Probi, a great Christian patrician family of enormous wealth, uprooted by the sack of Rome. Her father, Olybrius, a Roman and a senator, remained in Italy; but her mother Juliana, and her grandmother Anicia Falconia Proba,[1] widow of the great consul

[1] Perhaps the poetess of that name who dedicated a poem to Honorius.

[197]

Probus, fled with Demetrias to the supposed safety of
Africa, where the family, like many Romans, had considerable estates. Here they encountered the terrifying
Heraclian, Count of Africa,[1] who was making a fortune for
himself by selling refugee women as slaves, or permitting
them, if they were wealthy, to buy themselves off with
enormous ransoms. Proba was able to buy off her family,
and many others also among her acquaintance and connec-
tions who were in like case.

Demetrias was a lovely young girl with a magnificent
dowry, betrothed already to a most suitable bridegroom,
and her relatives felt that her renunciation must be celebrated
as it deserved; for renunciants, Jerome tells us, were commonly crippled or deformed, or dowerless, such as were not
likely to obtain husbands. Her marriage would no doubt
have been the subject of epithalamia like those of which
Ausonius and Claudian have left us specimens; so for her
renunciation the greatest pens of the Latin Church were
mobilized. We have Pelagius' letter and another by Jerome,
and between the two an interesting contrast. The opening
of Jerome's letter is a deplorable exhibition of what can only
be described as gush. With all reasonable allowance for the
elaborate, almost Chinese manners of that rhetorical society,
Saint Jerome's letter to Demetrias is a disgusting display.
Jerome, fulsome and in a genial mood, is far less tolerable
and respectable than Jerome vituperative and vitriolic; and
the reader can indulge in a melancholy reflection upon the
importance of rich widows and wealthy renunciants in the
Church, at that time as always, and upon the lengths to which
even distinguished ecclesiastics could go when the reversion
of a fortune or of a dowry was at stake. Let us hope that
Demetrias did not believe, any more than Jerome did, that
'every church in Africa danced with joy when the news of

---

[1] Stilicho's murderer in 408.

her renunciation was received', or that 'the news reached
to the remotest villages, to the huts of the poorest inhabitants. Every island between Africa and Italy put off her
mourning, and the ruined walls of Rome resumed in part
their ancient splendour, believing that Demetrias' vows had
restored the favour of God. One would think the Goths
had been annihilated.' There is much of adventitious interest
in the letter; her jewels, her make-up, her coiffure are
described among her sacrifices; she is warned against her
smart girl friends with their curls, their tight sleeves, expensive shoes, and shockingly low *décolletage*, which they
love to display in public. Even married women are to be
avoided, as much as the giddy girls, especially that more
insidious sort who are still fond of their husbands; the others
apparently are not so dangerous. Widows are safer as companions for her, and severe virgins, but even these may be
unsound, for there are always the *fausses dévotes*, outwardly
renunciants, who practise all kinds of indulgence, such as
taking baths. The rest of the letter is a dissertation upon
chastity in the usual patristic style; and it is impossible not
to wonder what a very young and possibly innocent girl,
undergoing perhaps the experience of a genuine religious
vocation, thought of the torrent of salacious detail with
which she and her kind, at these junctures, were apt to be
deluged by supposedly celibate old men professing to be
their religious guides.

Pelagius' letter to Demetrias is in quite another vein. It
is less interesting to a modern reader, for its lack of descriptive detail, salacious or other; it is dull, but it is at any rate
respectable. Neither Demetrias nor her family receive any
bouquets; she is properly warned of the gravity of her undertaking, she is to practise chastity, but not chastity only, there
are the other hard and homely virtues, *justitia*, *scientia*,
veritas and *sapientia*, and she is to avoid lying, swearing,
and backbiting, to hate nobody, and above all she is to find

in herself, in the freedom of the will, all power and capacity for good.

When Pelagius' letter to Demetrias, with its emphasis on free will, reached the Probi, it seems to have caused no surprise; no one detected in it any doctrinal unsoundness. Demetrias probably found it most edifying, and if she took its contents to heart she must have become a most exemplary little nun. Later, when the Pelagian controversy had begun to rage openly, it fell into Augustine's hands. He found it, of course, most pernicious: 'chastity is not in our own power or in the capacity of human nature,' he wrote to Demetrias' mother Juliana, 'it is a gift only of the grace of God'. While as for the story of Joseph and Potiphar's wife, used by Pelagius, as by many another both then and since, to illustrate resistance to temptation under difficulties, what a story, Augustine angrily exclaims, to tell to an innocent young girl![1] Pelagius, as a matter of fact, did not tell the story: the Probi were well-read people and it was necessary only to allude to it in passing, as too well known to need repetition in full; and as for the subject of the story, Pelagius, like many another pious author, was not afraid of Scripture. In any case, if Demetrias' modesty was regarded by Augustine as too frail a flower to stand the simplicities of a Bible story, how can he have expected it to sustain the shocks of Jerome's unsparing disquisitions, and many a passage in his own works?

[1] Orosius also expresses disgust on this point. *Apol.* xxxi.

VII

Pelagius had better not have gone to Jerusalem. His friendship with Bishop John, however it originated, brought him within the orbit of one of Jerome's most violent quarrels, that with Rufinus of Aquileia, which had included Bishop John; and though the quarrel was supposed to be over and done with long ago, for Rufinus was dead and the peaceable John had long arrived at amicable relations with Jerome, that jealous temper was always easy to inflame, and there was an immediate explosion. The connection, in Jerome's mind, between Pelagius and Rufinus cannot be explained with any certainty. Marius Mercator says that Pelagius got his doctrines from Theodore of Mopsuestia, through the agency of Rufinus, a Syrian monk; Celestius said that free will was taught at Rome by Rufinus, a Syrian. Rufinus was a fairly common name at that time, and the epithet Syrian seems to imply a distinction from any other Rufinus known to fame, and to preclude Rufinus of Aquileia. Jerome, however, seems to have assumed without question that Pelagius was a pupil of Rufinus of Aquileia, and that his arrival at Jerusalem implied a deliberate renewal of the old hostilities.

Jerome's quarrel with Rufinus of Aquileia was, like many quarrels of those days, about the reputed heresies of Origen, that mighty scholar who was so attractive to other scholarly minds and, with his broad philosophic outlook, so dangerous to their theology.[1] It was a popular pastime among the Fathers, when they wished to annoy one another, to make accusations of Origenism against any one found studying, or showing signs of having been influenced by, the works of this great author. Rufinus, Jerome, and John of Jerusalem had all, at some time, been students at Alexandria, where, in their native air, the works of Origen were much esteemed and studied, and both Jerome and Rufinus translated his books and quoted and praised Origen in their own works. But as the feeling against Origenism grew, there began to be some sensitiveness among those who were known to be students and admirers of Origen. Augustine himself at one time had accused Jerome of Origenism, and Jerome protected himself by putting the charge upon others in his turn.

Trouble first began in Palestine on the arrival in Jerusalem, many years previously, of a fanatical Egyptian monk, Aterbius, accusing both Rufinus, who was living on the Mount of Olives, and Jerome at Bethlehem, of Origenism. To defend himself Jerome took the offensive by summoning a friend Epiphanius,[2] bishop of Cyprus, a fanatical old heretic-hunter, who diverted the attack by concentrating it upon bishop John of Jerusalem and accusing him of Origenism in his own episcopal see.

Feeling in Jerusalem was quickly inflamed; both the bishop and the intruder fell to preaching against one another. Epi-

---

[1] Origen believed that all truth is one, and justified, retrospectively, the pagan philosophers. He believed that all sinners ultimately will be saved, including Lucifer, and he was vague as to the resurrection of the body and the origin of the soul, which he thought pre-existed its appearance in the human body.

[2] Author of a book, *De Hæresiis*. He had made mischief in Constantinople against Chrysostom, trying to implicate him in the accusations against the Tall Brothers. Originally he had been nearly inveigled by some Gnostic ladies in Egypt, who wanted to initiate him into their mysteries. He never got over his fright and hunted heretics passionately thereafter.

phanius called John a heretic and John called Epiphanius an
old dotard, which he undoubtedly was. Epiphanius, to
spite John, ordained a priest for the community at Bethlehem,
so that Jerome and his friends should be independent of
John and of his heretical, if legitimate, authority in his own
diocese.[1] There was now a clear rift between Jerusalem,
which included Rufinus, and Bethlehem, in the person of
Jerome. The quarrel with John eventually was more or less
made up, but with Rufinus it was never permanently healed.
Rufinus and his friend the great Melania[2] on the Mount of
Olives were too near Bethlehem for peace, and Jerome was
jealous of Rufinus' scholarship. There was an interchange
of violent polemics, which dislodged Rufinus from Palestine
and projected him to Italy. Jerome called Rufinus a scorpion,
and because he had a peculiar voice, a grunter,[3] and because
he was a well-to-do hospitable person, a hypocrite, a Nero
at home, a Cato abroad.[4] He even accused Rufinus of pur-
loining one of his books, and Melania was also loaded with
opprobrious epithets, she was as black as her own name.[5]
Even after Rufinus' death[6] the atmosphere in Palestine
remained inflammable, and into it walked the artless, rather
unobservant Pelagius, thinking he had found a safe retreat
from Goths, and from unfriendly Africans with their naturally uncertain tempers badly frayed by their prolonged local
controversies.

News of what was happening in Africa in 411 no doubt
reached Bethlehem in due course, and the arrival of Pelagius

[1] The victim was Paulinianus, Jerome's brother, who was seized
and bound and ordained with a gag in his mouth.
[2] See p. 101.
[3] *Grunnius*. This epithet is sprinkled freely through Jerome's work,
especially the prefaces to the *Commentary on Jeremiah*.
[4] Ep. CXXV.
[5] Melania was presumably derived from the Greek word for black.
Perhaps it also implied comeliness.
[6] A.D. 408.

in the neighbourhood must have aroused interest. Some time subsequently an inquirer named Ctesiphon, a relative perhaps of Demetrias and the Probi, asked Jerome, apparently quite innocently, for his views on the Pelagian question, and got in reply the famous *Letter to Ctesiphon*,[1] a most vigorous and erudite attack upon the assertion that man can live without sin. It is directed chiefly against Rufinus of Aquileia, who is deluged with a torrent of vituperation in which Melania, his companion, is included, and likened to the harlot Helena, and to Philoumena;[2] in fact the whole of her sex receives a handling which, from Jerome, it certainly did not deserve. Jerome does not economize his language: 'My temper rises and I cannot check my tongue,' he concludes, 'not against Ctesiphon, but against Rufinus, Melania, Pelagius and all his works.' And throughout there is scarcely a word of grace; it appears a couple of times very casually, with a very unsophisticated, indeed a very Pelagian meaning, as God's help to man in avoiding sin, not at all the meaning applied to it by Augustine.

Everything now seemed to favour a *rapprochement* between Bethlehem and Hippo. The quarrel between Augustine and Jerome had died a natural death, Augustine having long abandoned the hope of wresting the last word from the inexhaustible Jerome. They were both men of established reputation now; Jerome, as an old man, might even feel a little flattered by overtures, if they were properly obsequious, from the distinguished African doctor, now no longer to be regarded as the impertinent puppy whose ears he had boxed seven or eight years ago. There were, moreover, fresh topics of ecclesiastical conversation in Africa which seemed to demand some consultation between the two great churchmen: the origin of the soul, and the stimulating discussion

---

[1] Ep. CXXXIII.
[2] Helena was the friend of Simon Magus, Philoumena a sort of medium employed by Apelles, a follower of the heretic Marcian.

between Creationists and Traducianists, as to whether the soul is created at birth, or pre-exists the arrival of the human infant into the world, at what moment, precisely, the human soul entered the body, and what, if any, was its previous history.[1] It was a dangerous subject, as usual, and Marcellinus had written to Jerome for his opinion and had been referred by Jerome back to Augustine. In 415 Augustine wrote his book on *The Origin of the Soul*, leading up eventually to original sin and the guilt of infants, which he demonstrated to be difficult to reconcile with Creationism. The book was addressed to Jerome, and was intended as an overture; for the bearing of this question of the soul upon Pelagianism would test Jerome's attitude to Pelagius, without the risks of asking a point-blank question.

Most opportunely, also, there arrived at Hippo, in the early weeks of 415, an eager young Spanish monk called Paulus Orosius, a native of Tarragona, full of this and other controversial subjects, upon which he wished to consult Augustine; for Spain too was full of controversy and heresy, the Priscillianists having kept up a prolonged and courageous struggle there despite the execution of their leaders in 385. Origenist views had also got into Spain, and now the nature of the soul was engaging the Spanish ecclesiastics, instead of the more urgent and far more disagreeable duty of doing something to keep the Visigoths and the Vandals and other Germanic tribes out of their peninsula. They complained, indeed, that the Goths were nothing to the horrible perversions of Christian doctrine which were rife among themselves. From these debates came Orosius determined to gain a clearer light, and he so

---

[1] Behind Traducianism lay the fag-ends of Greek philosophy, transmigration of the soul, and the more blameworthy portions of Origen, even Gnosticism, but it fitted in better with the transmission of original sin and was more or less favoured for that reason by Augustine and the western ecclesiastics.

recommended himself to Augustine that the great African
decided to make use of him for his own purposes. Perhaps
Augustine had not yet seen Jerome's *Letter to Ctesiphon*,
and thought the atmosphere in Palestine needed stirring up;
or perhaps he knew all about the *Letter to Ctesiphon* and
thought the moment a good one, which indeed, for him, it
was. He sent Orosius loaded with his book on *The Origin
of the Soul*, with another letter on *The Nature of Individual
Sins*, a letter of introduction, and all Orosius' own searching
questions on these subjects, to Bethlehem, to sit at Jerome's
feet.

Orosius was without any of that grand indifference, that
dignified calm, which used to be associated with the Spa-
niards. Perhaps these qualities were brought to Spain later
by the Arab and the Moor; perhaps they were always the
admired exception rather than the rule. He was a fussy little
ecclesiastic, excitable, rash, and very stupid, a fiery partisan
incapable of understanding, or even listening to, any case
but that of his own side, and full of the true heretic-hunting
spirit, which was perhaps his most conspicuously Spanish
quality. He was not without learning and literary preten-
sions; he wrote, later, a history of the world, with a dedication to Augustine from himself as Augustine's pet house-
dog, entitled *History against the Pagans*, being history
indeed with a purpose, intended, on the model of Augustine's *City of God*, to show that paganism was the cause of
every disaster, as Christianity of every good in the world.
Pagan antiquity is a long series of calamities, in which even
natural catastrophes, eruptions of Etna, plagues of locusts
and monstrous births, such as that of a child with four hands
and four feet, are ascribed to a lack of Christianity. Once the
Christian era is reached all is peace, prosperity, and love,
with mild benevolent emperors; and the disorders of the
reigns of Nero and Caligula are a symbol of God's wrath at
the slow progress of Christianity in the world. The sack of

Rome, a Christian town, by Alaric, is a polite and bloodless affair, and the whole ends with the marriage of Galla Placidia, sister of the Emperor Honorius, to Ataulf, Alaric's successor, to the tune of holy wedding bells, and her peaceable return to Ravenna at his death. The history, sponsored by Augustine and having, it must be conceded, a wide scope and an easy way with a vast tale of events, had great estimation in the Middle Ages. It is to the credit of Alfred the Great, one of the more literary of our kings, who translated it for his subjects to read, that he got so tired of his author before the work was done that he left out large sections and inserted instead a geography of Europe of his own composition, and some interesting voyages by Norwegian and Saxon authors.

It will thus be seen that Orosius had an ardent and very simple mind: Augustine, in his letter of introduction to Jerome, emphasizes his eagerness to take the field against false doctrine. His energy was unquestionable, but, unfortunately, not his discretion; events proved that Augustine had made a very bad choice and seriously over-rated his man.

At Bethlehem Orosius, 'a poor foreigner', as he called himself, sat at Jerome's feet. He must have made excellent pace, for very soon there was anxiety at Jerusalem, and Bishop John decided that the Pelagian question must be investigated by a proper inquiry, and Pelagius' position made clear beyond further suspicion and doubt. That Orosius was recognized as the main instigator of the agitation, and the active representative of Jerome, is shown by John's invitation to him personally to come to Jerusalem to state his case. Orosius had arrived at Hippo early in 415, and in July of that year, having come to Bethlehem on the pretext of consulting Jerome on a quite different matter, he attended a synod at Jerusalem expressly summoned to hear his case against Pelagius.

VIII

Our knowledge of the proceedings at the Synod of Jerusalem is derived from Orosius' own somewhat confused account. Language provided an initial difficulty: the synod and its president, John of Jerusalem, knew only Greek, Orosius only Latin. Pelagius' language was Latin, but he understood Greek. So, to help Orosius, interpreters had to be employed, whom Orosius subsequently accused of incompetence and bad faith. Every opportunity, with great fairness, was given to Orosius for stating his case. He was allowed the first word, before Pelagius appeared; he gave his own *exparte* statement of the proceedings at Carthage, at which Celestius had been pronounced a heretic and excommunicated, and to define his case he read aloud a letter written by Augustine to the Pelagians in Sicily explaining their errors to them, thereby revealing who was behind him.

John now summoned Pelagius. His appearance, as described by Orosius, was not unattractive: a huge, tall figure, towering over the tribunal like Goliath (Orosius anxiously disclaimed any desire to liken himself to David), broad also and sturdy, handsomely dressed from head to foot, with complete confidence in himself; and his esquire,[1] Orosius says, stood by his side, ready to support him with all the armoury

[1] It is not clear who this was. Some have assumed Celestius, but if Celestius was present it is curious that he was not mentioned by name or questioned, and played no part in the proceedings.

of his heretical lore. To Orosius' disgust and surprise, Pelagius was invited to take a place among the presbyters just as if there were no charge against him, and he was asked by the tribunal to say whether or no he had really taught the opinions which Augustine had condemned. To this Pelagius made the incautious and not very helpful reply, 'What is Augustine to me?' The tribunal was a trifle taken aback, and Orosius clamoured that a man who thus blasphemed Augustine should be excommunicated. John, however, nettled by the repeated quoting of Augustine, replied that he himself was Augustine as far as that tribunal was concerned, meaning that it was for him, and not for Augustine, to adjudicate in that diocese. Orosius, missing the point, retorted angrily, 'Then if you are Augustine you should submit to his judgments.'

John now tried to make an end of this exchange of repartee; he asked Orosius whether the opinions in the letter which he had just read were referable to Pelagius or to some one else, meaning Celestius. Orosius said that Pelagius himself had taught that a man if he liked could live without sin, and to this Pelagius replied unequivocally that he had always held and taught this opinion and did not intend to deny it. This calm affirmation on Pelagius' part roused Orosius to fury; he called Pelagius a slippery reptile, an antichrist, condemned by the 'greatest writers in the Church, upon whose word all men hang'.

John paid no attention to this outburst, and invited Orosius, very properly, to become Pelagius' formal accuser. But Orosius, little jackal that he was, declined, appealing to the authority of the great men who were his backers; he refused to argue, or even to discuss texts of Scripture put forward by John which seemed to support Pelagius' views. Here Orosius, perhaps owing to the incompetence of the interpreters, lost the thread of the proceedings, and John tried in vain to make him accept Pelagius' position that a man can live without sin by adding the words *with God's help*.

Exasperated by Orosius' implacability, John then entangled him to the extent of making him seem to deny the efficacy of God's help. This was too much for Orosius, who, feeling the situation beyond him, suggested that since the dispute was between Latins (so far was theology already a matter of geography) it could not be settled in the East, but should go before some Western authority. John readily agreed to refer the question to Rome, where he believed that Pelagius still had friends; for Innocent I, who was now Pope, had been a friend of Pelagius before the coming of the Goths, and was still, as far as John knew, kindly disposed to him. Meantime there was to be a truce. Both sides undertook to hold their tongues pending the Pope's decision, and with an oath of peace the council broke up.

A letter was dispatched to Rome, but there is no indication that Pope Innocent made any reply. The letter might be many weeks on its way, and Innocent, though he might welcome any opportunity of asserting the competence of the Roman See in Palestine, was not a man to commit himself to hasty opinions. Pelagius was in high esteem at Rome, and Augustine's doctrine of grace was itself a novelty, not yet widely known in the Church, while his personal prestige rested principally on his reputation as the destroyer of Donatism, a trouble which had been confined to Africa.

The truce proclaimed at Jerusalem was not observed. Jerome and Orosius on their side accused Pelagius of continuing his propaganda, and Orosius said that John, meeting him six weeks later, disregarded his courteous greeting and gibed at him as the 'fellow who had blasphemed God's help at the tribunal'. It is hard to believe that the experienced John would give way to such a cheap gibe, and as he spoke Greek and Orosius Latin, he may have said nothing of the kind. Pelagius complained later that the campaign against him at Bethlehem at this time was never one whit abated, that it was even aggravated by two new arrivals at Bethlehem, a couple of Gallic bishops, Heros and Lazarus (of whom more will be heard later), who had been expelled from their sees in Gaul, with justification in the opinion of some for supporting the usurper Constantine.

By December of that year, 415, the truce was such a dead letter that it was found necessary to hold another synod without waiting for Pope Innocent's reply. Jerome still remained in the background; the active part was taken, or was intended at any rate to be taken, by Heros and Lazarus who lodged a complaint against Pelagius with the Metropolitan of Palestine, Eulogius bishop of Cæsarea. In December a council was held at Lydda, under the presidency of Eulogius, with a panel of fourteen bishops who included Pelagius' firm friend, John of Jerusalem. Orosius, though he was present, was no longer in the foreground; the Gallic bishops were evidently intended to retrieve at this council the failure of the previous attack.

As far as we know John was the only personal friend of Pelagius in the council, which even by his enemies has never been accused of bias towards him. It is impossible, however, not to feel that the Council of Lydda intended, from the very first, to acquit him. The Eastern bishops who composed it would be without prejudice against Pelagius' views, and indifferent to the opinions of Latin ecclesiastics, whose intervention in the East they probably regarded as superfluous and irritating. The Council has been accused of not having understood what the controversy was about, and indeed this was probably true, as it was true of Pelagius also. The point of the whole matter was what each party meant by the word grace: and both Pelagius and the Palestinian bishops certainly meant something quite nebulous and unimportant, such as God's help and guidance and a natural tendency in human nature, in which they had a laudable faith, to prefer good to evil.

As for Augustine's idea of grace, the Palestinians knew nothing of it, and as it was only in process of development, there was no reason why they should. To try to get Pelagius condemned in Palestine was therefore a poor piece of strategy; and once again the choice of agents proved unfortunate.

Heros and Lazarus, the Gallic bishops, made the worst error that litigants can make. Whether they lost courage, or were merely incompetent, or lazy, or merely thought of something more amusing to do, they defaulted at the hearing, on account, we are told, of the 'grievous illness of one of them'. Nowhere in the world do two men stay at home, because one of them is ill, when serious business is on hand, and the default seriously damaged their case. Their accusation was a paper one only, which was read aloud. Pelagius was asked a number of questions, to which he made replies which entirely satisfied the tribunal. On the testimony of the fourteen eastern bishops he was acquitted of heresy and pronounced an orthodox Catholic.

The only extant account of these proceedings comes from the pen of Augustine in a work entitled *The Proceedings in Palestine*, in which he concentrates all his forces to prove that Pelagius obtained his acquittal by means of lies. It is difficult to form a clear judgment of Pelagius' behaviour from Augustine's account, which is necessarily prejudiced and at second hand. His sources were Orosius' report of the trial, composed, as before, under difficulties occasioned by language, and a short account supplied by Pelagius himself. This was sent direct to Saint Augustine, and reached him before the other. Augustine, however, reserved his public comment till he had received the report of his own people, in the avowed expectation that Pelagius' report would be contradicted and proved to be false. Discrepancies, Augustine assures us, were there, but unfortunately he does not tell us what they were; the only passages which he quotes from Pelagius' report seem to agree excellently with that of Orosius. The sole specific charge that Augustine can bring against Pelagius is one of undue brevity: he 'huddled together' several points and questions and dealt with them in a single answer, instead of giving each with its reply separately. In this, Augustine says, he must have had 'some very special purpose', and insinuates that the opinions repudiated by Pelagius at Lydda were indeed those that he had believed and taught, and that he refrained from specifying them in order to conceal that they were his own. 'We may of course only be indulging in a suspicion,' Augustine adds, 'which is natural to man, and if so we entreat him to forgive us, but at the same time . . .' and so on to the conclusion that Pelagius lied, and that the synod, though it acquitted him, had condemned the opinions which Pelagius had taught, and regarded them as heresy.

It would have been better perhaps if Pelagius had not concluded his rejection of these debatable opinions with a rather pointed anathema on all *those who by spreading false opinions have excited odium against me*. The remark may have been justified, but it was not wise.

Augustine, in his book on the proceedings in Palestine, is at great pains to show that Pelagius not only hoodwinked his judges, but that the bishops helped Pelagius by framing their questions in such a way that they were easy to repudiate. The questions, however, were all read out from the document prepared by the prosecutors, and the Council was asked to judge Pelagius not upon his own writings, but upon the answers he should make to these questions. No fault, therefore, could be laid upon the conduct of the tribunal.

In the framing of their questions the accusers made a number of mistakes; they tried to lure Pelagius to repudiate eternal punishment for sinners, but the attempt to make an Ulsterman deny eternal fire to those whose religious views he dislikes proved, as it always must, quite futile. Pelagius readily replied that the wicked shall go away into everlasting punishment, adding, with pardonable relish, 'and he who thinks otherwise is a follower of Origen'. Two other charges, moreover, were based on forgeries which Pelagius was able to repudiate. First, by the alteration of three Latin words, they accused him of saying that *evil never entered into his thoughts*;[1] and Augustine has great difficulty in explaining away this false step on the part of his agents: perhaps, he suggests, they had been supplied with an incorrect copy of Pelagius' works. But if this was true, considering for whom they were acting in the attack upon Pelagius, it is impossible not to wonder whence that copy came, and who was responsible for tampering with the text.

The second forgery was a perfectly fatuous letter to a widow unnamed, published anonymously just before the Synod of Lydda, ascribed by many to Pelagius, and a cause of great excitement among the anti-Pelagians. It might have been a genuine letter addressed by some Father or other to one of the celebrated widows of the time, but it is not in the least like anything Pelagius ever wrote; its fulsomeness most closely resembles the style of Jerome's letter to Demetrias. Augustine and his supporters, however, were convinced, on what grounds we know not, that Pelagius had written it, and they included it in the documents for their case. A single sentence, torn from its context, was quoted to convict him of an extravagant piece of flattery. The recipient of the letter is supposed to say: 'Lord, thou knowest how pure and free from guile, unkindness or greed are the hands I stretch out to thee, how honest and free from falsehood are the lips with which I supplicate thee.' In the text these words were rendered quite innocuous by a preceding clause: '*Deservedly can a man stretch out his hands to thee in prayer who can say: Lord,*

---

[1] 'Malum non cogitandum quidem' was altered to 'malum non in cogitationem venire'.

thou knowest . . . etc.'[1] The letter, even without alteration,
was indeed silly, but there was no evidence that Pelagius
had written it. 'Such words are nowhere to be found in my
books,' he replied to the synod, 'nor have I ever at any time
said such things.' And when pressed to anathematize all who
hold these opinions Pelagius added the justifiable but pert
rejoinder: 'I anathematize them as fools, not as heretics, for
there is no doctrine in the matter.' Augustine, in the *Proceedings* cannot relinquish Pelagius' guilt on this point; his
informants had believed for some four years that Pelagius
wrote the letter, and so his disclaimer must have been a
lie, and from this not very comfortable position Augustine
takes refuge in a lengthy disquisition on the difference
between heretics and fools, arriving eventually at the por-
tentous if irrefutable conclusion that all fools are not heretics,
but all heretics are fools.

The accusers then proceeded to lay upon Pelagius the
entire series of the six heretical dogmas which the Synod
of Carthage had formulated and brought against Celestius.[2]
These Pelagius repudiated; he had never enunciated any of
them, in the written or the spoken word, and had no responsibility for them. His outlook, and doubtless his reason-
ing capacities, were too limited to grasp that in the mind of
a theologian they must be regarded as directly resulting from
his own teaching.[3] For the satisfaction of the synod, who
demanded the formality, he pronounced anathema on all who
hold or ever held these opinions.

For this anathema Pelagius had been charged with equi-
vocation. He certainly had referred in his commentary to
the opinions of 'those who repudiate original sin', but he
had not put them forward as doctrine. He seems to have

---

[1] It seems probable that this was part of a current formula in use
at the time, to express self-abasement: it appears in a letter of pious
admonition by a British bishop, Fastidius, to a widow, some decades
later. See p. 240.
[2] See p. 188.   [3] Especially No. 3.

been quite incapable of relating them to his own position, and with a strange indifference, turning a blind eye, almost, to theology, he refused to be drawn into theological dialectics. He would repudiate any views disliked by the Church, provided he was not asked to give up his free will.

There were some further questions relating to Celestius, upon points not even included under the six condemned headings of the Carthage formula, and these Pelagius repudiated unhesitatingly, in fact rather contemptuously. One of them, as to whether grace is bestowed arbitrarily or according to merit (this was to agitate the Church later), plunges Augustine into a dissertation in which appear the beginnings of his own extreme ideas of election and predestination. He tries to show that the synod was trying to make Pelagius say that the bestowal of grace depends upon election, not upon merit, and that it thus displayed a belief in predestination. But in the absence of any certainty as to what the Palestinian bishops meant by grace, and as they had probably never heard of predestination, it is not easy to discover what they were attempting here to decide. To the whole of this part of the accusation Pelagius replied 'I say again, that these opinions even according to their own showing, are not mine, nor, as I have already said, am I to be held responsible for them. The opinions which I have confessed to be mine I maintain are sound and correct; those which I have denied to be my own, I reject . . . pronouncing anathema on every man who opposes and gainsays the Catholic Church.'

Pelagius was acquitted. The synod had, of course, at the same time condemned most of the opinions which are now associated with his name, but it left him in triumphant possession of the two points to which alone he attached any value, free will and the capacity of man to avoid sin. To Pelagius' thinking it might have anything it liked if it but left him those.

In his simplicity Pelagius thought that the campaign against him must now be relinquished, and his own anxiety (as usual) seems to have been lest he had not made his position sufficiently clear, for he followed up his acquittal with further works in which it is restated most unequivocally. He sent an account of the trial to Augustine, and a letter which he wrote to a friend, intended for public perusal, eventually found its way to Augustine, who preserves extracts from it. Into this, in the course of its travels, the word 'easily' had crept into the sentence 'a man is able to live without sin, and *easily* to keep the commandments of God, if he chooses'. The word 'easily' horrified Augustine, and puzzled him too, for it was nowhere to be found in the report of the tribunal which he had received from his own people, who would hardly have overlooked such a damning utterance. Very likely if the letter was genuine it might in the course of its travels have been improved upon, not by Pelagius' enemies but by injudicious friends, over-eager to advertise their master's triumph.

Pelagius was indefatigable; in the same year, 415, he wrote his *De Libero Arbitrio*,[1] a further assertion of his well-known views on free will. To Albinia and her son Pinianus and his wife Melania the younger, friends both of Pelagius and of Augustine, Augustine later wrote a grave warning against Pelagius' duplicity in this book: but his quotations show that the book was confined to general ethics and took no account at all of the theological points that had been raised at the trial. Pelagius' last work, *The Declaration of his Faith*, addressed to Pope Innocent, contains, after a perfectly orthodox affirmation of the doctrine of the Trinity, yet another unabated assertion of the freedom of the will, with a mild corollary that the will needs always the help of God. He also sent Innocent copies of all his other works to

---

[1] Extant only in fragments in Augustine's *De Gratia Christi*.

enable the Pope to judge their orthodoxy for himself, with a covering letter in which he complains that people are still accusing him of refusing baptism to infants and of denying the grace of Christ.

'Let this letter absolve me in the eyes of your Holiness, in that I have always said that we have a free will to sin and not to sin, and that divine grace will assist us . . . that all men have this power of free will . . . but Christians have the aid of grace. . . . Those are to be judged and condemned who, with a free will to bring them to the faith and to win the grace of God, make an ill use of this freedom. . . . This was always my opinion before I was subjected to persecution. . . . Let them [his enemies] read the letter which I wrote twelve years ago to the holy Bishop Paulinus, which in thirty verses treated of nothing but grace and its help, and declared that we can do no good without God. . . .'

After years of persecution and two solemn councils of the Church Pelagius had not the faintest notion what the controversy was about.

The persecution was by no means ended. There was fresh trouble which Pelagius, in his letter to Innocent, asserts had its immediate source in Bethlehem. 'Jerome', he wrote, 'had some spiteful grudge against me, and the two bishops [Heros and Lazarus] and a young man from Spain [Orosius] attacked me, although the bishop [John of Jerusalem] had required them to observe silence regarding me, and the Holy Synod had confirmed my orthodoxy.' In 417 Jerome published his *Dialogues against the Pelagians*, a rather feeble imitation of the Socratic method of question and answer, in which an imaginary Pelagian named *Critobulus* defends Pelagianism, but under cross-examination by an imaginary *Atticus* is led on to make a thorough fool of himself. Jerome also resumed his old abusive attacks upon Bishop John, calling him an Arian who had concealed his heretical views in order to become a bishop and 'roll in luxury'. John's supporters retaliated with a raid upon Jerome's dovecot at Bethlehem; they beat some monks and nuns, burned some cells, and, according to Augustine, one deacon was killed. Jerome and his faithful Paula and Eustochium fled to a fortress, where, as usual, they relieved their feelings with the pen, and wrote to Pope Innocent to complain of the outrage.[1]

Innocent was not greatly excited by Jerome's appeal; he was a statesmanlike person, anxious to be impartial; he wrote, however, to Bishop John to point out that these disorders did not reflect much credit upon his conduct of his see. He also wrote rather coldly to Jerome that 'dissension has never done any good in the Church'; and, since Jerome's complaint was unusually vague and inexplicit, he added that he could take no steps in a matter in which nobody was accused by name, and that if Jerome would name the aggressors action might be taken against them. It is a good letter, worthy of a great Pope, and it achieved its purpose, for Jerome seems to have relinquished the matter. Pelagius, perhaps out of consideration for John, seems to have left Jerusalem, for a time at any rate: Jerome compares his departure to the flight of Catiline. Thereafter hostilities between Jerusalem and Bethlehem gradually fizzled out, and very soon, in that arena, no more is heard of the Pelagian controversy. The next round in the struggle was fought between Africa and Rome.

[1] Jerome himself had approved of violence in religious disputes when the Bishop of Alexandria, Theophilus, beat the monks of Nitria.

IX

Innocent's letters to Jerome and to John show that he was disinclined just then to take either side in the Pelagian dispute; he preserved for a time a neutrality which was not at all to the African taste, and wrote to Aurelius and Augustine most impartially. Augustine was disturbed at the Pope's neutrality and at the sight of the East settling down in placid satisfaction with the acquittal of Pelagius, indifferent to African opinion. There seemed to be no hope of unity if the East was to be allowed to regard itself as entitled to form its own opinions in matters of doctrine, and if African opinion was to have no currency beyond Africa.

At the close of 416 two councils were called, at Carthage and in Numidia, including between them practically all the heads of the African Church, with the purpose of condemning the Pelagian doctrines and of defining the African position regarding sin, grace and the fall. In result three letters were sent to Rome from Augustine and Aurelius, intended to leave no doubt in any mind about the dangers to the unity of the Church and to the authority of Rome inherent in Pelagius' view of grace, and also to galvanize the reluctant, pacific Innocent into taking decisive action—on the African side of course. This appeal to Rome is made much of in later times by ardent Romans to prove that, at this early date, the See of Rome was already head of all the churches. It meant, as the sequel shows, nothing of the kind. The purpose of the Africans, who were in real anxiety, was to flatter or, if necessary, bully Rome into conformity with their own views; and they were ready to say anything that might induce that desired result. To be flattered is always gratifying, while even to be considered worth bullying is better perhaps than to be utterly ignored, and African shrewdness was rewarded. Innocent, in a personal question, could be fair-minded and statesmanlike, but as an ambitious champion of the Papacy, one of its inventors in fact, he was not proof against appeals which might increase its prestige. In his replies to the several letters from Africa he referred to the 'time-honoured custom' of invoking the authority of Rome, while, as a biographer[1] of Augustine has pointed out, 'his delight at the novelty of the proceeding floods every page of the letters'. He confessed himself to have been completely convinced by their arguments, he endorsed the views of the African synods, upheld their condemnation of Pelagius, and pronounced excommunication on Celestius and Pelagius until they should come to a better mind.

Once more the controversy seemed at an end, this time to the satisfaction of Augustine and the anti-Pelagian party: the findings of the Council of Lydda were apparently reversed by the success of the African manœuvres. But, as often in the Pelagian controversy, decisive results were short-lived, and an argument which depended more on personalities than principles was at the mercy of human vicissitudes. In March 417 Innocent died, probably before Pelagius' *Declaration of his Faith* with its covering letter and enclosures could reach him. And Bishop John of Jerusalem, Pelagius' great friend and supporter, also died, and with the death of his principal ally, and of the powerful instrument against him with which his persecutors had now provided themselves, the situation lost its definition and became rather confused.

Innocent's successor, Zosimus, was a Greek, and naturally

[1] J. MacCabe, *Saint Augustine and his Age.*

in sympathy with the eastern section of the Church, untroubled by any jealousy for the prestige of the Roman See. He also owed his own elevation to the Papacy in part to the friendship of Constantius, commander of the army in Gaul, who had captured Constantine, the British usurper, at Arles, and turned Heros and Lazarus, the unsuccessful accusers of Pelagius, out of their sees. Thus he had every personal reason to be favourable to Pelagius, and desired, perhaps, being a small man in the shoes of a greater, to take an independent line of his own. He had also received from bishop Praylius, John's successor at Jerusalem, Pelagius' new book on free will, and perhaps also the letter which Pelagius had addressed to Innocent; at any rate he made a display of independence by instituting in Rome an inquiry into the heresy on his own account, a step which, after all, was precisely what the Council of Jerusalem, the first to examine Pelagius in Palestine, had unanimously demanded. He summoned, not Pelagius, but Celestius, who happened to be in Rome, as the original object of the African denunciations, and Heros and Lazarus, to present their respective cases before him. Celestius, who seems to have been in the unfortunate situation that he attracted the odium and attacks of the anti-Pelagians without enjoying much personal support from the Pelagians, had been in Constantinople vainly trying to arouse interest in his cause in that capricious and usually controversy-loving public. But the Constantinopolitans seemed to have found at last a heresy which bored them and they refused to be interested in Celestius.

On the accession of Zosimus Celestius had come at once to Rome, glad to find a place at last where his presence seemed not unacceptable, and he made, on his arrival, a declaration of submission to the Pope. When the inquiry opened Heros and Lazarus, as usual, failed to appear and their case again went by default. Celestius' defence was heard: he refused to retract the opinions for which the Africans had condemned him at Carthage, and also repudiated the accusations brought against him by Heros and Lazarus, a position which seems not quite logical. Zosimus and the tribunal, however, were satisfied; and though no definite verdict was given, Zosimus wrote the Africans a letter in which he showed no intention at all of submitting to their dictation, or of taking the field against Pelagius. Over any other signature the letter would be praised for its moderation and common sense, for in words almost identical with those in which the Emperor Constantine had addressed other Africans in another controversy[1] more than a couple of generations before, Zosimus informed them that 'these complicated questions and silly arguments destroy the faith rather than fortify it, and proceed from an idle curiosity'.

He also invited the Africans to send representatives to Rome to present their objections against Pelagius, mentioning by name Paulinus the Deacon, the very man who, eight years before at Carthage, had been the formal accuser of Celestius. Paulinus, rather pusillanimously, refused to go to Rome, and, as far as we know, the Africans made no effort to put in a personal appearance. Encouraged by their inaction, Pelagius' supporters in Rome and Italy seem at last to have bestirred themselves: they threatened to abandon him if he abandoned his teaching, and they made the Roman synod renew its sittings. Various documents and quotations from Pelagius' writings were read aloud and, as Pope Zosimus afterwards told the Africans, the council almost wept at the thought that so holy and excellent a man had been condemned. In a further letter he informed the Africans that Pelagius and Celestius had been acquitted and approved, and Heros and Lazarus condemned and excommunicated.

The African, or rather the Augustinian, retort to these spirited proceedings at Rome was a couple of fresh councils,[2]

[1] Between Athanasius and Arius.
[2] At Carthage.

which reaffirmed the previous condemnation of Celestius
and warned Zosimus, in a most patronizing way, to beware
the guile of the heretics. Their tone was now quite different
from that accorded to Innocent, for Zosimus was not worth
flattering as Innocent had been, and it was galling to have
exaggerated the prestige of Rome to gain Innocent and then
to have to endure the paltry, puffed-up Zosimus. There were
other ways than flattery available at need to bring an in-
subordinate Pope to heel. Meanwhile synods could always
be held to focus general attention and keep the game alive.

The second of these two councils met on May 1st, 418 at
Carthage. On April 29th, everybody, except perhaps Augustine and his intimates, was startled by a letter from Zosimus,
written on March 21st, which seemed to foreshadow a change
of front, to be intended to prepare them for an eventual
capitulation. Zosimus' decision, it seemed, was still in re-
serve: fresh material had reached him which seemed to show
the matter in another light. The change of tone, since his
last communication to Africa, is complete, and naturally it
took some of the sting out of the proceedings of the council.
The African bishops, however, persevered with the Pope's
education by formulating and sending him a series of nine
canons[1] on original sin and grace, to show him what was
and was not safe for him to believe; and a permanent sub-
committee remained in session, to keep an eye on the progress
of affairs, while the inevitable delays elapsed, consequent
upon the slow means of transit of those times.

When Zosimus' letter arrived the principal movers in
the African proceedings, Aurelius bishop of Carthage and
Augustine, knew that there was no further need for anxiety,
and that their case was won. On April 30th, at the very moment
when the second council was assembling at Carthage, the
Emperor Honorius, from his retreat at Ravenna, addressed
a decree to all the Prætorian Prefects, denouncing Pelagius

---

[1] Called *The Canons of Carthage.*

and Celestius and their doctrines as dangerous and false, deploring the disturbances caused by heresy in the imperial city, and ordering both Pelagius[1] and Celestius to quit it forthwith.[2]

Both to the Church and the Christian world at large must be accorded the credit of being astonished and disgusted at the decree. It produced a reaction in favour of Pelagius and against Augustine; for never, either then or now, has the latter's part in the affair been in doubt. The decree was called both a *rescript* and a *reply*, and for many reasons Augustine could be assumed to be its instigator. We have, however, the explicit admission of Honorius himself, who blandly admits in a subsequent letter to Aurelius and Augustine that the decree was issued at their request.[3] It seems a humble posture for a Roman emperor to obey the dictates of provincial ecclesiastics in Africa, but Honorius was not a very masterful personality; insignificant, futile, half-forgotten in his retreat at Ravenna, he was flattered, most probably, by the appeal, and was glad to have an opportunity to over-rule the Pope.

For the second time in a few years, imperial intervention had been invoked in ecclesiastical affairs and, though the immediate result was not a bloody persecution as in the case of the Donatists, the principle of penal action by the civil authority in a religious quarrel gained further support. Christians of later days have looked back with gratitude to these two precedents. As a modern ecclesiastical historian has said, 'the bloody pages of mediæval history rise before us when we dwell upon Saint Augustine's later ideas'. So indeed they may, but in justice to Augustine it must be

---

[1] Pelagius was probably still in Palestine.

[2] The text of this document is quoted at length by Baronius (*Annales Ecclesiastici:* ann. 418), and in P. Quesnel's collection in Migne lvi, pp. 490 and 959. It is referred to by several contemporary authors, Marius Mercator, *Comm.* 3, Julian, *Contra Catholicos*, Augustine, *Epistle to Valerius*, and others.

[3] Migne, LVI. 43.

remarked that, though he advocated the use of persecution to suppress heresy and himself called in the emperor's aid, he was not the inventor of the principle. From the time of Constantine the emperors had perforce been dictating to their subjects what they should and should not believe.[1] Many were the edicts against the sects in those first Christian reigns. Manichæans, Montanists, Macedonians, Eunomians, Apollinarians, Arians, Pneumatomachians, Encratites, Apotactites, Saccoforians, Hydroparastates, Fryges, Pepyzites, Sabbatians, Priscillianists, Donatists, and Mathematicians were the constant objects of repressive decrees, were deprived of their property, expelled, and called the most uncivil names. And once imperial intervention began it had no end; with truly royal delight in detail the emperors are found deciding questions of the minutest practical kind. There are decrees to prevent women from outraging God and man by shortening their hair,[2] and ecclesiastics from keeping in their houses ladies whom they called their sisters.[3] From the first day of Toleration the process was inevitable; the emperors could not have left the polymorphic heresies and their internecine battles to follow their courses unrestrained, and even had they not been invited must in the end have intervened.

Zosimus made no attempt to rebel against his masters. He followed suit, as indeed he needs must do unless he was to provoke a violent schism, with a circular called the *Tractoria*,[4] to all his bishops, containing under several headings a condemnation of the alleged Pelagian teaching, which they were required to sign. Many of them, indeed the majority, submitted and signed; but there were places where, through a genuine devotion to Pelagianism, or a certain

---

[1] See pp. 13, 278.
[2] *Codex Theodosianus*, XVI, 2, 27.
[3] *Codex Theodosianus*, XVI, 2, 44. Jerome complains of these 'sisters'; the relationship evidently was quite a frequent one.
[4] See W. Bright, *Age of the Fathers*, ii, 212.

indifference to the Emperor or to the Pope, the *Tractoria* was disregarded and the condemnation was not signed. The attempt to force submission, as usual, stimulated opposition, and consolidated a heresy that might very easily have died away and been forgotten.

Among the admirers of Pelagius, even if there was submission to authority, there was difficulty in understanding why he had been so persecuted, and the more courageous of them, people of sufficient distinction to have a right to be answered, wrote to Augustine for an explanation.[1] Their inquiries produced a torrential polemical output in which Augustine not only attempted to deal with Pelagius but formulated and developed his own peculiar ideas on sin, grace, and the fall, leading eventually to the sinister and unfortunate doctrine of predestination.[2]

Zosimus made a feeble effort to revenge himself upon the Africans for his coercion by asserting Roman authority in a case of local discipline in Africa in which a bishop, Urbanus, a pupil of Augustine's, had on his own authority excommunicated a priest. The attempt was not taken very seriously, and before the year 418 was out Zosimus was dead, and the appointment of his successor engulfed the capital in the disorders of a schism.

Little more is heard of Pelagius himself. At Antioch in 418 he was summoned to appear before the bishop to answer once more for his views. In a synod of which we have no details, but which was no doubt profoundly influenced by the Western decrees, he was finally excommunicated and refused admission to the Holy Places. He must now have realized his defeat. Thenceforward he is heard of no more.

---

[1] Saint Paulinus of Nola; Dardanus, Prætorian Prefect of the Gauls; Optatus bishop of Biskra; Anicia Juliana, mother of Demetrias; and the distinguished family of the Cælianhill, Albina, Pinianus, and his wife Melania the younger.

[2] *De Gestis Pelagii, De Gratia Christi.*

We do not know what became of him, where he went, or lived, or died. In the words of his Benedictine biographer, 'there is a great silence about Pelagius'. We have no reason to suppose that anything much happened to him, for had any sudden fate overtaken him in the hour of defeat his enemies would hardly have failed to advertise the workings of divine justice. The silence is so complete that we can only conclude that he was hidden, as the objects of persecution sometimes had to be hidden in those days, in a quiet retreat among friends, in Palestine perhaps, or more likely in Britain. For his enemies it must be said that all they wished for was that he should be silent; and when he ceased to be heard of, though the controversy still raged, they did not seek him out.

★ X ★

The *Tractoria* proved an effective advertisement for the heresy. It travelled about the Roman world, and in places where Pelagius had never been heard of it had to be read and signed; obscure Pelagians who might never have declared themselves were now compelled by conscience to come out into the light. In Italy eighteen bishops defied it, and at Aquileia, among the friends of Rufinus, there was a sturdy opposition which openly attacked Augustine. The leader of the Italian opposition was Julian of Eclanum in Apulia, a distinguished young man, son of Augustine's rather tedious friend and correspondent Memorius, and a friend of Saint Paulinus of Nola. He was a scholarly person, a philosopher, as well as an expert theologian, and he thought nothing at all of Augustine's newfangled mysticism, of his notions of sin and human nature, which he regarded as immoral, fatalistic, and as imputing injustice to God. He was the typical clever young man, irrepressible, devoid of respect or pity for his elders, and he did not care what he said about Augustine. He called original sin a vulgar catchword imposed on the Church by a deliberate conspiracy, a piece of pestilential orientalism, savouring of Traducianism and of Manichæanism, both condemned by the Church. And he wrote four books against Augustine's views of marriage as injurious to morals, for he had been married himself, very happily, and had taken holy orders only upon the death of his wife.

He put into the attack an energy and venom equal almost to Augustine's own. He wrote to the Pope, demanding a re-hearing of Pelagius' case, and to Valerius, an official at the Court of Ravenna who was a strong *point d'appui* of the anti-Pelagian movement, and to the bishop of Thessalonica, that outpost of Roman interests on the fringe of the East. His writings were widely read and caused some stir. Their principal effect was to evoke the last group of Augustine's anti-Pelagian works; in which his views on marriage, on grace, on original sin and the nature of the soul, reach their extremest form, and the doctrine of predestination is finally enunciated. It was a strange effect of Pelagianism, to drive Augustine farther and farther along the path of his argument to its only logical conclusion.

There was a ding-dong battle of treatises between the two men, with nothing to choose between them, and a good deal of public support for Julian's side. Zosimus in 418, however, excommunicated Julian and his friends, and Valerius at Ravenna kept the court consistently anti-Pelagian. The re-hearing was refused and Julian left Italy, first for Constantinople, where he tried, but like Celestius failed, to gain support, and then for Cilicia, where Theodore of Mopsuestia, that independent-minded person who, according to Marius Mercator, was the original source of Pelagianism,[2] seems to have provided a refuge for the exiled Pelagians. Here Julian continued the controversy for a time, but Theodore eventually tired of his refugees and their campaign, and submitted to the findings of the Council of Antioch, which condemned Pelagianism. His mind was busy with other, larger themes, the Incarnation and the nature of Christ. These were subjects worthier of his bold and subtle mind and far more fascinating

---

[1] *Against the Two Letters of the Pelagians; On Original Sin; On Marriage and Concupiscence; Against Julianus* (four books, unfinished).

[2] In 416 he published a book 'Against all those who say that men sin by nature and not by will'.

to the Easterns in general than the simplicities of Pelagian ethics. Theodore developed these themes, and by 428, when he may himself have died, the East was engulfed in the Nestorian controversy, christened after Nestorius, but derived in all probability from Theodore's speculations.

Julian, and some of the surviving Pelagians, obtained some further protection for a time from Nestorius, the future heresiarch, who was newly created Patriarch at Constantinople. But Nestorius was already being attacked for his own views, and after some hedging, not finding the Pelagians conducive to a reputation for orthodoxy, he too decided against them. Marius Mercator, an African layman, who seems to have established himself at Constantinople as an eye of Augustine to watch heretical possibilities there and guard against any attempt by the Pelagians to win over the patriarchate, produced his *Commonitorium super nomine Celestii*,[1] an *ex parte* description of Pelagianism intended for the Pope in particular but also for congregations and monasteries and for all whom it might concern. The work, valuable indeed to later ages for its record of the Pelagian controversy, served its purpose and decided the East against the Pelagians, who were finally condemned all over again by the council which condemned Nestorius at Ephesus in 431.

In the West, despite the *Tractoria*, the Pelagians gave Augustine no peace. There were bishops even in Africa who were shocked and alarmed at the new doctrine of predestination, and in Rome there were publications, some of them anonymous, actually attacking Augustine,[2] who was driven to compose further letters and treatises.

In Gaul the Pelagian question was regarded with an in-

---

[1] Migne, xlviii.
[2] An anonymous work called the *Prædestinatus* defended Augustine but attacked predestination.

dependence of mind that was beginning to be characteristic of the transalpine countries. There were objectors to signing the *Tractoria*, and Galla Placidia, reigning at Ravenna as regent for the young Valentinian III who had succeeded the usurper John in 425, was driven to request the Prætorian Prefect of the Gauls to threaten some Pelagian bishops into submission. Among these Gallic Pelagians were some very estimable people,[1] and even among those who had signed the *Tractoria* there were many who were not disposed to regard an acceptance of the whole of Augustine's position as comprehended in that act. Predestination was something entirely novel in the Church, it had not been heard of before, and the Gauls did not like it at all. They attached no importance to the Africans, whom they had never seen and who were a very long way off, and the harshness of the idea offended their native geniality. In their opinion Augustine was guilty of both inhumanity and innovation, two things distasteful, on the whole, to the Gallic mind. As for doctrine and Church tradition, they had churchmen of their own to lead them, perfectly qualified to teach them what they might believe.

If there was not an open attack on Augustine, there was a critical atmosphere, especially in the Provençal monasteries, where the more acute intelligences seem, at that time, to have been gathered. In these houses great men were reared and developed, Vincent, Honoratus of Arles, Hilary of Arles, Patrick of Ireland, Germanus of Auxerre, men to whom the Church in later ages has looked back with pride; and here the Gallic church acquired some of those qualities, both in learning and in the capacity to govern and to civilize, that enabled her later to face the herculean task, which she performed with such surprising and impressive success, of making civilized Frenchmen out of the blood-thirsty, blood-curdling, and occasionally cannibalistic barbarians

[1] Sulpicius Severus was among them, see p. 25.

from beyond the Rhine. In these houses free will versus predestination was freely argued as an intellectual exercise, without rancour or acrimony, and it is pleasant to picture the Riviera of those days dotted with communities like Fréjus and Lérins given over to philosophical and ethical discussions of a kind that would not be encouraged on the *Côte d'azur* to-day.

John Cassian was a champion of free will. His position, explicitly set down in dialogue form in his *Conferences*,[1] is adroitly fathered upon a highly respected elder, that same Abbot Chæremon whose discourse on chastity so baffled the translators: 'For we should not hold that God made man such that he can never will or be capable of what is good, or else he has not granted him a free will. . . .', and he had also his own views on grace. While admitting its indispensability for salvation, he added a modification, which was both original and important, that its efficacy, that is to say salvation, must depend upon the *manner* in which grace is received. The result is to retain both liberty and uncertainty in each individual case: a man can accept or reject grace, and can fall away even after receiving it, and yet always receive it again. There is no predestination here, and salvation remains within a man's free choice, while grace remains the prerogative of the Church, who alone can dispense it. The combination is a stroke of genius, preserving as it does the liberty and dignity of human individuality, while leaving to the Church a power and control denied her both by complete freedom of the individual, and by predestination. It was known, in later times, as semi-Pelagianism, also as Massilianism, having been sponsored at Marseilles. The Provençal monasteries adopted it, and their powerful influence might have made it the ultimate position of the Roman Church. It had, however, the drawback that it made a man's first turn to God depend on free choice, not

[1] See p. 73.

on grace preventing, and so the Church could not accept it as a whole. But it left its mark on Church doctrine, and predestination, the true Augustinian doctrine, was abandoned and almost forgotten, till it was resuscitated, surprisingly, by reformers and dissenters, and by all sorts of people who, from both extremes of criticism,[1] needed a stick with which to beat the Church.

Here and there a few voices were raised for Augustine. Hilary,[2] a monk of Marseilles, who had once been his friend and companion, appealed to him to intervene with the intractable Gauls and got, in reply, the treatises on *Predestination* and on the *Gift of Perseverance*. It was rash at any time to provoke that voluble pen. But treatises served only to increase both the opposition to Augustine in Provence, and the Gallic determination not to be tyrannized over by any foreigner in the matter of their faith.

Prosper of Aquitaine, a pedant and a partisan of Augustine, with some of the acidity peculiar to pedants, tried to wake up the Gauls against the semi-Pelagians, but got very little support. In 432 he wrote a whole book[3] against John Cassian, but nobody paid any attention to it; and his efforts against Vincent,[4] the great Abbot of Lérins, in whose dislike of predestination he detected symptoms of Pelagianism, failed altogether. Vincent's great work, his *Commonitorium* on which his reputation rests, denounces all heresy, all innovation, all doctrine not directly derived from the prophets, the Scriptures, and the time-honoured traditions of the Church. What is ancient must be right, conversely all innovations must be wrong. He pours obloquy on all the well-known heretics, including Pelagius, and though he does not

[1] The Lutherans, for instance, and, in the opposite direction, the Jansenists.
[2] Not the Bishop of Arles, nor the celebrated Bishop of Poitiers.
[3] *Contra Collatorem.*
[4] *Responsiones ad Capitula Objectionum Vincentianarum.* Vincent's 'objections' are no longer extant.

mention Augustine, there was no doubt in the minds of churchmen that the attack was intended to include Augustine and his predestination. As a defender of Church authority and tradition Vincent was too precious to lose, and the Church, wise in such matters, has decided to overlook his attitude to the great African, and also anything Pelagian in his sympathies, for the sake of his appeal to tradition. His famous canon, that new ideas must be tested by their faithfulness to tradition, has been of incalculable service. It is somewhat negative for a church that may be compelled to progress, and as Cardinal Newman remarked, it was better fitted to ascertain what is *not* the doctrine of the Church than what *is*. But it has certainly served; 'quod semper, quod ubique' has been repeated by churchmen through many ages, and by people who never suspected that it was originally directed against Saint Augustine of Hippo and his revolutionary ideas.

Events were impending, however, which must terminate these stimulating intellectual pastimes, for the Africans at least: fortune took a strange way to deliver the Western Church from their doctrinal extremes. In 430 Augustine died, and that year the Vandals landed in Africa. Numbers of African Christians were massacred or fled into the desert to the monks, and the remainder were too much occupied in maintaining their Catholic doctrine against their Arian conquerors to trouble about predestination.[1] The Vandals have had in later times the thanks of devout Catholics for their unintended service to the Church of Rome in ridding her at this stage, without trouble or expense to herself, of her predestinarians. Latin theology and Latin culture, through the barbarian age, found a refuge in Gaul; and with Gallic churchmen in the ascendant semi-Pelagianism settled down

---

[1] The so-called Creed of Saint Athanasius was probably composed a century after his death by African theologians in need of a document with which to confront the Vandals, who were Arians.

peacefully in Gaul with even a tendency, notably in Provence, towards full and complete Pelagianism. This was corrected in 529 by the Council of Orange, which reaffirmed prevenient grace but ignored and hushed-up predestination. The Council of Orange settled these points for many centuries to come, and its findings were referred back to and reaffirmed in 1546 by the Council of Trent.

Gaul was not the only western refuge for moderate opinion and for toleration. In 404, with the withdrawal of the Roman eagles, the Roman authority faded from Britain. There was no longer a Prætorian Prefect to enforce imperial decrees, and if they were heard of or read in Britain they were certainly not heeded. The *Tractoria* may have reached Britain or it may not, but there was no one to oblige her bishops to sign it or to depose any who did not. Cut off from Europe by her preoccupation with Saxons and Picts, she was outside continental movements and controversies, and was learning once more to be, and to be regarded as, an island. Both emperor and Pope became the foreigners they have always been in English history. It is significant that where imperial authority did not function the Pope did not imagine that papal decrees had any currency either; and British bishops seem to have been regarded in Rome as beyond direct control. Interference, if any, must be by argument and persuasion, by missions sent over to preach, not by decrees or threats or penalties. Britain, ecclesiastically at any rate, got on very nicely without Rome and was busy developing her Church in her own way, with her own peculiar saints, and her peculiar ideas of liturgy and of Easter,[1] derived from the old, un-

[1] The Celtic churches kept the old date of Easter Sunday based on the eighty-four years' cycle of the Passover, which had been the first usage in the Church. It fell earlier than the later nineteen years' cycle introduced by Augustine of Canterbury.

[237]

reformed Roman usage. She had a native indifference to theology, and an indigenous belief in the importance of conduct and of good works. Even Ireland seemed nearer than Rome, and as relations between Britain and Ireland grew closer behind the barrier of the Saxons which divided them from the Roman world, the unorthodoxy of the British was passed on to the Irish Church. And if the Saxon barrier was also a pagan one, it was because the British, with excellent common sense, refrained from converting the Saxons,[1] preferring to ensure their damnation in the next world whatever success or prosperity might attend them in this. Later, when a great Pope decided that these undisciplined islands with their British saints and pagan Saxons must be brought within the jurisdiction of Rome, Augustine of Canterbury found his thorniest task not in the conversion of simple pagans but in inducing the British bishops to abandon their peculiar practices and procedure, and conform to those of Rome.

The first use the British made of their insularity was to go, in the eyes of the continent, dangerously astray, and one of their earliest errors was Pelagianism. In the decades that succeeded what was intended to be the close of the Pelagian controversy churchmen on the continent saw with alarm a snug little nest of Pelagians flourishing safe and uncorrected beyond those narrow seas, which seem to have more power than many a mightier ocean to isolate and divide.

Pelagian literature must have reached Britain early in the career of the movement, in the first decade, perhaps, of the fifth century. In Pelagius' time, as we know, there was a good deal of coming and going between Britain, Rome and the Holy Places. There were the regular pilgrims, and people might make a long stay abroad for education, or for religious purposes. Pelagius' books, as the work of a distinguished

---

[1] Bede, *Ecclesiastical History*.

Briton, no doubt went straight back to Britain as they were published; and might well recommend themselves to the simple-minded, theologically guileless British. When Pelagius was branded as a heretic, and the persecution of the Pelagians began, Britain must have been a natural refuge for any one who wished to adhere to his teaching. Prosper of Aquitaine[1] says that Pelagianism reached Britain by certain heretics, enemies of grace, who were of British origin; and there was a man named Agricola,[2] not expressly described as British, but with a name that any Roman Briton might be proud to own, son of a Pelagian bishop Severianus, who corrupted the British Church with the slow poison of his false doctrine.

There are some fragments of literature which seem to come from British Pelagians. Fastidius, a British bishop, perhaps of London, wrote a tract on piety and virtuous living, addressed (not surprisingly) to a widow. It was included, at one time, among Augustine's works, but is now regarded as tainted with Pelagianism. To any one not on the look-out for such a taint it seems a harmless work enough, if a trifle dull, except for some little glimpses of life in Britain at the beginning of the fifth century. The recipient is urged to practise all the virtues, and is warned that charity out of ill-gotten gains is useless and can have no effect in removing the guilt of the deeds by which the ill-gotten gains were won. She is to avoid behaviour such as that of the snobs, the rich and haughty aristocrats, who bring up their children to the world and its vanities, neglecting the proper obligation of Christian hospitality to chance-comers, and disdaining, with their white and dainty hands, to wash the feet of the poor. When not engaged in almsgiving and succouring the poor, she must read and pray so assiduously that no one will ever find her otherwise than kneeling, or with a good book in her hand.

[1] *Chronicle* and *Contra Collatorem.*
[2] Bede, *Ecclesiastical History.*

There is some doctrinal vagueness in the letter, which has led to a suspicion of Pelagianism, and there is a quite unexplained passage which takes us back to Pelagius' trial at Lydda, and may have some bearing on his behaviour there. Fastidius uses, with verbal exactitude, but without ascribing them to Pelagius or any one else, the very words which, deprived of their context, Pelagius was accused at Lydda of having addressed to another widow.[1] It can only be concluded that they were a traditional or accepted form of prayer in local use in some section of the Church unfamiliar to Augustine; it is possible even that they go back to ancient Greek religion, to a formula inscribed over the entrance to temples or recited on entering.[2]

There are also some anonymous letters with Pelagian characteristics, in one of which the writer, who seems to be a Briton abroad on a pilgrimage, reproves his parents for their objections to his journey. If God is everywhere, they seem to have said, why should it be necessary to run the risks of foreign travel to find him? Against this objection the pilgrim urges that if it is true that God is everywhere, in France, in Saxonia, and among the barbarians, then there can be no danger anywhere, everywhere it must be safe to go. He had intended to reach Antioch, but adds, in a somewhat apologetic tone, that he has been detained in Sicily by religion, that is to say by a noble and pious lady, a widow as usual, who has convinced him that God is to be found there just as well as at Antioch.[3]

[1] See p. 215.
[2] See an epigram from the Supplement to *The Palatine Anthology*: Mackail, 5, xvi, and note.
ἀγνὰς χεῖρας ἔχων καὶ νοῦν καί γλῶτταν ἀληθῆ
εἴσιθι μὴ λουτροῖς ἀλλὰ νόῳ καθαρός.'
[3] Caspari, *Briefe, Predigten und Abhandlungen aus den letzten jahrhunderten des Kirchlichen Altertums*. Caspari concludes that the letter is British because Britain is omitted from the list of countries where God is to be found and must therefore be the godless country from which the writer has fled.

Pelagianism seems at last to have become so flagrant in Britain that her continental neighbours decided to interfere. Some one called Palladius,[1] about whom we have no previous knowledge, drew Pope Celestine's attention to it, and in 429 Germanus, the great bishop of Auxerre, was sent to frighten the independent islanders back to the fold. He was accompanied by Lupus bishop of Troyes, another great bulwark of northern Gallic Christianity, and with a party of ecclesiastics they set out that autumn for Britain from some Channel port.

They had a bad crossing, but arrived safely at what their chronicler[2] very properly calls the greatest and most important of all islands. Crowds gathered round the visitors wherever they went. They preached against Pelagianism in the churches and outside them, meeting at first no opposition. Later the Pelagians, fearing to lose their case by default, challenged the visitors to meet them in public contest. A great debate was staged at Verulam, with a great crowd shouting and applauding on each side and occasionally threatening violence. The visitors claimed the victory, as also in a subsequent competition in miracles; and later Germanus is found leading the British against a combined invasion of Saxons and Picts in the north, triumphing over them in the celebrated 'Hallelujah' victory, in which the shouts of 'Hallelujah' so frightened the heathen that they fled, leaving enormous booty on the field. Germanus and Lupus returned to France covered with glory, after a stay of two years.

It is a little disappointing, after all this, to learn that sixteen years later, about 447, Germanus was again called to Britain, to deal with a fresh outbreak of Pelagianism. Further miracles

---

[1] Not the author of the *Lausiac History*.
[2] Constantius, *Vita Sancti Germani*. This Constantius was a Gaul, a friend and correspondent of Sidonius Apollinaris. The story is told more briefly, by Bede: *Ecclesiastical History*.

were performed, and the mission was so successful that the British, Constantius assures us, a little prematurely, never again relapsed into heresy.

Ireland seems to have been the next resort of the heresy. Palladius was sent to Ireland by Pope Celestine, to convert the heathen and to be the bishop of the Irish believers, an indication among many others[1] that there were Christians, before the mission of Patrick, in Ireland. Perhaps there were Pelagians too, for there is more than a hint of the Pelagian controversy in one of Patrick's professed motives for his Irish mission, namely that he was anxious about the Irish infants, who were being allowed to die unbaptized. Indifference at this period about the baptism of infants justifies a suspicion of Pelagianism. If the snakes cast by Patrick out of Ireland included Pelagianism, their extermination was not, however, very complete. In Ireland Pelagianism simmered on, scarcely aware perhaps that it was a heresy. In the seventh century John, Augustine's successor at Canterbury, had his attention drawn to an outbreak of Pelagianism across the Irish Sea, as also to the uncanonical date of Easter, which the British churches still persisted in keeping earlier than the Roman Church.[2] He did not succeed in checking Pelagianism in Ireland, for Ireland became a repository of Pelagian literature, and in Ireland Pelagius' works, especially the *Commentary*, were unashamedly copied and read. When, in the ninth century, the Vikings sacked and burnt the Irish monasteries, the monks fled to the continent taking what books they could salve with them, and in continental houses, as at Saint-Gall in Switzerland, an Irish foundation, the work of copying continued. Copies of the *Commentary* are found in many of the older libraries of Europe, in Germany, Italy and France; and sometimes, if the text was in the old Irish script, it was erased to enable the valuable

[1] See p. 160.
[2] See p. 237, note.

parchment to be used again, and the existence of the vanished manuscript was remembered only in the catalogue of the library. Often enough, on the continent, the *Commentary* appears without Pelagius' name; for it could be circulated with greater safety and tranquillity without a name which had caused so much trouble. Awkward passages, sometimes, were omitted, or pieces added from other authors, to the torment of subsequent scholars. Its anonymity led in the end to some strange ascriptions: unsuspecting editors included it in the works of other authors,[1] and, by the most ironical of all strokes of fate, in those of Jerome himself, and Pelagians could read their favourite author under some spurious but unimpeachable name. Erasmus, though he included Pelagius' *Commentary* in his great edition of the works of Jerome, was the first to cast doubt upon the alleged authorship, and eventually scholars identified the true author of a work which masqueraded so long and so successfully under the name of one of its most vigorous opponents. An exception to the general anonymity of the work is in Ireland, in the Book of Armagh of the year 808,[2] in which Pelagius' prefaces and 'arguments' to the Epistles of Saint Paul are included under his own name.[3]

The extreme form of Saint Augustine's predestination faded away, as we have seen, after his death, and Pelagianism was whittled down to semi-Pelagianism, or Massilianism. In a world of violence and disintegration the Church could not afford any standpoint that did not make her indispensable and also permanently accessible, and her adroit combination of bits of Augustinism and Massilianism miraculously made her both. Predestination would merely have deprived her of the power, which she held as a monopoly, of dis-

[1] Ambrosiaster, Pope Gelasius, Sedulius Scotus, Primasius. See Souter, *Introduction to Pelagius' Commentaries*.
[2] Now in the library of Trinity College, Dublin.
[3] Zimmer, *Pelagius in Ireland*.

pensing and of bestowing the sole means of salvation where she chose, and thenceforward she consistently frowned on any attempt to revive it. It raised its head occasionally in the Middle Ages, to be swiftly crushed. Free will, nevertheless, and the fascinating controversy between it and determinism, had remarkable vitality. Thomas Bradwardine,[1] the great Oxford scholar, found free will being so openly advocated that he gave a series of lectures against it which eventually appeared in a vast work *De Causa Dei contra Pelagium*; and the question could be openly discussed by the Canterbury Pilgrims.[2]

Predestination was eventually revived, very strangely, by the Protestant Reformers, who discerned its possibilities as a weapon against the Church, and those whom Augustine would most fiercely have condemned appealed to his authority and quoted his own words to defy her. Henceforward the history of predestination was a mad game of battledore and shuttlecock, as reformers of different types took it up. Luther, himself originally an Augustinian monk, adopted it as part of his defence of the rights of the individual against the oppression of the Church, which was purveying for profit that salvation which was a man's inalienable right; and Erasmus, who could not follow Luther in his revolt against Church authority, withstood predestination for that and for other more rational reasons. Over free will he fought with Luther one of the battles of history, incurring the charges of being a Pelagian and a pagan; for both accusations can be brought against supporters of free will. The Calvinists, preferring the gloomier aspects of predestination, dwelt upon damnation by predestination rather than salvation by election; and the Lutherans, to maintain themselves against the Calvinists, were forced to mitigate their predestination

---

[1] Edward IV's secretary, and later Archbishop of Canterbury.
[2] See the '*Nun's Priest's Tale*'.

and the Lutheran Church eventually abandoned its once extreme predestinarian position.

The controversy had a remarkable vitality; it simmered on through the seventeenth and eighteenth centuries and is not yet completely dead. Predestination was not even the monopoly of the Protestant reformers, for in the sixteenth century the Jansenists, as extreme Augustinians; took it up, to be downed in the end by the worldly-wise, Church-defending Jesuits. The Articles of the Church of England enacted by Parliament in 1562, which are those of Edward VI considerably remodelled and re-written under and partly by Elizabeth on a broader basis, with the object of excluding as few people as possible, achieve a miracle of vagueness, especially upon original sin, free will,[1] and predestination. Elizabeth herself detested predestination,[2] and Article XVII which looks predestinarian at first sight, in fact defines predestination and describes the effects for good and evil which it may produce, but omits to say whether it is to be believed or not, and has been shown to admit of the whole of the contradictions to be found in Scripture on this subject.[3] Strict predestination has now been left to a few sectarians; and as for free will and the rest of Pelagianism, who would be so bold as to deny that the majority of well-disposed Anglicans have followed, as indeed in an age of nationalism they should, Augustine's British antagonist and are at heart Pelagian heretics to-day?

[1] Free will is not even mentioned in Article X which bears its name.
[2] 'Predestination is not and never has been the doctrine of the Church of England.'—Elizabeth to Archbishop Whitgift.
[3] E. C. S. Gibson, *The Thirty-Nine Articles*.

IV
THE SAINT
Gregory of Nazianzus

'*How charming is divine Philosophy,*
Not harsh and crabbed, as dull fools suppose,
But musical as is Apollo's lute,
And a perpetual feast of nectared sweets,
Where no crude surfeit reigns.'

I

'Avoid women and bishops', was an old saying of the desert fathers, to be regarded as just a piece of their customary cynicism were it not reiterated very fervently by John Cassian,[1] a person too eminent and too sincere to be suspected of a taste for cheap gibes or meretricious *bons mots*. Of bishops Cassian must have had experience in Gaul at any rate, where we know they were often great country gentlemen, sophisticated and worldly, living in splendid houses, panelled and painted and richly furnished, with fine horses and equipages, and gorgeous clothes made and embroidered for them by the 'dear widows and kind virgins' of their flock. But the Gallic bishops were probably not much worse than many of their compeers at any time, saints in lawn, as Pope called them. Bishops and women have been railed at through the ages, though not always in the same breath, by those people, the eternal puritans, to whom authority is at least as distasteful as the world, the flesh and the devil.

The standard of asceticism demanded of bishops has not, as a rule, been high. Saint Jerome[2] complained that bishops were elected by congregations not always from the best motives; too often they were people who could be relied on to encourage and patronize the theatre and the shows, or they were chosen for their wealth or rank, for their ancient

[1] See p.p. 25, 233.
[2] Ep. 69.

lineage, or their new fortune, just wire-pullers or snobs. And Ammianus Marcellinus, a pagan himself, was horrified at the pomp and swagger of the Bishop of Rome in his public appearances; why could he not emulate his own country clergy and live in a manner more becoming to his profession?

This contempt of bishops cannot, at so early a date, be ascribed to jealousy on the part of people who themselves had not been called upon to fill a lofty office; for it was joined with a very general reluctance on the part of many of the most suitable people to accept bishoprics when they were offered.[1] Many were the unwilling bishops of those times, for in an age of rapid ecclesiastical expansion the demand for bishops was enormous, and the press-gangs positively were needed to supply them. Small isolated communities must have their bishops, to keep them from wavering, or from falling into the ever-insidious heresies; every town of any size had its bishop, and sometimes towns of no size at all, when, as sometimes happened, it was convenient to create a bishopric to fortify one side in a controversy or a schism.[2] Locally a bishop had far less prestige than attaches to that respectable title now, but among his peers he had full status, however small or non-existent his see; he could vote at councils, and must take part in controversy, for the thorns of theological differences marred the comfort of most episcopal thrones. So the more conscientious the nominee for a bishopric, the less, as a rule, did he wish to be elected, and the more extreme the measures he might adopt to escape. Generally, when once the sacrifice had been made, the victim justified the choice of his electors by becoming a most ad-

---

[1] There had been a rush for holy orders when Constantine exempted the clergy from decurial responsibilities. Later this was rescinded and members of curiæ were not permitted to take orders.

[2] The *chorepiscopi*, village bishops, had full status: by the Council of Laodicea it was forbidden to appoint bishops for villages, but this was disregarded.

mirable, distinguished bishop. Synesius, the philosopher of Cyrene,[1] was one of these, and in the next century Sidonius Apollinaris, the Gallic *littérateur* and dilettante, was found in the end a heroic shepherd of his people, sustaining their hearts against the Burgundian invaders, even to eating mice in a siege.

Most unwilling of all the unwilling bishops was Saint Gregory of Nazianzus, a person so fundamentally out of sympathy with everything which constitutes a Church, so indifferent, hostile even, to ecclesiasticism and all its activities, that the wonder is that he ever became a saint at all. But he had the gifts which the times needed. The blood of martyrs was no longer required, and the Church had professional ascetics enough and to spare. Gregory can be counted among the ascetics, but his asceticism was never extreme, nor his principal claim to the attention of his fellows. He had the gifts which that controversial age valued, a subtle and highly-trained intellect, and a pen and a tongue too, equipped with all the arts of rhetoric. From his youth he chose philosophy as his profession, and literary composition was the only form of practical activity which he could endure. Much as he hated and shirked the demands of ordinary life, he cannot be called slothful, for, despite a host of interruptions and disturbances which perpetually snatched his leisure from him, his literary output was enormous, and his earthly monument a mountain of admirable, if entirely theological prose, and a mass of undistinguished, and also mainly theological verse.

His career was a long, almost unrelieved struggle against what looks like a conspiracy on the part of circumstance and his contemporaries to make him a bishop. Over and over again they seemed to have defeated him, and as often he slipped through their fingers till the next time. Once they

[1] Synesius has left a long letter to his brother fully explaining all his philosophical objections to holding a bishopric.

succeeded in elevating him to the episcopal throne of Constantinople, but not for long; from that high eminence he escaped, or rather fell, not perhaps with perfect dignity; and at the end of his life, which for those times was a reasonably protracted one, he attained that peace and seclusion to which through all distractions and disturbances he had never ceased to aspire.

Of his personal opinion of bishops Gregory made no secret. 'There is a danger of the noblest of all offices becoming a by-word among us. For promotion depends not on virtue, but villainy; and the sacred thrones fall not to the most worthy but to the most powerful. . . . Physicians must first study the nature of diseases and painters must gain experience in handling colours and in drawing; but a prelate is easily found, without serious training, with a reputation of recent date, sown and sprung up in a moment.'[1] In his poetry he goes still farther:[2] the ordinary crowd of bishops, he said, appeared to him 'as if a herald had summoned the scum of mankind, liars and perjurers, bullies, the malicious and the quarrelsome, the insatiable and the rapacious, cheats, drunkards, and devourers of the people', and more to the same effect, for Gregory's resources in invective were enormous. For himself he would have no part in an office that was so strangely filled, he would 'avoid it like the fires of Sodom'.

Gregory might abuse the bishops, but his aversion to becoming one was based on better reasons than prejudice; he was quite unfitted for such a position and he knew it. A bishop's life, then as always, was one of ceaseless bustle and stir, of controversy and politics. By his own open profession and by nature he was a philosopher, for philosophy was still regarded as a trade to which a man might give his life. He was a Christian, of course, but he conceived of Christianity

---

[1] *Panegyric on Basil.*
[2] *Historical Poems,* XIII.

as the ancients did their systems of philosophy, less as a principle for the conduct of ordinary life than as the proper occupation and object of life itself. It set a man apart from his fellows, even above them; exonerated him from the ordinary cares of business, of family, of a livelihood. 'My principal business is to avoid business', he once wrote. He called Christianity Divine Philosophy, and himself its sophist, using the word in its oldest, its once respectable meaning, as a master, a teacher of a craft, the sense attached to it before Socrates attacked the sophists in the state to which they had then fallen, and before Aristophanes had made fun of them. In Gregory's time, amid the general confusion of words with thought and the popular craze for rhetoric, for verbal gymnastic and display, for everything which had once brought the sophists low, the sophists had returned to honour again, for those same meretricious qualities which had provoked Socrates' contempt. Gregory could join in the verbal gymnastic himself, and was an excellent performer when he chose; but he knew what dangers lay in the lure of words, and that many of the sophists were mere wind-bags. Rhetoric, he complained, had invaded theology, and theologians played with words as jugglers play with pebbles, to deceive the eye with quick changes, showing off before audiences as if they were rhetoricians. 'The antithetic style, like a fell disease, has infected our churches, and babbling is mistaken for culture; like the Athenians in the Acts, we do nothing but hear or tell some new thing.'

There was nothing shocking, in that age, in the fusion of theology and philosophy, or in Gregory's philosophic pose. Theology had long been capitulating to philosophy, and it was precisely his capacity for speculation which gave Gregory his value to the Church. He was born into an age in which, to the better sort of minds, it seemed that the time had come for the last word to be said in a controversy which had raged for a couple of generations; and Gregory, for the eastern portion of Christendom, was called upon to say it. The controversy between Catholics and Arians had had everything to recommend it to the sophisticated minds of that age, who were loth indeed to relinquish it. Both sides could claim a foundation in Platonism; the Trinitarians, or as they called themselves, the Catholics, derived their difficult conception of the Trinity from the later Platonic dialogues, while the Arians could claim for their interesting equation of Christ to the Platonic *Logos* the same respectable origin.[1]

Speculation on such attractive subjects was not easily to be relinquished by refined minds bred in the schools; and the crude attempt of the Trinitarians at the Council of Nicæa to force, with the emperor's assistance,[2] their hard-and-fast, but extremely difficult formula upon their adversaries had only a fleeting success and brought half a century of embittered controversy. The successors of the Emperor Constantine, with the exception of Julian, were all, by accident or early education, on the Arian side, and even Julian, if he tolerated a Christian, preferred an Arian to a Catholic. Ultimately, the capture of Gratian and of Theodosius by the bold and determined Bishop Ambrose of Milan won the day for Catholicism in the West. Meantime in the East, throughout the middle of the fourth century, Arianism flourished and had the upper hand, not at all impeded by its own tendency to break up into sects and fine shades of definition inside the main group. It had evolved no exclusive dogma, nor made any disciplinary attempts to enforce unity. Its intellectual appeal in the argumentative Greek world, addicted as it was to dialectic and verbal hair-splitting, was

---

[1] The alternative name for the Catholics was *Homoousians*, because they held that the Son was of the *same* substance as the Father; and for the Arians, *Homoiousians* for their belief that the Son was of *like* substance to the Father.

[2] Constantine was president of the Council, and in addition to Government hospitality there was a good deal of military display.

enormous; it could only be met by an argument more interesting, more subtle still. Here came Gregory's peculiar genius with miraculous opportuneness to hand. To him the Trinity, as defined at the Council of Nicæa, was a conception to match the ancient philosophies; it demanded, and defeated, the highest effort of the human brain. To contemplate it was the worthy occupation of a lifetime, and to defend it with the utmost literary skill at command the sublime duty of the scholar. His expositions of the nature of the Trinity have never been superseded. Perhaps they have not always been understood: but their reputation has been none the worse for that. They breathed fresh life into the crestfallen Catholics, inspiring them ultimately to rout the Arians and to banish them from the high places in the Church. Catholicism triumphed, and the Church, seldom slow to appreciate her great men when they have furthered her progress in the world, forgave him his rudeness to her ministers, his contempt for her organization and machinery, and conferred on him the honorary degree of 'theologian', and the title of 'saint'.[1]

Gregory has other claims to our attention and our gratitude now. He was one of the earliest of autobiographers; he inherited, with the rest of the classical tradition, the Roman habit of self-expression, the art of cultivating his private life in literary form, in poetry, letters, and epigrams. He had a great circle of friends among the governing classes, both civil and ecclesiastical, in Asia, and the letters he bestowed upon them, both for business purposes and in an ordinary friendly way, rank with the epistolary flowers of all time. His poems are of humbler literary status; but between the two he has left us rich in information about himself and about the world and the society that surrounded

[1] The Council of Ephesus called him Gregory the Great, but tha title was subsequently reserved for another and perhaps more obviously suitable candidate, in the Western Church.

him. He is a little querulous always, a born kicker against the pricks, unburdening himself upon paper of all the grief and rage a man must feel who knows what he wants to do with his life and is perpetually compelled to do something quite different. He would have made an excellent Anglican bishop of the eighteenth or nineteenth centuries, or an admirable university don at any time. In any but a paper controversy he was out of place, an actor wrongly cast, making a sad mess of his part, wretched himself because he well knew the ineptitude he was displaying. So, at any rate, he has told us; we can believe him or not as we like.

II

Gregory was born in Cappadocia, about the year 330[1] of our era, at Arianzus, the country estate of his father, also called Gregory, who was bishop of Nazianzus.[2] His nationality must remain in doubt, but Greek seems to have been the family language and most of his relatives had Greek names. In Cappadocia the question of race has always been obscure, as often in Asia Minor, that most confused of countries, which has been in contact with so many civilizations without ever producing one of its own, and whose inhabitants, like most populations when described by ethnologists, always seem to have come from somewhere else.

In spite of her name and geographical position, western Asia Minor belongs, spiritually, to Europe; her shores are a part of that encircling Mediterranean seaboard whose civilizations were the precursors of our own. For sea-going, enterprising peoples, the sea is not a barrier but a link, and civilizations arose and flourished around the Mediterranean and communicated with and influenced each other. In the hinterlands behind the coasts, where the deserts and the mountains begin, there civilization ended, there were the barriers; beyond them were the barbarians, the Persians and

---

[1] He was about forty-five when his father died in 374.
[2] Nazianzus survives to-day as Niseni, a miserable place with some Byzantine ruins, but no remains of Gregory's date. (Sir W. Ramsey, *Historical Geography of Asia Minor.*)

the Medes, the Scythians and Cimmerians, the Troglodytes
(the swiftest of living men), the Garamantians, the Atarantians
who have no names, the dog-faced creatures, those also
whose heads do grow beneath their shoulders, and those
without heads anywhere; all remarkable in their way and interesting to the curious, but not really human. On the coasts of
Asia Minor the Greeks flourished and spread, in a brilliant
maritime climate, amid grand mountains and rivers with
romantic and unforgettable names, Sangarius and Cycnus,
Caïster, Hermas and Mæander. In the centre of Asia Minor
rises a great, somewhat sinister plateau, partly salt-desert,
partly a country where shepherds find, rather surprisingly,
a living for their flocks. It climbs eventually towards the
east to great mountain ranges, Taurus and Anti-Taurus, and
falls again to the valleys of the Halys and the Euphrates.
Beyond are the Armenian mountains, the Medes and Persians, and the strange nations of the east, Sogdians, Sagar-
tians, Hyrcanians, Bactrians, the Anthropophagi, the cannibals that do each other eat, Indians and what not.

The Ionian Greek, busy along his coasts, content with
his own civilization, gave little thought to his eastern hinter-
land with its unharvested deserts, till the Persians, natural
landsmen, undismayed by a great continental expedition,
found it a useful means of access to the Greek world, and the
Ionians found themselves paying tribute to Susa. This has
been one of the age-old differences between the Asiatic and
the Greek, that the Greek finds a real, if somewhat vague,
frontier on dry land, while the Asiatic can move indefinitely
on land and is brought to a halt only by the sea. Cleomenes
of Sparta stoutly refused the lures of Aristagoras, who
invited him to Susa, when he discovered that he was being
asked to take Greeks to a place three months' journey from
the sea; and Herodotus remarks on the clumsiness of Aristagoras, who had hitherto manœuvred with extreme skill, in
revealing the true nature of his plan before Cleomenes had

given his consent. Eventually Alexander flung the Persians across Anti-Taurus, and the resulting vacuum of Asia Minor was filled by the kingdom of the Seleucids, who made of it an outpost of the Greek world. Over the central and eastern parts of the country, with their strange mixture of inhabitants speaking uncouth languages and worshipping strange gods, they cast a veneer of Hellenism, apparently without great difficulty, for the natives had acquired but little from their Persian neighbours and seemed to have a natural aptitude for Western culture. The Seleucids began the civilization of the central plateau; and the Romans, the true successors of Alexander, eventually merged it in the full provincial system.

Cappadocia,[1] on the mountainous eastern edge of the plateau, toward the borders of the Persian and Armenian kingdoms, seems to have been first a Hittite stronghold; later Darius included it in the satrapies, and Cappadocians were in the army of Xerxes. Alexander never conquered it, and its kings played adroitly between Pompey, Cæsar and Antony till their dynasty died out and Tiberius made it a Roman province, a useful bulwark against the Persians. Its population, called sometimes Syrians, sometimes the white Syrians,[2] seem to have felt very little sympathy with their near neighbours the Persians, and when they eventually acquired a civilization it was that of the Seleucid kingdom to the west of them. Civilization reached them late, an imported article, Hellenistic and Græco-Roman, complete and ready for their use; and it must have been entirely superficial, the property and privilege of the wealthier classes, who were *nouveauxriches* in their attitude to culture, attaching an exaggerated importance to letters and the refined arts.

Cæsarea, the old capital of Cappadocia, and the other chief

---

[1] Herodotus omits it from the list of countries paying tribute to Cyrus.
[2] Strabo.

towns Archelais and Tyana, like all the cities of Hellenistic
Asia Minor, developed a vigorous Hellenism and flourishing
schools where the Greek language, letters, philosophy, and
science were taught. The rhetoricians of the later Greek age,
even at Athens, were frequently from Asia Minor, from
Bithynia, Pontus, Lydia, Cilicia, and Cappadocia, educated
in the Grecian culture in their native towns. And when
Christianity, newly liberated, invaded the intellectual classes,
there was a cultured society ready to receive it, and men of
breeding and sophistication to provide leaders and teachers.
Cappadocia, by some curious conjunction of circumstances,
was rich in ability in the fourth century and gave a fine
population of bishops and Fathers to the Church, not always,
it must be admitted, of the most orthodox shade of doctrine.
They were intellectually energetic and also subtle, in love,
like so many Asiatics, with dialectic and debate. They are
regarded, indeed, by a good Roman Catholic historian,[1] as
upstarts and adventurers, people of inadequate training and
experience who rushed in where angels fear to tread. This
seems ungrateful, for the Church owes them Gregory of
Nazianzus and Basil the Great; even if they did at the same
time produce the regrettable George, the bacon-factor, the
schismatic and violent bishop of Alexandria, and Eunomius
and Apollinarius, each the sponsor of a heresy bearing his
name. The Cappadocian bishops certainly made a great impression on their contemporaries; the Cappadocian delegates
at the dedication of the Emperor Constantine's great new
Church of the Holy Sepulchre at Jerusalem cut a fine figure
and impressed every one by the purity of their theology and
their talents for oratory. Even George, the bacon-contractor,
had a large and valuable library, part of which was purchased
at his death by the Emperor Julian.

Among themselves the Cappadocian ecclesiastics and
their friends and relatives lived as people will who are some-

[1] Duchesne.

what isolated from the centre of their own civilization, and are surrounded by a simple peasant population. They had to depend on one another for cultured intercourse, and like all small societies they quarrelled, intrigued, and talked scandal, in their case mostly of a theological kind. But community of interest and the possession of their Greek and Christian culture held them together, with a conscious superiority which amounts to affectation and snobbery: they were blue-stockings, *précieux ridicules* almost.

For the rest of the Cappadocians, the peasants, shepherds, and humbler classes, opinions were divided about them. Some regarded them, with the Cilicians and Carians and other peoples beginning in Greek with a K, as completely worthless, whilst others prized them for their industry and purchased them, in Roman times, for slaves. Isidore of Pelusium compared them to the giants of antiquity for their vices,[1] excepting of course those of the southern portion of Cappadocia which gave Basil and Gregory to the world. Like other non-Ionian people of Asia Minor, they were not averse to brigandage when occasion offered, and that, as we shall see, in classes of society superior to peasants and shepherds, who in hard times and remote places may be expected to indulge in such activities. But they were not as bad as their neighbours the Isaurians[2] who systematically raided monasteries, lay in wait for travellers whom they robbed, kidnapped or beat, and were generally regarded as beyond public control.

Gregory's father, Gregory the elder, bishop of Nazianzus, was a Cappadocian country squire, a considerable landowner at Arianzus[3] in a district not famous for any peculiar advan-

[1] There was always something fabulous about Cappadocia; the Romans believed that in Cappadocia even the mules were fertile and could breed.   [2] See page 130, note 2.

[3] Sir William Ramsay identifies Arianzus with the Turkish Gelvere, where till recently relics of Saint Gregory were preserved and shown in the church.

tages of climate or soil, yet providing its owner with what passed for wealth. Its climate ran to extremes; as in most places at high altitudes far from the sea, it blew both very hot and very cold. Basil, in a letter of somewhat elephantine pleasantry to Gregory, gibes at its cold and its mud in winter and its raging heat and dust in summer, and calls it the nastiest place on earth, the very sewer of the whole universe. It had occasional shortages, as when Gregory, in expectation of a visit from Basil, found himself in a dearth of greenstuff, and wrote urgently to the bishop of Iconium to beg a gift of vegetables, which were plentiful in his district. 'For you,' he wrote, 'who know Basil when he is full and philosophical, would not like to see him hungry and cross.' But the Gregories were rich enough to enable Gregory's mother Nonna to indulge in extravagant charity, and his father to build the church at Nazianzus almost entirely out of his own pocket. This church, which has entirely disappeared, was one of those late Roman buildings of which so few have survived. According to Gregory it was an octagon, faced outside with stone, inside with marbles of local origin, quite as beautiful, he assures us, as the fashionable foreign ones and, we can well imagine, much cheaper. It must have been domed, and inside were two tiers of columns, one above the other, and mosaics and more marbles, and there were great windows, filling it with light.[1] It was the scene of many incidents of Gregory's life, some of his greatest orations, his unwilling ordination, and his still more unwilling episcopal consecration.

Gregory the elder seems to have been the very antithesis

---

[1] The light is unusual for a building of that time: among the few extant examples are the Mausoleum of Diocletian at Spalato and the Lateran Baptistry, the former about fifty years earlier, the latter about fifty years later, than this church. A description of the building of a fourth-century church is to be found in Gregory of Nyssa, Ep. XVI. Eusebius describes Constantine's buildings at Jerusalem in his *Life of Constantine*.

of his son: he was weak in theology and rhetorical gifts, but had some strength of character.[1] In his secular days he had been that rare phenomenon, a Roman official who did not peculate; and as a bishop he defied the Emperor Julian when he came to Nazianzus to seize the churches, boiling with rage against him, and threatening personal assault. As will be seen, he could bully and browbeat his son.

His wife, Nonna, was a lady of great spiritual force, with a man's heart and mind in a woman's body, her son tells us, yet full of womanly kindness and Christian charity. She could never be induced to take the hand of a pagan, and she was never known to spit in church. She obtained all her desires by prayer, her children, who were all born to her in her middle age, and the conversion of her husband. She died upon her knees in prayer. Gregory compares her to Sarah for the advanced age at which she was reputed to have had children, but her age was probably always much exaggerated, and one is tempted to suspect that a saintly reputation coupled with a venerable appearance did duty, in those times, for a birth certificate.[2] She had three children, Gregory, Gorgonia, celebrated by Gregory in a funeral oration,[3] and Cæsarius, a brilliant and interesting person, more worldly-minded than his relatives, who became court physician at Constantinople.

The Gregories, exemplary as they seem at first sight, are a cause of grave distress to the extremer champions of celibacy for the clergy. For here we have the elder Gregory, a person in holy, even episcopal orders, living a normal family life

---

[1] Before his conversion he had been a Hypsistian, a sect which worshipped Zeus Hypsistos in the form of fire and light, probably a form of Zoroastrianism.

[2] She was reputed to be over ninety when her husband died in 374. Gregory was then forty-five at most and may have been less, which would make her over forty-five when her first child was born.

[3] She refused medical aid after a carriage accident, preferring to restore herself by prayer.

with both wife and children, unquestioned and unashamed, in the midst of his congregation.

It has been suggested, to save the old bishop's credit, that his children were born prior to his ordination and that his subsequent life with Nonna was one of a purely spiritual felicity. Unfortunately we have his own word, uttered in pardonable pride, that he had been in holy orders longer than his son had been alive.[1] Bishops in these times very commonly had sons; Saint Paul allowed them to have wives, so they had but one apiece; and Saint Jerome, who has something acid to say about most things, has a sharp word for the characters of bishops' sons, so presumably they had them. As for Gregory himself, he boasted that he had a bishop for his father; and the Cappadocians were not only undismayed at the paternity of their bishop but took it for granted that in such a family a bishopric should be hereditary, and that an excellent father should be succeeded by his equally excellent son.[2]

[1] See page 328, note. There was an unsuccessful attempt to force a clause about celibacy of the clergy upon the Council of Nicæa. Later, men who already had wives were excluded from the episcopacy.

[2] Popular election was a quite usual method of appointing a new bishop, and might be contradictory to the selection made in a synod called for the purpose, as in the case of Saint Martin of Tours. Attempts were made, as at the synod of Gangra, to stop the method of popular election, but without success.

✶ III ✶

Gregory, as becomes such a person, was a grave and studious child, fonder of books than of playing with other boys, and preferring serious books to amusing ones; at least such is his own account of himself. He was a poetic child, and once dreamed that two lovely women stood before him, with damask cheeks and dewy lips, but modestly veiled of course, and told him that they were Chastity and Temperance come to stablish him in these virtues for life. The bright vision never left him. Gregory practised a modest, unobtrusive asceticism; and he was chaste, if we do not force too far a word of which the precise significance, in patristic times, is none too clear.[1]

Gregory went to school at Cæsarea, the old capital of Cappadocia, where he first met Basil, known to us as Basil the Great, who was ultimately to dominate his whole life. Basil was Gregory's junior by some years, and though he made an impression on Gregory at school, the friendship did not mature at this stage and their ways parted for a time. In his early teens Gregory, accompanied by his young brother Cæsarius, went to Cæsarea in Palestine, which had a famous school of rhetoric, presided over by Thespesius, a

---

[1] See pages 326–7. Chastity admitted of degrees. Paulinus of Pella regarded himself as severely chaste and on the high road to absolute purity when he confined his attentions to the ladies of his own domestic staff; and took it as a sign of special approval on the part of Providence that he was spared, in these relations, the embarrassments of paternal responsibilities.

florid rhetorician of the usual type, whom Gregory celebrated later, in an epigram, as of the purest Attic quality.
Cæsarea, however, was not to complete their education.
Soon Cæsarius left for Alexandria, the foremost medical
school of that time, to study medicine, and five years later
Gregory joined him. But, perhaps through the influence of
Thespesius and his pure Attic teaching, Gregory was inspired by an obstinate purpose from which he could not
be deterred. His goal was Athens, and his one object to
shake off Alexandria and get himself to Athens as quickly
as he could. The reason he gave later in life for this contempt
of Alexandria was the desire to avoid the wiles of the sophists
and the entanglements they spread for the young men's feet.
But Athens even more than Alexandria was given over to
the sophists, her learning was entirely pagan, and she had
no ecclesiastical reputation whatever; while Alexandria had
a sheet-anchor for the faithful in the great Athanasius, protagonist in the Arian-Catholic controversy, who was bishop
there at the time. Alexandria, as a place of education, was
superior to Athens by far. She was seething with ideas, even
if not all of them were good ones, and though she had
decayed somewhat from the great days of the Ptolemies she
still had her contribution to make to philosophy, to science,
and to religious controversy. But Gregory could see nothing
in Alexandria and would have none of her. With an obstinacy
that was fundamental in his character he was set on Athens
and to Athens at all costs he would go.

He was not alone in his craving for Athens; others looked
to her still as the fountain-head of all literature, art, and
thought. She still had the intellectual prestige which the
Romans had not grudged her, had indeed industriously
cherished whilst they systematically looted her works of art.
Her university still had teachers, rhetoricians of course, with
reputations that could vie with those of the dazzling, more
recent centres of learning in Syria and Egypt. But in fact

the inspiration of Athens had long been spent. The Ilissus ran muddy and low, and the bird of Athena was dead or flown, having, like all good birds, done her duty and sent a flourishing brood to nest and multiply over the whole earth. But in this last age of the empire people clung to the belief that so holy a place must still be haunted, and that Ilissus ran clear beneath the planes. Sometimes they were disappointed when they got there. Libanius of Antioch, who was contemporary with Gregory, refused the fairest heiresses of Syria when they were offered as an inducement to him to stay at home, saying that he would rather see the smoke of Athens than kiss the white hands of a goddess. But when he reached Athens he was shocked at the low standard of teaching and the rough behaviour of the undergraduates. Half a century later Synesius of Cyrene, travelling through Greece on his way to present a petition at Constantinople, cursed the ship's captain who brought him to Athens; for Athens, he said, retained nothing but her great names, and a few monuments such as the Painted Portico; but even that had lost its paintings, which the Consul[1] had carried off long ago. Gregory, however, was not disappointed. Perhaps Athens with the Acropolis still intact, and her Hadrianic glories still in bloom, was good enough for a Cappadocian boy; or perhaps, at Athens if not at Alexandria, he was that sort of traveller who brings with him in his own heart what he intends to see. At any rate he remained there for ten years, to leave only when calls from home were too insistent to be ignored, with a homesickness for Athens for ever in his heart, and a sigh, and he was fond of sighing, for his lost mistress always on his lips.

Gregory was lucky to reach Athens alive; in his eagerness he made the journey too early in the year, and was overtaken by one of those storms of Homeric fury and duration which punctuated the precarious lives of the navigators of those

[1] Sulla.

times. Gregory prayed, and the sailors, Æginetans, were terrified and, to make matters worse, let the water-butts break and lose their water with a lurch of the ship, so that they were like to die of thirst even if the wind and waves abated. A Phœnician vessel, however, handier in such adventures, contrived to pass them a cask of water, and the ship and her company came safe to Rhodes and then to Ægina, in sight of the Acropolis at last.

Among the professors who still upheld the fame of Athens were two rhetoricians, Himerius and Prohæresius, whose reputations, as great as they were undeserved, linger on in the pages of their pupils whom they had trained in the gentle art of panegyric. Of Himerius' work sufficient fragments remain to assure us that it was compact of everything which least deserves the name of Attic and is most repugnant to our severe modern taste. It is preposterous stuff, verbose and tawdry, loaded with Homeric quotation and mythological allusions. His colleague, Prohæresius, whatever his literary style, was at any rate a handsome figure of towering height, with splendid silvery hair. The two of them made up for their lack of literary simplicity by following the good old Attic tradition of moderation in their dress and way of life; unlike the majority of the sophists who even at Athens used to paint their faces and wear jewels and wigs, habitually driving abroad in sumptuous carriages with silver harness and trappings, indulging every kind of foppery in order to advertise the popularity of their lectures in terms of the wealth they derived from fees.

Gregory studied under both these men, and adored them both. Of Prohæresius he says that even his unprepared discourses could shake the world, and when he died dedicated several epigrams to him, in one of which he mourns that there is nothing left to bring students to Athens any more. The Emperor Julian, who was a student at Athens for a while in Gregory's time, also praised Prohæresius to the length of telling him that his speeches equalled those of Pericles, with the advantage that he did not use them to stir up strife among the nations, a fair if somewhat unusual comment upon Pericles.

In his daily life at Athens Gregory assures us he lived very quietly, kept himself to himself, and took no part in the rowdy undergraduate life. The Athenian students had fallen away somewhat from the exalted character they had in Hadrian's time, when, inscriptions tell us, they never rioted or fell out in their cups, but were faultless all the year through. There had even been an occasion when the Roman Senate voted them a golden crown for their exemplary behaviour, which included taking pity on the old catapults, rusted and out of repair, and having them repaired at their own expense; for the duties of a student at Athens preserved to some extent the tradition of the *ephebi* of olden times, and were military and civic as well as academic.

In Gregory's time they had a positively systematic rowdyism, with a repertory of elaborate 'rags', and were divided into violent factions in support of rival professors. Whenever a ship came in they used to lie in wait for strangers intending to become students, and kidnap and carry them off into the country to lonely places or to the houses of patrons of individual professors, where the victim was imprisoned till he agreed to attend the lectures of the particular teacher advocated by his captors. This partisanship was neither so innocent nor so intellectual as it may seem, for the victims were apt to be the richer young men among the arrivals, and it was obviously convenient for students who could not pay their fees to bring their professor others who could. The party system seems to have been so strict that it was difficult after such an adventure to be transferred to a different professor; and Libanius, having been caught in this way and enrolled with the wrong professor, was reduced to pursuing his studies alone without a teacher of any kind.

To Gregory it seemed that the students at Athens had run quite mad after rhetoric, and that their rivalry over the professors was like that of the crowd at a race-meeting, who lose their heads about their fancy even when they have scarcely a shilling to put on. The rival gangs of students even came to blows in the streets. Young men of every nation were in Athens then, Syrians, Egyptians, Asiatics; and the partisanship had some nationalist feeling, the gangs would rally round a professor who was their compatriot. Prohæresius, a Bithynian, was backed by the Bithynian students, with supporters from Pontus and the neighbouring cities of northern Asia Minor. Sometimes, when the rival factions clashed too violently, the professors chose the better part of valour and stayed at home, preferring to give their lectures indoors rather than venture abroad in the streets. When Libanius first heard of the fighting in the streets he was inclined to respect the students for facing danger in defence of the honour of their professors, but when he came to Athens he soon had enough of such exhibitions of academic chivalry.

The 'rags' were of a more normal ' 'Varsity' type. These tended to crystallize, as such things will, into tradition, or rather, into the drearier kinds of practical chestnut, to be played off upon the uninitiated. Regularly the freshmen were captured and marched in solemn procession to the baths, where suddenly a pretence was made that the establishment was shut and must be besieged. There was a mock assault, a tremendous uproar, and the freshman was expected to be horribly frightened; but eventually the doors were opened, the party entered, and the rather pointless proceedings ended very tamely, not with the ducking which would seem reasonable in such a place, but with the liberation of the victim and his admission as an initiated member of his university. There was conflict also between town and gown, and some bullying, as when a poor pedagogue, a teacher of a humble kind much inferior to a professor, was tossed in a blanket by his class. Gregory seems to have avoided these rougher kinds of sport, but he was no prig and submitted to the freshmen's 'rag' with a good grace.

When he had been at Athens for some little time Basil arrived, and as a compatriot and old schoolfellow Gregory naturally took him under his wing. Gregory remembered Basil as a boy of great promise at school, and now the early promise seems to have been realized in an impressive, distinguished young man. Gregory's generous admiration was immediately evoked, and he felt it his duty to protect Basil from the crudities of undergraduate wit. He obtained, for he seems to have been popular enough himself, Basil's exemption from the kidnapping and sham fight at the baths, a kindness which was the kindling spark, Basil records, of their life-long friendship, that marriage of true minds which survived many tempests and, on Gregory's side at least, lasted to the edge of doom. But the exemption from the 'rag' was a mistake, for Basil was considered a prig and the two young men found themselves isolated and laughed at. Some Armenian students one day resolved to take Basil down a peg by drawing him into an argument from which, as a raw freshman, he should have been unable to extricate himself, and Gregory, who was present, thought the game a fair one, or at any rate only a game; he even took the part of the Armenians in order to uphold the honour of Athenian learning. Later, as the argument developed, it appeared that the freshman was not so green as the Armenians expected, that he was even getting the upper hand, and Gregory began to realize that the Armenians, for their part, were arguing, not in fun, but in serious spite. Like many another he perceived that the Armenians are 'not at all a simple race, but exceedingly crafty and cunning'. So he threw them over, to be told, of course, that he was a turncoat, and both he and Basil found themselves for a time cold-shouldered in their university. Gregory was not too serious about the affair, but Basil was deeply wounded and found Athens but an 'empty happiness' and the tone of the students unworthy of so great a place; and Gregory, not for the last time in his association with Basil, had to exercise all his arts of persuasion to mollify his hypersensitive friend. Eventually their unpopularity blew over, but it had settled their habit of living together, somewhat apart from others. Henceforth in Athens they lived in semi-seclusion: their mutual bond, Gregory says, was comparable to that of Orestes and Pylades, and was renowned even beyond Athens. 'Two souls we were in one body . . . as time went on we acknowledged our mutual love, and that philosophy was our purpose. We were all in all to one another, house-mates, mess-mates, in close intimacy.' This was no ordinary passion, Gregory hastens to assure us, of Athenian boys: 'Love which is godly and under restraint, since its object, the soul, is imperishable, not only is more lasting itself, but the fuller its vision of beauty grows the more closely does it bind to itself and to one another the hearts of those whose love has one and the same object.' No one can write or speak thus of love who has not steeped himself in the *Phædrus* and *Symposium*, and no one who, in the days of his impressionable youth, has felt and tried to live these two dialogues of Plato, as Gregory seems to have done, will ever get his two feet quite firmly on the common earth again. So the two young men lived for what they called philosophy, with a real, if rather vague Christian basis, undisturbed by the surrounding pagan atmosphere of the city. On the contrary, these pagan surroundings served, by contrast, to confirm their enlightened faith; Gregory boasts that they were like salamanders unscathed in the fire, or like Alpheus, the Arcadian river which flows, uncontaminated by the salt water, through the ocean to Syracuse in pursuit of Arethusa. And in the fervour of their youthful enthusiasm they dedicated themselves to philosophy for life.

This vow, which by their later correspondence seems to have been a serious one, was regarded quite differently by the two young men. Gregory really thought that he and Basil would spend their entire lives in that kind of academic, scholarly retirement which was easy to realize at Athens, or in any university atmosphere, but scarcely anywhere else. Basil's ideas were more practical, and if he believed in the contemplative life, he thought of it as organized in conformity to a discipline, and compatible also with some attempt at self-support. His development of these ideas led eventually to the monastic system of the Greek Church.

As the years passed—and at the ancient universities, as in some continental countries to-day, there seems to have been no time-limit to a student's career—the two young philosophers, no longer so very young, acquired considerable prestige, and were expected to set up as professors. Gregory might have been glad enough to prolong indefinitely his Platonic honeymoon with his friend; it was Basil who decided that the idyll had lasted long enough, for Gregory was thirty and Basil about twenty-eight. Athens, however, had no wish to part with them, and when news of their impending departure leaked out there was a demonstration accompanied by violence almost. Everybody, their fellow commoners, the professors, even the city fathers, crowded round them, begging them to stay. Basil, as always, was inexorable and left; Gregory, more persuadable, was induced to stay a little longer, till he grew tired of explaining to the inquisitive Athenians why he and Basil had parted, and tired also of living without his friend. So, deciding not to risk further demonstrations, he escaped by stealth.

✴ IV ✴

Gregory's homeward journey took him first to Constantinople, not out of any curiosity to see the new capital of the world (indeed, he liked it no better than Alexandria, for it was in the hands of the Arians), but because Constantinople lay upon the land route to Cappadocia, and he did not care to go to sea again. And a surprise awaited him there; for almost simultaneously Cæsarius arrived from Alexandria, having come to seek his medical fortunes about the court.

Cæsarius had been in Alexandria for ten years and was now more than qualified as a doctor; he had distinction in mathematics and astronomy also, and he was handsome, his brother tells us, with an attractive voice. The reputation of the Alexandrian medical school at that time was such that it was sufficient recommendation for any doctor to be able to say he had been there;[1] but Cæsarius must have been exceptional, for immediately upon his arrival at the capital the most tempting professional offers were made to him, a public practice under the state, a seat upon the imperial council, and a wealthy heiress to wife. No ambitious young man could be expected to resist these dazzling proposals, and Cæsarius probably had no intention of doing so. But he was a gracious person and gave in to his brother's urgent entreaties that he should go back with him to Nazianzus to

[1] Ammianus Marcellinus.

visit their aged parents; for Gregory could not understand the attractions of a worldly, luxurious capital where both emperor[1] and bishop were Arians, and the orthodox Catholics were oppressed and despised.

But Nazianzus could not hold Cæsarius: before long he was back in Constantinople, where the high position previously offered, and let us hope the charming heiress also, still awaited him. He became one of the foremost physicians of his time, giving his medical services free of charge to the state; and though, as a Christian, he refused to take the oath of Hippocrates, he was entrusted by both high and low with their most precious invalids, and successive emperors cherished him and treated him as a friend. He is not one of the great figures of history, but he remains one of those attractive personalities who occasionally stray, accidentally, into its pages to reassure us that life has often been more tolerable, and people more respectable, than historians, with their natural preference for the more dramatic figures, the more disastrous and sensational happenings, have cared to admit.

Gregory meanwhile seems to have accepted the duties and responsibilities of the eldest son of his father's house. The elder Gregory, the bishop, was by this time about eighty-five, Nonna about eighty, and they looked to Gregory as parents have commonly looked to their unmarried daughters, rather than their sons, to abandon every personal ambition and stay at home to mind the house during their lifetime. Gregory found himself obliged to take charge both of the family property and of his father's household, tasks for which he had neither aptitude nor taste. The boredom and distress this donnish, not very young man must have endured, torn from the infinite philosophic leisure of the Athenian atmosphere, and plunged into a whirl of petty concerns, are only too easy to imagine. But to imagine them

---

[1] Constantius was Arian; Julian, his successor, pagan and anti-Christian.

is unnecessary, for Gregory has told us all about them repeatedly and at length.

There was a mass of disagreeable business, interviews with magistrates and tax-collectors; it was necessary on occasion to appear in court, and Gregory groaned at these soiling contacts, for the courts were corrupt,[1] and the rich man, whether right or wrong, was sure to win his case. And as for domestic servants, they are neither submissive to bad masters nor loyal to good ones.

The folk of Nazianzus, with their Asiatic respect for Greek culture, undoubtedly had high hopes of the bishop's son, fresh from the seat and fountain-head of all learning. He was pressed to give public rhetorical displays, to open a school of rhetoric; but he professed to have outgrown the vanities of rhetoric, and if he gave a rhetorical display or two, 'danced', as he called it, for their amusement, he did it out of good nature, to indulge his friends.

For himself he had but one purpose, the pursuit of philosophy. He would have liked to escape from the world altogether, to some kind of retreat, but his present filial responsibilities did not permit of that, and he had to content himself with making the irksome duties of housekeeping into an ascetic exercise. Gradually he began to find that filial duty to an ageing bishop extended beyond assisting him with his household to sharing in the cares of the diocese.

Basil, meanwhile, had gone home to Cæsarea and, still free to follow his ideas, had been to Syria and Egypt to see what the ascetics and solitaries, the so-called philosophers, did. His sharp eye had penetrated beneath the surface and noticed the failures and the terrible cost of success in that exacting profession. Like Pachomius,[2] he decided that the human spirit

[1] Ammianus Marcellinus corroborates this sad estimate of the law courts of the Eastern Empire: the advocates, if their business was slack, would employ *agents provocateurs* to stir up disputes and litigation.

[2] See page 52.

flourishes best in society and under discipline, and that asceticism was the means to an end, not the end itself. With a handful of companions he set up in Pontus a community after his own heart, and here he expected Gregory to join him. Gregory was distressed that family claims held him from his friend, but was not to be led away. Basil showed some impatience at Gregory's filial scruples, and to appease him Gregory offered a compromise: 'I will not fail you altogether; if you will accept this offer, I shall be with you half the time, and half of it you will be with me . . . and so my parents will not be disappointed, and I shall not be without you.',

But Basil was as unaccommodating as Gregory was conciliatory, and would have no half-measures. There is a correspondence, in the best rhetorical style, in which Basil praises Pontus in exaggerated terms and belittles Nazianzus, while Gregory tries to turn the tables on him. 'Laugh at my place if you like,' wrote Gregory, amiable as usual, if a little nettled at Basil's contempt for Cappadocia, 'pull it to pieces whether in earnest or in fun, I do not mind. . . . Everything that comes from you is dear to me, whatever it is. . . . Well I admire your Pontus, and your Pontic fogs, and your retreat, which is about fit for an outlaw, and the hills hanging over your head, and your refuge beneath, a regular mousehole, which you dignify with the names "abode of contemplation", "monastery", and "school", and the wild beasts which test your faith, and your thickets of wild thorns, and your crown of steep mountains, with which you are not so much crowned as imprisoned, and your confined air, and the sun which you long for but can only espy as through a chimney . . .' and much more to the same effect.

No serious ill feeling resulted from these little bouts of rhetorical sparring, which were but mutual exercise of those tricks of the professional game they had been at such pains to acquire in their youth. Gregory visited Pontus occasionally, where Basil's little community lived in rather rudimentary conditions, employing no labour, and doing everything for itself. Gregory took his share in the tasks and in building the cells, and in a later letter he laughs over the rough time they had. The garden was badly managed and unproductive, and the food was dreadful; there was nothing but broth and some very hard bread which nearly broke Gregory's teeth; in fact they were saved from starvation on one occasion by Basil's mother, who, with motherly contempt for the young men's notion of doing for themselves, arrived in the nick of time with a supply of food. But Gregory loved to be there, and seems on one occasion to have made his escape there for about three years, when suddenly the elder Gregory was found to have made one of his theological mistakes. All unsuspecting he had subscribed, as a good Nicene Catholic should not have done, and a loyal subject should, to the Arian creed which the Emperor Constantius imposed upon the frightened bishops at Rimini, and called upon all the bishops of the empire to accept. The too loyal bishop found himself in disgrace with his flock and with the neighbouring monks, who, like all the hermits and solitaries of those times, kept a sharp eye on their neighbours' doings, and liked to have a finger in every pie.

Gregory had to leave Pontus in a hurry to patch up matters for his father in the diocese. His soothing presence soon reduced the hurricane, as he calls it, to the merest summer zephyr, with the aid of a majestic oration which he composed and delivered in his father's defence; for there was nothing in those days like a good dose of rhetoric to pacify ruffled feelings, and an audience probably did not then exist which could resist the compliment of a fine piece of oratory, composed especially for its benefit.

Gregory's intervention had other results, less satisfactory to himself. He had been obliged to acquit himself at last in the way the Nazianzenes had always desired, and to his father's wish for his assistance was now added their evident determination that he should not only help, but eventually succeed, his father in the bishopric.

Gregory was dismayed, and might have fled again to Pontus had not the bishop and the people betaken themselves to the usual remedy in such a case; they seized Gregory and ordained him by force. Unfortunately we have no details of the incident; but Gregory's disgust, as usual, is not left to our imagination, it is perpetuated, at proper length, in his verse. He took a temporary and quite useless revenge, and fled to Pontus, only to be recalled by the bishop, who could command the priest, even if as a father he had no authority over his son.

There were some further bickerings between Gregory and the Nazianzenes, and he relieved his feelings by trying to preach at them; but they would not listen to him till he composed and delivered a proper apology, and at last he accepted his fate, and settled down at Nazianzus to perform the mixed duties of assistant bishop and of family prop and pivot at home. He had plenty of time, however, for writing, which was now a first duty to the faith. The Emperor Julian, whose passion for literature and delight in meddling in scholarly matters made him a peculiarly ingenious enemy of the Christians, forbade them to hold teaching positions in the schools and universities. The challenge was precisely one that Gregory could take up. If there was to be nothing but pagan teaching in the schools, then Christian scholars must provide their own book-learning to teach the young Christian idea how to shoot, and train it in speaking and writing. A vast proportion of Gregory's literary output both in prose and verse was a direct retort to the imperial insult to the intellectual capacities of the Christians.

His personal horror of Julian found expression in the two invectives[1] which reflect more credit upon his resources in

[1] *Contra Julianum*, I, II.

abusive language than upon his Christian charity. From beginning to end there is no sparing the lash; Julian's campaigns, his literary and sophistical efforts, are all manifestations of his diabolical possession and even his personal appearance does not escape. He is that serpent, that apostate, that Assyrian, who filled the whole earth with wrath and threats, and extolled malice and iniquity to heaven. His holy and august predecessors on the imperial throne, including the shade of the late blessed and pious Constantius[1] (who as an Arian would have been greatly surprised at receiving these bouquets from Gregory), are invoked to bear witness to the enormities of the monster, the anti-Christ Julian. Gregory even invades the realm of military strategy, in which he can hardly have been at home; he arraigns Julian's conduct of the Persian campaign, accusing him of having taken the advice of a traitor when he brought the ships from the Euphrates through Trajan's canal to Ctesiphon, and burnt them there to make his army fight the better, because when its own supplies were destroyed it would be fighting for its food.[2] Finally, Julian's death is represented as a vengeful murder, and the Almighty is heartily congratulated upon the death of his arch-enemy. If these two works were begun, and wholly or partly composed, during Julian's lifetime, it must be assumed that they did not reach the public, at any rate, till after he was dead.

[1] Athanasius had said that Constantius was worse than Saul, Ahab, and Pilate.

[2] The account given by Gregory is partly true, but the ships were burnt after the abandonment of the siege of Ctesiphon, not before; and if they had not been burnt it is not clear what Julian could have done with them. They could not be carried over land, nor towed indefinitely up the Tigris or the Euphrates. See also Libanius, *Funeral Oration for Julian.*

Cæsarius meantime continued to distinguish himself at court, and if the unorthodoxy of Constantius disturbed him he did not allow his feelings to interfere with his professional career. But if he was at ease, the family at Nazianzus were not, for in their position as leaders in religious circles in Cappadocia it was awkward to have a relative in office in an Arian court, especially since the old bishop had had to be cleared of a suspicion of heresy. And when Constantius died, and Julian, the avowed enemy of the faith, succeeded him, there were audible murmurs.

Nazianzus was a small place, a cathedral town, where everybody knew and talked about everybody else's business, and when Cæsarius' unprotesting acceptance of his new master was discovered, the bishop's family were made to feel uncomfortable. 'You have given me sufficient cause to blush for you,' Gregory wrote to Cæsarius, 'and to you, who know me better than any one, I need hardly explain how much I was distressed. . . . I wish you could have heard what others, both our relations and people outside the family who know us (Christians of course, I mean . . .) were saying about us both . . . "Fancy a bishop's son taking a post in the army, running after power and advancement, given over to money, to amassing wealth (when the fires[1] are being kindled for all men and all are in peril of their souls). . . . How can the

___
[1] i.e. of persecution: for Julian was expected to make things uncomfortable for the Christians.

bishop rebuke others who go astray when his own family deprives him of the right to accuse any one." Every day we have to hear remarks such as these . . . and worse.'

Cæsarius evidently did not mind the remarks; without quarrelling with his brother he remained at his post, respected and unmolested by Julian, who seems to have indulged for some time in a kind of good-humoured give-and-take upon religion with his Christian physician. Eventually, however, as was usual at Constantinople, the argument acquired a sporting character and a public debate between Julian and Cæsarius was staged. Julian, vain of his skill in dialectics, no doubt thought he could make short work of the arguments of the Christian doctor; but Cæsarius was too clever for him. Julian was badly beaten, and suffered a humiliating public discomfiture, while the triumphant Cæsarius, a little incautious perhaps in the hour of victory, made before the emperor and the audience a formal confession of faith. Julian could not put up with defeat: though the contest was intended to be a purely sporting one, he indulged a petty spite and dismissed Cæsarius from his various posts, thus forcing him to seek the retreat which his brother had been advocating.

Cæsarius may have visited Nazianzus, but when in 363 Julian died, he returned to public life under Valens as Quæstor of Bithynia. We have no comment from Gregory till four or five years later, when an earthquake destroyed Nicæa, the beautiful capital of Bithynia, in a night. Large numbers of the inhabitants perished, and Cæsarius by mere chance escaped with his life. Gregory was not slow to point the moral. We have a letter urging Cæsarius not to ignore the warning, to leave the world and come home, and Cæsarius, unnerved perhaps by the earthquake, would have returned; but he never saw his father's house again. He died the following year, and was brought in death to Nazianzus to be buried there with great honours, not least among them a formal funeral panegyric spoken by Gregory at the tomb.

Gregory could forgive Cæsarius now; for his scoldings had been due in reality to love, to admiration for his great gifts. Had Cæsarius been an ordinary mediocre person it would have mattered less how he spent his time. 'I will confess to you that I think it a better and grander thing to be in the lowest rank with God than to win the first place with any earthly king. Nevertheless I cannot blame him, for inasmuch as philosophy is the greatest, so also is it the most difficult of professions, which can be undertaken only by the few. . . . I was distressed . . . that a man so fitted for philosophy should be obscured by the inconsistency of public life, like the sun behind a cloud.'

The panegyric, with its classic formality and Christian intention, shows the confusion which occasionally resulted from the attempt to be both Grecian and Christian at one and the same time. The language echoes the traditional lament of the pagan Greek for the brief flowering of youth and life, for the shadow which is the inevitable end, while the Christian must look to the resurrection of the body and everlasting life. Gregory wavers between these two poles of sentiment, at one time seeing himself as the mourning figure of a Greek funeral stele or vase, his panegyric, like a votive garland, in his hand, at another repudiating the pagan despair, and yet returning in the same sentence to a quite untheological notion of immortality.

The confusion is not peculiar to Gregory, nor even to his age; it is inherent in all classic revivals. The English seventeenth-century writers held the same divided allegiance, and were as ready at any moment to celebrate the prophets as the Olympian gods, to entertain nymphs as angels. Milton loved Parnassus as well as Sinai; and Gregory, gazing across the dark river at the dim shore beyond, seems quite uncertain whether that dividing flood is Jordan or Styx.

The death of Cæsarius brought Gregory other troubles.

[283]

'Alas, my poor brother, what power thou hast for my undoing,' he cries. Cæsarius' property was left to the poor, with
Gregory as executor; and his death was the signal for the
appearance of a host of creditors, mostly, but probably not
quite all, fraudulent: slaves, friends, and people unknown
before. Gregory calls them all dogs. They even laid hands
unceremoniously on the dead man's effects and looted his
house. Gregory sought the easiest, if not the most sensible,
way out of his difficulty. To avoid disappointing the poor
he made up the supposed deficiencies and paid the imaginary
claims out of his own pocket, only to find, in result, that the
creditors, like the French vipers when a price was put on
their heads, multiplied instead of diminishing. He was
obliged in the end to appeal to the Prefect of Constantinople
for protection.

◄ VI ★

Gregory's dream of the philosophic life was fading. Basil had given it up, even without the excuse of family calls on his time. Perhaps his energetic, ambitious nature had never intended to bury itself in any monastery. His model community was a piece of practical research; and he encouraged Gregory's loyalty to their old philosophic ideas of seclusion, so far as he could be of assistance in working out the experiment. As his own ambitions developed, he had no pity for the suffering, protesting Gregory, immersed in the cares of the world, and seems to have decided to plunge him yet farther into them by making use of him in his own career. That career was now taking a definitely ecclesiastical turn. Some years previously, with proper and fashionable reluctance and protest, Basil had been ordained priest. He had apologized to Gregory, who must needs forgive him, 'for I too was forced into the priesthood, never having wished for it myself. . . . It would have been better had this not happened . . .' and soon Basil is found to be acting as assistant at Cæsarea to Eusebius, Archbishop of Cappadocia.[1] Eusebius was gentle and old, needing an assistant now, and likely before long to need a successor. As might be expected, a quarrel soon arose between the mild bishop and his ambitious, not very meek assistant, in the course of which Basil retired to Pontus,

---

[1] Eusebius himself had been an unwilling bishop suddenly consecrated by his enthusiastic fellow citizens.

in dudgeon or disgrace or both. Gregory, a friend of Eusebius as well as of Basil, was appealed to by both sides, but could take no part but Basil's in a controversy. 'If you love Gregory you must love Basil too,' he wrote to Eusebius, 'for if you honour me and disgrace Basil, it is as if you were to stroke my head with one hand and slap me in the face with the other.' Peace, however, was made, and Basil returned to Cæsarea. In 369 Eusebius died, and there arose at last the important and thorny question as to who should be his successor. Cæsarea was an archbishopric and a formal election must take place, for which all the provincial bishops must be assembled. Basil was far from popular and there were other candidates, some supported by the excitable Cæsarean populace who, having made their last bishop, were much inclined to make the new one too. Basil's proceedings at this juncture have puzzled his admirers, but are not really difficult to understand. He decided that the two Gregories of Nazianzus, father and son, whose support he could count upon, must at all costs be got to Cæsarea for the election, not only for their votes but for the great influence which their universal popularity and prestige must exert in his behalf. There were difficulties, however, for the elder Gregory was very old and ill, and the younger, with his profound dislike of ecclesiastical foregatherings, might refuse to attend.

To meet these difficulties Basil concocted the clumsiest, the most unpardonable of schemes. Gregory, who had not yet heard of Eusebius' death, received an urgent message that Basil was ill and must see Gregory before he died. Gregory set out in haste for Cæsarea, to discover when he had got half-way that the summons was a hoax and his friend in the best of health. Justifiably furious at the abuse of his loyalty and love, he went straight back to Nazianzus and wrote briskly to Basil: 'Do not be surprised if I say something unexpected which no one has said to you before, for I have always thought you . . . honest rather than cautious. . . . You have summoned me to the metropolis at the moment when a council has been called to elect a bishop, and your pretext is seemly and plausible indeed—you pretend to be very ill, positively at your last gasp, and to long to see me to say a last farewell. I do not know what your object can have been, or of what use my presence could be in the matter.'[1]

The situation, however, was too serious for the indulgence of personal pique; for a new archbishop must be elected and the Gregories saw that without their aid Basil would be passed over. Cæsarea was in an uproar and Basil's enemies took care that the Gregories should be invited in terms which made it clear that their presence was not wanted. They sacrificed respectively their own infirmity and recalcitrance and not only went to Cæsarea themselves, but raised other bishops friendly to Basil to do likewise. Basil was elected; but it was neither a very dignified nor a creditable business. In the great funeral oration which Gregory delivered as a memorial to Basil after his death, the steps that led Basil to the throne of Cæsarea are discreetly and generously passed over; the gratifying result alone is mentioned.

Basil showed his gratitude to the Gregories in a clumsy, egotistical way. He seems to have expected Gregory to come over to Cæsarea to help him in the archbishopric; but Gregory, unworldly as he was, could show on occasion an admirable common sense in other people's affairs. If Basil had been elected, as every one knew, by the efforts of his friends at Nazianzus, he must not appear incapable of holding his position without them. 'I rejoice', he wrote to Basil,

---

[1] It has been thought by Basil's defenders that his purpose in attempting to get Gregory to Cæsarea was to have him elected, and that Gregory also thought so. But it is clear from subsequent events that Gregory would not leave Nazianzus in his father's lifetime, and from the letter Basil's intentions seem indubitable.

refusing his invitation, 'that you have been placed on that lofty throne. . . . Yet I did not rush to you instantly, nor shall I, even if you yourself urge me. My first reason was to safeguard your dignity, lest you should seem to be collecting partisans, out of ill temper and bad taste, of which your slanderers would probably accuse you. . . .'

Basil now accused Gregory of indifference, and of belittling his needs and difficulties. But Gregory was firm, though distressed that his friend should think him callous. 'What a word has escaped the barriers of your teeth . . . how dare you say such a thing. . . . Do you not know me as you know yourself, you eye of the world, and voice and trumpet and palace of learning? Your affairs trifles to Gregory! What then on earth could any one admire if Gregory admires not you? . . . Or are you vexed because I am acting in accordance with philosophy, for, by your leave, philosophy, and philosophy only, is higher than your conversation.'[1]

The trumpet and palace of learning are compliments in the fashion of those times, but there is a brisk little sting in the word philosophy. Had they not both, once upon a time, vowed themselves to philosophy? Gregory had a right to that particular gibe, for if he had deserted philosophy he had two aged parents as his excuse, while Basil had acted from ambition, had resumed, in Gregory's words, the burrs of the world, including an archbishopric, of his own free will.

The burrs were indeed sticking to Basil: they seemed to flourish on the soil of Cæsarea, for no sooner had he begun to live down the troubles of his own election than the imperial Government, in its callous way, indifferent to the agitations of churchmen, proceeded to reorganize the provincial administration for its own ends. Cappadocia was divided into two provinces, Prima and Secunda, with Cæsarea as civil capital of the former, and Tyana of the latter.

[1] Ep. XLVI.

The question now arose whether the ecclesiastical functions in Cappadocia were divided also, whether in fact the arch-bishopric of Cæsarea now had jurisdiction over the whole of the old province or over Cappadocia Prima only. Basil characteristically held that the secular administration had no bearing upon the ecclesiastical, and that he still had authority as archbishop over the whole of the old province. But the opposite view was very naturally held by the bishop of Tyana, Anthimus, who now saw himself as primate of Cappadocia Secunda. The situation was delicate enough from a disciplinary point of view, but tithes also were involved, and Anthimus decided to retain the tithes due from his part of the province. Some rumour of the dispute reached Gregory, and Basil received as usual a letter full of philosophy and admonishments, which perhaps he may be pardoned for finding a little superfluous in a situation which might mean that tithes in kind would have to be collected by force.

'I hear you are being troubled by this fresh innovation', wrote Gregory, 'and worried by the usual sort of sophistical interference on the part of the authorities. . . . I have no fear of seeing you behave in your troubles in a manner un-becoming to a philosopher. . . . If you think it well I will come myself and I shall perhaps be able to give you some assistance by my counsel. . . .'[1]

Counsel was not what Basil wanted, but he accepted the offer of help. Anthimus was actually mounting guard over the tithes, pigs and chickens and the like, which were de-posited by the peasants and farmers at a station in the Cappa-docian mountains, and Gregory was somehow prevailed upon to lead an expedition to bring the livestock away. He cut a poor figure as a cattle-lifter. Anthimus set an ambush in a defile where Gregory's party must pass on their way to fetch the spoils, and there was a skirmish in which Gregory himself was wounded, though not severely, and he and his

[1] Ep. XLVII.

companions were routed. He returned home to Nazianzus, infinitely disgusted, almost shaken at last in his loyalty to his friend.

That loyalty had to stand further tests, for Basil's difficulties seemed inexhaustible, as also his habit of making use of Gregory at every turn. Between Cappadocia Prima and Secunda, whose frontiers were not clearly drawn, there was a debatable land where Anthimus amused himself by asserting his authority over a negligible and scantily-inhabited country. Basil conceived a stratagem, military rather than spiritual in its inspiration: he decided to create bishoprics at the frontier villages, regardless of their insignificance and lack of population, and to place in them bishops favourable to himself, to act as a bulwark against Tyana and its aggressive prelate. To one of these bishoprics, without warning, he appointed Gregory.

The appointment was a shock to Gregory. His aversion to public office was well known, and the see selected for him was Sasima,[1] which was nothing but a traffic station at a crossing of three main roads, a tiny squalid village without water or verdure, important only as a halting-place for travellers and caravans and in consequence full of pack-animals and vehicles, of shouting and cursing, of noise and dust. Gregory not inaptly asks Basil whether fifty bishoprics under him were not enough that he must add to them this one also. Sasima, moreover, was close to Tyana, and would be in the thick of any further hostilities; its dreariness and isolation would be relieved only by raids, frights, and broils.

Basil's action has been the subject of much argument: his defenders have accused Gregory of pride and self-conceit in refusing a Christian duty laid upon him by so great a man. But it must be remembered that Basil was not yet Basil the Great; and though he was archbishop, he was but newly-made, and that by the favour and influence of the Gregories.

[1] The second syllable is long: Sasīma.

Sasima was an insult to a man of Gregory's intellectua
quality, and only a narrow self-interest on Basil's part can
explain the appointment.

Gregory seemed inclined to ignore his bishopric; and to
break his resistance to it Basil came to Nazianzus and consecrated him in person.[1] Gregory bent his neck, he says, to
the imposition, but not his will. He was obliged to submit,
as to his archbishop, but he delivered in the church at
Nazianzus a discourse full of sorrow, even of reproach, and
quite devoid of spiritual submission.[2] He had been trapped
a second time into a holy office and felt only humiliation,
and no obligation at all to submit himself to the imposition.
Consecration he might not escape, but Sasima was an outrage which no just man should tolerate. He never went there,
he never 'consummated', as Gibbon says, 'his spiritual union
with his disgusting bride'.[3]

'Do leave off speaking of me as an ill-educated, rough,
unfriendly person, unworthy even to live,' he wrote to Basil,
who had shown resentment when Sasima remained bishopless
and undefended from his rival, Anthimus, 'because I ventured
to show that I was quite aware of the way in which I had
been treated. . . . My conscience does not reproach me with
having been unkind to you in anything either great or small,
and I hope it never may. I only know that I saw I had been
deceived . . . too late, indeed . . . and I throw the blame
upon your throne, as having suddenly lifted you above yourself. . . . Now I will plainly speak out my mind, and you
must not be angry with me. . . . I will not take up arms, nor
will I now learn ways which I did not learn in former times
. . . nor will I face the bellicose Anthimus. . . . Fight him
yourself, if you wish . . . or look for some one else to fight
him when he seizes your mules. . . . Give me before all

[1] *Carmina de se ipso:* XI, 386 *seqq.*
[2] *Oratio* IX.
[3] Gibbon (Bury), iii, 144.

things quiet. Why should I fight for sucking pigs and fowls, and those not even my own . . .?'¹

The tirade is perhaps more violent than serious. Gregory could not be quite serious about Sasima; it was after all a joke, if a bad one. His next letter is almost flippant:

'You accuse me of indolence and sloth because I would not accept your see of Sasima, nor . . . become an occasion for your controversies, like a bone thrown to dogs. My principal business is always to keep clear of business and, to give you some conception of my good qualities, I take such a pride in peace and quiet that I regard myself as a pattern to all men of this sort of virtue. If only the world would copy me in this the Church would be free from broils, and the faith, which is used by every one as a weapon for their private differences, would not be torn in sunder.'²

Gregory hoped that Sasima would blow over; but if he was ready to forget it, others were not. Anthimus came in person to Nazianzus in the hope, perhaps, of winning over the Gregories, by impressing and wheedling them, or of engaging them to negotiate for him with Basil. Gregory did make some overtures about settling the frontier line between the two Cappadocias, only to be blamed by Basil for wanting to treat with Anthimus at all. The squabble, for it was scarcely a quarrel, simmered on for a time, and, as often in such cases, it was the aggressor, Basil, who was offended, and the victim, Gregory, who must apologize and pacify. But there could be no permanent breach. Basil could not really do without Gregory; to rely on his moral support had become a habit, and his prestige in Asia was immense, an indispensable asset to an ambitious man of uncertain popularity.

After these agitations Gregory contrived to retire from Nazianzus to a retreat or monastery in the hills, where he achieved a period of peace lasting some months at least. But

¹ Ep. XLVIII.
² Ep. XLIX.

both Sasima and solitude were ceasing to be serious possibilities, for the aged Gregory was becoming increasingly incapable and his son soon found himself discharging all the functions of the bishop of Nazianzus. And a bishop of character and practical acumen was needed in times that proved disastrous at Nazianzus. There was a hailstorm and a drought, and the townsfolk were threatened with famine and financial ruin. In such a crisis they looked to their bishop, not in those days for charity or a subscription list, nor even for prayer, but for a fitting and apposite rhetorical display; and here Gregory was qualified indeed to content them, for the Nazianzenes, so long as they could have a first-class sermon when occasion required, did not much mind what it was about. There were political troubles too. Valens, whose sympathies were Arian, was rumoured to be threatening to destroy Nazianzus in punishment for its adherence to Nicene orthodoxy;[1] and Gregory pleaded successfully for the town before his friend Optatus, the Provincial governor.

Then, at last, in 374, the aged bishop of Nazianzus, a reputed centenarian, died, followed a few months later by his wife, the equally holy and almost as ancient Nonna. Gregory had always regarded their eventual death as the natural term of his obligations at Nazianzus, and seems still to have believed that he could be free. There was, of course, the last of his filial duties to perform, the funeral oration with which a rhetorician must mark his parents' passing. The oration on his father, a panegyric in the stilted manner of the times, is none the less an expression of perfectly genuine affection, of almost too tender-hearted grief, unqualified by any personal relief at his own release from filial obligations. As a person so obstinately fixed in one idea, Gregory must be conceded a most unusual degree of generosity in his treatment of those who stood between him and its realization.

---

[1] Or perhaps for forgetting to pay its taxes.

Freedom, however, was a prize still dangling just beyond his reach. To the Nazianzenes the old man's death meant the elevation of his son to the bishopric, to the full title of what he had long been in fact. There was no movement to elect a new bishop and, as Nazianzus could not be left bishopless Gregory found himself staying on from month to month as acting bishop, without any definite decision or plan. A severe illness saved him from his obvious fate, and when he was sufficiently recovered he made his health a pretext for withdrawing at last from Nazianzus and the world, to that seclusion he had desired so consistently and so long. The chosen refuge was a monastery dedicated to Saint Thecla, in a remote spot, Seleucia in Isauria, where he hoped he might be hidden from Nazianzus and forgotten by the world.[1]

[1] See page 129.

★ VII ★

Gregory was at Saint Thecla's for more than three years, an adequate holiday, by all reasonable worldly standards, from the fatigues and commotions of this mortal coil. Whether he seriously believed that he could make his retirement a permanency we do not know, and it is impossible to guess to what extent he followed the movement of events, political and otherwise, in the outside world. But in January 379 his peace, or whatever of it he contrived to attain among the monks—and monasteries can be disappointing in this respect—was shattered rudely by a quite unforeseen blow, by the death of Basil, untimely, for he was barely fifty years of age. In the pain and shock of his loss Gregory forgot all the agitation his friend had caused him, forgot Cæsarea, Sasima and Anthimus, all the squabbles, insults and intrigues, and recovered in death the Basil he had lost, of late, in life.

Distance and illness kept Gregory from Basil's funeral, and he regretted, for once, the remoteness of his retreat; but he should have been glad to be spared what amounted to a shocking exhibition of popular hysteria at the obsequies. The whole of Cæsarea, Gregory proudly tells, regardless of nationality, not excluding even the Jews, turned out to see the *cortège* pass, and the press of those who crowded round the bier, to catch a glimpse or touch the draperies of the dead saint, was so violent that many were crushed to death, funeral victims, Gregory grimly adds, in one of his pagan relapses, fortunate to be allowed to enter paradise in company with so great a man.

Gregory's pen could well make up for his personal absence. His funeral epitaphs for Basil are characteristic examples of his prowess in elegiac verse, which was not his happiest literary vein. Basil is loaded with conventional encomiums, hackneyed and meaningless. He is described as the ornament of Cappadocia, the eye of the faith, the pillar of the priesthood, the mouthpiece of sounding truth, his voice the glory of the thunder, and his life of the lightning, and a dozen other absurdities which in the fourth century passed for pretty enough conceits. Worthier, however, of Gregory and of his subject is the funeral panegyric delivered some time subsequent to Basil's death, composed of all the best that Gregory could put into such a work.

It is in full form; for, to honour Basil, Gregory would not be sparing of the conventional trophies and garlands which must adorn such a piece. It opens in the accepted manner with the proper complement of classical allusions, of tags and scraps of ancient mythology; for Athena's nursling must show that he can practise, when occasion requires it, all the time-honoured literary tricks. And if here and there our taste is jarred, or the juxtapositions seem utterly grotesque, or there is a descent into dismal bathos or startling anti-climax, we must remember the force of current fashion and the demands of popular taste.

'What family can boast so many, such distinguished generals, governors and court officials, or so many men of wealth, of lofty position, of public honours, of oratorical distinction? . . . They quite dwarf the grandeur of the Pelopidæ, the Cecropidæ, the Alcmæonidæ, and the Heracleidæ[1].' The education of this Christian divine, pre-eminent

[1] 'If you want to make a funeral oration on a man', said Saint Jerome, 'begin by digging up all his ancestors.'

[296]

among the founders of monasticism, cannot be mentioned without comparisons to Achilles in the cave of the Centaur, and to the careers of Orion and Actæon. Basil and Gregory in the days of their mutual love at Athens are likened to Orestes and Pylades, and Basil is compared to Rhadamanthus and Minos, those ancient symbols of human equity and justice. The façade is baroque in the extreme, but the work is a historical monument of the first importance. As a human document its sincerity is proved by the perfectly frank and just allusions to the Sasima affair, which is not mentioned by name but is clearly dealt with; for in an account of Basil by Gregory it could not with any honesty be left out. 'I am afraid that I myself was treated as a mere appendage to this scheme. By no other term can I readily describe the position. Greatly as I admire his whole conduct, of this single particular I find it impossible to approve, for I must acknowledge my feelings in regard to it. . . . I mean the change and faithlessness of his treatment of myself, a cause of pain which even time has not obliterated. For this is the source of all the inconsistency and the tangle of my life, it has robbed me of the practice, or at any rate the reputation, of philosophy. The defence which perhaps you will allow me to make for him is this, that his ideas were above human interests. . . .'

The panegyric was considerably delayed; it must in any case have taken some time to compose, and it was not de- livered till perhaps the second anniversary of Basil's death, when Gregory was able to go to Cæsarea to speak it in person with proper formality at Basil's tomb. For strange things had happened to Gregory in the meantime. Within a few weeks of Basil's death he had perpetrated the most glaring and flagrant inconsistency of his whole life, and was involved in one of its worst entanglements. Before Easter that year, 379, he had exchanged the chaste shades of Saint Thecla, not for Nazianzus or any other probable or explainable destination, but for Constantinople, where eventually he was to occupy the patriarchal throne.

This change of purpose, inconsistent as it seems with everything Gregory had ever professed, is startling, for he was far from being the sort of person to profess humility all his life and then snatch at the first gilded opportunity. Nor was he weak or vacillating by nature, indeed he could be obstinate to a fault. But where appeal could be made to his friendship, his loyalty, or his public spirit, as we have seen in the cases of his father and of Basil, he was persuadable. In this instance his help was very urgently demanded; he was appealed to as the only person available who was also qualified to render a very important service to the Church, that of leading and restoring the down-trodden Catholic party at Constantinople.

Since the reign of Constantius, the persecutor of the Catholics, the Arians had had the upper hand in Constantinople. There had been some very violent passages there between the two parties, riots, massacres, murders, conflagrations, with the advantage in the end to the Arians, who had maintained their supremacy with some degree of peace. Not that they objected to controversy confined to words and to the pleasures of argument, for speculation and dialectic were always dear to the Greeks. What the Arians most objected to in the Catholic party was their intolerant totalitarian desire to force the uncompromising formula of Nicæa upon everybody, and to terminate discussion. Among themselves, if they were not universally tolerant, the Arians admitted an enormous amount of variation in the nuances of doctrine which they would tolerate about the Trinity. There were innumerable sects of Arians, from extreme unitarians, as they might be called, through the Semi-Arians to small local groups such as that which went by the name of the Crumb-Arians, followers of a Syrian baker of a speculative turn, who had his fancies about the Trinity. The

Arians had a good Greek respect for argument, and a desire
that so pleasant an occupation should not be abated.

There was intellectual, if not spiritual, stimulus in the
Arian sects, and Constantinople was a congenial atmosphere
for them. Gregory says that the citizens made a sport of
divine matters; indeed, they were a people to whom everything was apt to become a sport. Everywhere in the city
theology was the theme of small talk, at dinner-parties, at
funerals, and 'even in the women's quarters'. The subtlety
and animation of common conversation in the city has been
immortalized by Gregory of Nyssa, a fervent Catholic, in
his contemptuous and much-quoted remark that the city was
'full of mechanics and slaves who are all of them profound
theologians, and preach in the shops and in the streets. If
you desire a man to change a piece of silver, he informs you
in what respect the Son differs from the Father, if you ask
the price of a loaf of bread, you are told that the Son is inferior to the Father, and if you inquire whether the bath is
ready the answer is that the Son was made out of nothing.'[1]

There is a touch of snobbery in Gregory of Nyssa's tone,
as indeed in the attitude of the Nicene Catholics in general
towards the Arians; for to them their creed was an esoteric
doctrine, the property of a privileged few, to be imposed
upon the unquestioning multitude. It was not for bakers,
money-changers, journeymen. But it is impossible not to
admire a populace who could enjoy the finer shades of theological speculation, and employ them as a diversion to
sweeten the daily round.

Quite suddenly, towards the year 380, after several decades of favour, something too unaccountable to be likened
to a tide began to turn against the Arians. Probably, by one
of those series of slow repercussions for which the civil unity
of the empire provided an uninterrupted course, it had its

[1] Gregory of Nyssa, *De Deitate Filii et Spiritus Sancti*. See J. B.
Bury, Appendix IX, to Gibbon, vol. iii.

motive source in Ambrose, the great bishop of Milan, concentrating, far away in the West, his entire energy, his bold and domineering personality, towards the final victory of the Catholic cause over the Arian throughout the empire. He had taken possession of the young emperor, Gratian; and when a successor was needed to Valens, who fell a victim to the Goths at Hadrianople, Gratian chose Theodosius, a natural ruler and organizer, born of Catholic parentage, with possibilities as a great champion for Catholicism, once he could be got to submit his violent, autocratic spirit to the great bishop of Milan. Valens, in some kind of superstitious panic, just before his death recalled some of the banished Catholic bishops of the East, and their appointments were ratified by Gratian. Gradually the Catholics began to recover courage. In 379 a synod at Antioch reaffirmed the doctrines of Nicæa, and in the winter of that year an illness 'of the sort called clinical' frightened Theodosius, who was at Thessalonica, into baptism, which he received from the hands of Acholius, the local bishop, a Catholic, and no doubt awaiting his opportunity. In February 380 Theodosius, shouldering with true imperial suddenness his responsibilities as a Catholic emperor, issued an edict exhorting his Eastern subjects to follow the faith taught by the Apostle Peter to the Romans.[1] The wording of the edict was not very tactful as a message to the Eastern sections of the Church, which were never very concerned to uphold the prestige of Rome, but they were prepared to overlook for the present Saint Peter's alleged occidental preferences in consideration of this sudden and quite unexpected improvement in their fortunes.

Up to 379, however, the Catholics of Constantinople had so lost their morale that they were drifting away from their theological allegiance and joining the Arian congregation, since no one took any interest in them or seemed inclined

[1] *Codex Theodosianus*, XVI. 1, 2.

to help them. They appear to have been without a leader, and Demophilus, the Arian bishop, an orator of some distinction, was without a competitor. When, however, the accession of Theodosius revived the hopes of the Catholics their first thought was to find a leader, and they looked very naturally towards Cappadocia, that remote theological oasis in which the pure spring of Trinitarian orthodoxy had flowed steadily through all the troubled and dangerous Arian years. Basil, a natural leader of men, was dead in the very moment when he was needed. There seemed to be no alternative but Gregory, and to Gregory came envoys to Saint Thecla's, to entreat him to come to Constantinople and lead the reviving Catholics. Entreaties were necessary indeed; for Gregory put forward every reason he could think of, both bad and good, to defend himself; his bad health, his poverty, his poor appearance—a bald, fragile elderly man, incapable of cutting the sort of figure that the Constantinopolitans were accustomed to look for in their bishop.[1] But the envoys persisted, and finally accused him, very justly, of shirking his duty to the suffering Church. That was the argument that fetched Gregory; but before accepting finally he bargained that, should his efforts in the Catholic cause at Constantinople be successful, some one other than himself should occupy the episcopal throne, one of the four loftiest in the world,[2] which would presumably become vacant.[3]

[1] *Orat.* XXXIII.
[2] The other three were Rome, Alexandria, and Antioch.
[3] This stipulation rules out the accusation which has been made against Gregory that he broke his resolve out of ambition and place-seeking. Cardinal Newman suggests that as Basil was dead, and Gregory thought it his duty to do what Basil would have done.

The Catholics at Constantinople, a small and timid congregation, lacked even a meeting-place, and Gregory's first act was to convert the ground-floor of a private dwelling, the home of relatives of his own, to the purposes of a chapel. He called it the Anastasia, the Resurrection, to symbolize not only the ultimate Christian hope, but also the resuscitation of the Catholic faith at Constantinople. The site of this chapel was covered later by a church, and finally by the mosque of Mehmed Pasha; and students of Church history still gaze upon the spot and picture Gregory preaching there upon the finer points of Trinitarian theology to a tense and eager audience. For here those great orations were delivered, so justly admired through all ages of the Church, which established Gregory's reputation and won the throne of the Eastern Church from the Arians.

Gregory's next task was to stop the quarrelling among his flock; for they seem to have been an exception to the general rule that the presence of a common enemy is conducive to unity. Perhaps, as members of an argumentative race, these unfortunate Constantinople Greeks were reduced to practising their natural talent upon one another. And to silence their arguments and speculations on subjects which, as a professional philosopher, he considered beyond their paltry intelligences, Gregory poured over them a deluge of his best eloquence in the form of the five great orations commonly

called 'theological', as chiefly concerned with a description
and definition of the Trinity. They were aimed, ostensibly,
at the Arian foe; but Gregory could use them deftly to rebuke
his own congregation and, by an exalted treatment of the
theme, to bring home to them their unworthiness to handle
such sublime conceptions. No one, however indifferent to
theology, who reads these works can fail to be moved by
the depth of feeling which inspires them and by the beauty
of the words. In poetry Gregory could be tawdry and
commonplace; in prose, feeling could lift him above the
impedimenta of a too carefully-studied literary style to the
heights of genuine literature.

The Catholics of Constantinople had, as it turned out,
done very well for themselves. The acquisition of a fine
speaker immediately advanced their prestige in a place where
speaking and listening to speeches were principal objects
in life. Gregory's ascetic appearance, his unfaltering tread
through the mazes of theology, and his fluent but not florid
rhetoric, were all that the most pampered, sophisticated
audience could desire; and the humble Anastasia resounded
with the whole-hearted applause which the responsive congregations of those times were eager, and indeed encouraged,
to accord to their preachers.

Soon the curious, the novelty-seekers, in whom Constantinople abounded, were finding their way to the Anastasia, and after them the *amateurs* of rhetoric, and the
weaker, wavering Catholics who had gone a-whoring after
the Arians because the Catholics could not provide an
attraction while the Arians could. Demophilus, the Arian
bishop, a rhetorician himself, began in the course of only a
few weeks to realize with alarm that he had a rival. As his
congregation began to fade away the fact had to be faced
that the Arians had no longer the monopoly of religious
entertainment in the city.

Constantinople was a place where, once things began to

move, they moved quickly. Not all the Arians were triflers at the command of every new celebrity; they had their loyalty even in error, and they were not going to see their leader's prestige challenged without striking a blow on his behalf. There was a sudden return to the mob violence which had been a feature of the old rivalry between Catholics and Arians. On Easter Eve 379, but a few weeks after Gregory's arrival in the city, an angry horde of men and women of the Arian congregation, accompanied by a troop of beggars, the parasites of their charity, rushed from the Great Church,[1] where the midnight office of that season was in progress, and made for the Anastasia. Like a Bacchic rout, Gregory says, they broke in, like mænads, corybants and fauns, a nightmare of paganism revived. They threw the congregation into confusion, beat and hustled them and threw stones; Gregory himself was wounded, but only superficially. He was, however, disinclined to take a very serious view of the affair, partly because stones were traditional instruments of martyrdom since the earliest days of faith, and partly because the Arians, with such a confusion as they had in their minds on the important subject of the Trinity, could hardly be looked to for anything but confusion in their behaviour. But there had been a breach of the peace, which the police could not overlook. Like all policemen in all ages they liked to make an arrest. In an officially Arian town they preferred not to arrest an Arian, so they seized Gregory and, after keeping him for some time in the cells, took him before the magistrates. Magistrates, from the days of his estate management at home in Cappadocia, Gregory could never abide; and to have to answer in court for his part in a common brawl wounded his soul. Nothing, however, came of this encounter with the law, for the magistrates probably knew perfectly where the blame lay. Gregory himself credits his release to uneasiness on their part as to what the emperor, whose Catholic sym-

[1] The predecessor of Justinian's Saint Sophia.

pathies were known to everybody, might have to say in the matter.

The fuss blew over for the moment. Gregory made no attempt to have his persecutors restrained or punished. To friends[1] he wrote that he thought that injuries should be forgiven, but that at the same time he could not help thinking that a little punishment would do the Arians good as a deterrent from future outbreaks.[2] In church he delivered a fine, and not at all forgiving, oration against the Arians, detailing their outrages and atrocities, their cruelty to the Catholics, their rudeness and violence towards himself and, crowning all their enormities, their abominable beliefs about the Trinity.

Gregory's friends did not put their faith in sermons alone. A deputation waited on Theodosius at his headquarters at Thessalonica (he was engaged in the Gothic war) to remind, him that the Arians were flourishing quite undisturbed in his own capital and molesting his Catholics behind his back. There was no immediate result, for Theodosius, who was a soldier first and a Catholic afterwards, thought the Goths must be settled with first. But the hint was not wasted: action was merely postponed for a more convenient time.

Bad as the Arians were, from a Catholic point of view they were the accepted, the time-honoured foe for whose destruction Gregory had come to Constantinople. More complicated and more disturbing were the divisions of the Catholics themselves. There was a difference of opinion, not wholly theological in its origin, sometimes called the schism of Antioch, about the succession to the bishopric there. An old bishop, Paulinus, needed an assistant who should ultimately succeed him, and the strongest candidate was a former

---

[1] One of them was Theodore, a friend of his from Arianzus, later bishop of Tyana, who seems to have accompanied him to Constantinople.

[2] Epp. LXXVII, LXXVIII.

bishop, Meletius,[1] who had once been deposed for Arian tendencies. There was enough of Arian-Catholic rivalry here to rekindle the old conflagration in a new and highly personal form, and soon the trouble had spread throughout the East, and it was necessary for every one to declare themselves on one side or the other. Meletius, however, was not strictly an Arian, he was not more than a semi-Arian, and he succeeded in recommending himself to some of the Asiatic Catholics, including the theological purists of Cappadocia, and had won over the great Basil himself. The situation was therefore confusing; for Athanasius, the great Catholic leader at Alexandria, had supported Paulinus and should have settled the allegiance of the Catholics upon the side of Paulinus but for the support given to Meletius by the Cappadocians. For Gregory the position was difficult, for as leader of the Catholics in the Arian stronghold he would be expected to side with Paulinus and Athanasius, whereas his personal allegiance was with any party which had won Basil's commendation. Actually the dispute bored him acutely: it was a rivalry of personalities, not of principles, and had nothing to do with religion or philosophy. His congregation, however, were far from bored by the new phase of an old controversy, and eagerly took sides. Gregory preached a couple of magnificent sermons on the subject of peace, with some temporary effect. But neutrality is always mistrusted by the contentious, and Gregory suffered the fate of all neutrals, who in the long run find themselves without the confidence of either party. He was also the victim of something which no saint should be called upon to endure, a bad practical joke.

There was a person called Maximus the Cynic, a fraud whose success is difficult now to explain in the light of our

---

[1] The schism of Antioch is sometimes erroneously called the Meletian Schism; but the Meletian Schism proper was another older tale connected with Jerusalem.

information about him, which we owe entirely to his dupes after they had found him out. He was an Egyptian, and had been a professional Cynic, practising the Cynics' traditional mode of life. On being converted to Christianity he became an ascetic, continuing to wear the Cynics' costume, the short soiled tunic, long hair, and the time-honoured wallet and staff. He was in fact just that mixture of *poseur* and ascetic to which the Alexandrians, with the philosophers on the one hand and the hermits on the other, were quite accustomed; and he had borrowed something from the rhetoricians too, he was a fop with a painted face, hair both long and short, light and dark, curled and straight, and some of it false. Gregory says he was a kind of man-woman, and hints at the darkest possibilities.

He had travelled considerably, had founded a community of virgins at Corinth which he had been obliged to quit hastily, and he had been whipped out of other towns and been a fugitive from the law. After all this it seems strange that he could impose upon anybody, but he successfully hoodwinked Gregory and some other harder heads, such as Athanasius, Peter bishop of Alexandria and, eventually, the great Ambrose of Milan.

Peter of Alexandria was an opponent of Meletius in the Antioch affair and, casting an anxious eye upon Constantinople, he wondered whether Gregory as a Cappadocian and perhaps a sympathizer with Meletius was a proper person to be leading the Catholic revival in the Arian stronghold. He has been called a busybody for interfering in Constantinople, but after all Alexandria was the one great Catholic see remaining intact at that moment in the East, and he may have thought that he had in consequence a special responsibility. He decided that the position wanted watching, and sent Maximus to Constantinople to report on Gregory's orthodoxy and to find out how the land lay. Whatever Peter intended, Maximus' object was most certainly to supplant

Gregory as bishop, and eventually to become patriarch of Constantinople himself.

It may seem to our eyes that Maximus was a curious choice for such a task; but to a world accustomed to cynics, ascetics, and rhetoricians he would not be so conspicuous nor look so odd as he would to us. And there can have been few moments in the entire history of Constantinople when, in the diversity of races and variety of costumes that have adorned her streets, an outlandish dress, a painted face, or a little false hair could produce a sensation or even a mild comment.

All went smoothly at first. Maximus ingratiated himself at the Anastasia by his exaggeratedly devout behaviour and his vehement applause of Gregory's discourses. Gregory received him kindly, and admitted the ex-philosopher to his house and his conversation. There was some talk, after a little while, of a return to Egypt, and Gregory bestowed a farewell panegyric upon Maximus[1] which is more creditable to his good nature than his common sense. Perhaps, with his passion for philosophy, Gregory was a little too appreciative of the flattery of an ex-philosopher.

Maximus, however, did not return to Egypt; over-rating his apparent popularity he decided to strike at once. He was reinforced by some Egyptian ecclesiastics who arrived by the corn-ships from Alexandria in the nick of time, and by their crews also. Money to gain further supporters was wheedled somehow out of an ecclesiastic from Thasos who had been entrusted by his congregation with a large sum to buy them Proconnesian marbles to adorn their church; the over-trusting Thasians never saw their money again, nor did they ever receive any marbles. A midnight entry was made into the Anastasia, which was empty and unguarded, and Maximus' supporters proceeded to consecrate him bishop. The first step in a consecration was to crop the candidate if

[1] *Orat.*, XXV.

he had not already parted with his hair at some previous
stage of his ecclesiastical career, and Maximus' hair seems
to have caused some delay in the proceedings, for between
the false and the real there was a great deal of it to be removed. The false came off readily enough, but the real was
still incompletely shorn when dawn brought the usual people
to the church for the first office of the day. A crowd soon
gathered, and the priests and people drove Maximus and his
friends from the church, to complete their rites in a private
dwelling, the house of a play-actor, a most fitting refuge, as
Gregory drily observes. Maximus' party had still enough
optimism, when all was completed, to renew their attempt
on the Anastasia, with the object of presenting their man to
the people as a fully fledged, or rather, cropped bishop. But
they had misjudged their public; the congregation were,
after all, mostly Greeks, and the affair of the hair was too
much for them. This time Maximus had to face a roar of
hearty laughter, which spread from the congregation to the
streets, echoed round the city, and sent him packing in
ignominious flight. It was the only possible ending to such
an episode, and it restores our somewhat wavering respect for the Catholic mob of Constantinople. It also leaves
us wondering why, in all the strange accidents of the early
centuries of Christianity, among the Greeks at any rate, that
reassuring, wholesome laughter is not more often heard.
Perhaps the laughter, often enough, was there; and if we
fail to catch its echo we must blame historians, who have
always preferred the anguish of the past to its mirth, and
love to dip their pens in tears.

Maximus and his friends showed a remarkable tenacity.
They appealed to the emperor, who was still at Thessalonica,
but Theodosius knew a fraud when he saw one and gave
them short shrift. They retired to Alexandria, where they
consoled themselves for a time by stirring up trouble against
bishop Peter. The principal result of Maximus' proceedings

was to draw the attention of Theodosius to Constantinople
and to remind him that even the Goths must not monopolize
the entire energies of an emperor who has the squabbles and
rivalries of Christians still upon his hands.

Gregory was in great mental distress. He and his flock
had been made to look very silly, and in their rather weak
position in that city of sharp eyes and ribald tongues it was
no comfortable thing to look a fool. His flock seem to have
murmured to some extent against him, and his friends fearing some revulsion of feeling, or perhaps wishing to make
it appear that his safety was threatened, mounted guard over
him day and night.

His own inclination was to disappear. Once more his
inner voices told him of the joys of solitude and the dangers
of being entangled with the world. The rumour of what was
passing in his mind spread abroad, and immediately there
was one of those sudden lurches of feeling so characteristic
of the Greeks and so common in Constantinople. Gregory
suddenly found the Anastasia packed to overflowing with
a crowd that would not disperse till he had reassured it that
he would pity it, and stay. 'If you leave us,' cried a voice,
a heavenly voice perhaps, or perhaps just a member of the
congregation, 'then the Trinity will leave us also.' He took
a short holiday by the sea, which usually comforted him,
but like himself it was unquiet and only tormented him the
more; the tireless surf flung the pebbles and weeds and shells
up the beach only to drag them all back again, and only
the rocks stood still. He returned to the Anastasia and tried
to restore his injured self-esteem by a great oration on
Maximus and his own mistake. The oration is not of his
best, it is too explanatory and self-excusing, but it no doubt
relieved his feelings and did something to restore his prestige
as an orator at least.

Fortune, for the Catholics, now quite suddenly took an
extremely brilliant turn. A few months later Theodosius,

aroused perhaps by the Maximus affair, entered Constantinople with his army, free, through the death of Fritigern the able and astute Gothic leader, of immediate military preoccupations, though the Gothic war was not by any means ended. Theodosius was an admirable monarch, Gregory justly observes, equal to the exigencies of the times, but a little inclined to use force rather than persuasion. He sent immediately for Gregory, and informed him that the Almighty had accorded to him and his congregation the consecrated places in Constantinople. He also sent for Demophilus, the Arian who was still in fact bishop, and told him that he must accept the creed of Nicæa, or disappear. To the credit of Demophilus be it recorded, and he has won but scant applause for it from succeeding ages, that he refused to make a false confession. He departed from the city, and with a small following continued to conduct holy worship according to his lights in a humble meeting-place outside the walls. The sacred buildings of Constantinople were then handed over to the Catholics, who were not a little dazed by this arbitrary and unlooked-for turn of fortune, and somewhat afraid of reprisals from the discomfited Arians. But the Arians could do nothing but stand and gape, angry and helpless (though it seems they did make some verbal protest to the emperor), while the soldiers of Theodosius took possession of their buildings. It was done in the name of theology and the Trinity; but it was none the less a military *coup d'état*, and Gregory aptly remarks that a crowd behaves better if there is an armed force visible.

The triumph of the Catholics, indeed, was clouded with doubt: they were perhaps the sport of a royal caprice, which might be forgotten in a moment; or the emperor's attention, and his soldiers, might be called off elsewhere, when the Catholics would be in an awkward situation. Gregory himself was positively disappointed. To be in a heroic minority, persecuted, suffering for the Trinity, was for him far more comfortable than to lead a military triumph, a revolution almost, owed to the swift stroke of an emperor equipped with armed persuasions. But there was nothing to be done about it, and Gregory must have felt like the sorcerer's inexperienced apprentice who, having raised the devil to do his bidding, found him clumsy and violent and, when no longer needed, impossible to dismiss.

Finally a public enthronement of Gregory was staged, to take place in the Great Church; and Gregory had to walk in procession with the emperor beside him, surrounded by guards, through Constantinople, which, with its vast crowd silent and cowed, looked what in fact it really was, a captured city. In the church he had to face an enormous, dense congregation largely composed of soldiers, for Theodosius left nothing to chance. It was an impressive scene, if also, for a theological triumph, an incongruous one; and Gregory felt extremely weary and rather frightened too, for the sky was black, and the basilica dark as night within, giving courage to the Arian crowd without. No doubt they thought that heaven was frowning on the proceedings and, remembering perhaps a former ceremony of reinstatement, hoped for a similar sequel and that the ignominious death of Arius might be avenged. But the frown passed, the clouds suddenly dispersed, a blaze of sunshine lit up the dark interior of the church, and the congregation broke into tempestuous clapping and cheers, instantly recognizing the sign of divine favour. The women, too, overstepping, Gregory thought, all womanly decorum, joined in the general acclamation, and they all called upon Gregory for a speech; for surely the occasion should have been crowned by one of his sublime oratorical displays.

But poor Gregory was quite unequal to the occasion: his voice failed him, and he could only ask the people to restrain themselves and remember that the occasion was one for thanksgiving, not for rhetoric, to which Gregory says, they wholeheartedly agreed. But one feels, as the congregation must have felt, that an opportunity had been missed, and a colleague of his, Gregory of Nyssa perhaps, had to round off the proceedings with a few brief unprepared remarks.

Theodosius, having handed over Constantinople to the Catholics, expected them to be able to carry on without further assistance. Fear of the emperor kept back open violence, but the situation was full of discomforts; the Catholics could not all behave with restraint in the hour of victory and, in a city which now contained the imperial court, Gregory had to witness his flock swarming round the palace anterooms seeking favours and places, and to hear their grumblings because he was not himself busy in the same direction. Gregory made no change in his own ways; as usual he remained out of sight, where indeed he may have felt more comfortable, for he had not a permanent guard and his friends were still a minority in a hostile population.

The Arians, however, contented themselves with verbal recriminations, some of them perfectly justified, such as that the Catholics, having now possession of all the churches in Constantinople, had neither congregations to fill them nor money to staff them or keep them in proper repair. The Great Church, however, was regularly full, with a vast crowd of all kinds of people, of all shades of doctrine, assembled to hear those matchless orations which Gregory now delivered there instead of at the Anastasia, fascinating his audience, silencing criticism by the pure beauty of his language and the finished perfection of his style, which in that town served better than superior numbers to maintain the prestige of a party.

Gregory's position had one serious technical flaw. He had been enthroned by the emperor, but he had not been elected bishop, and in so far as he was a bishop at all he was bishop of Sasima in Cappadocia. Theodosius seems to have been aware of this and, swift, practical and, in such matters, incurably optimistic, he decided to call an ecclesiastical council to settle the point and certain other little theological problems which were outstanding, such as the schism of Antioch, which was still tearing the East asunder.

The council, to which all the bishops of Asia, Africa, Syria, and Illyria were invited, was summoned to Constantinople in the spring of the year 381. In May the council assembled, but it was far from complete, and was not a little tinged with partisanship in the Antioch affair. The Asiatics and Syrians who arrived were all of the party of Meletius in the Antioch schism; for the partisans of Paulinus, knowing well that the council was expected to elect Gregory as patriarch, and regarding him as a supporter of Meletius, made one pretext or another to stay at home. The Alexandrian and Egyptian bishops, remembering Maximus and the discomfiture which had overtaken him and their schemes, also stayed away, on the pretext that bishop Peter was dying and that they were busy round his death-bed; and the Illyrians, including even bishop Acholius of Thessalonica who had baptized Theodosius, awkwardly placed as they were halfway between East and West, kept a cautious eye on Rome and contrived to be absent; for Rome, they knew, had taken the side of Athanasius and Paulinus, and might be opposed to the elevation of the dubious Gregory. Certain semi-Arians, moreover, who had been invited, discovering on their arrival that they would be expected to reaffirm the remorseless Trinitarian doctrines of Nicæa, packed up and left almost before the council had begun its sittings; and to complete the general perversity, Meletius himself was placed in the chair.

The first piece of business was to declare the consecration of Maximus the Cynic null and void, and to elect Gregory bishop of Constantinople. Still maintaining his customary attitude of resistance and protest, Gregory was duly enthroned, with all honours, in the Great Church. And then, when all seemed harmony and accord in this disappointingly small and most surprisingly unanimous council, Meletius, the president, the bone of schismatic contention, died.

The presidential chair was easily filled by the appointment of Gregory; but very unfortunately this extremely partisan council expected that Gregory would succeed the late president not only in office but in spirit, and that he would prove as ardent a Meletian as Meletius himself. There had been an agreement, some time before, that, when either Paulinus or Meletius should die, the bishopric should revert to the survivor. Paulinus should now therefore remain in undisturbed possession of his bishopric; but when Gregory proposed, as became a respectable chairman, that the agreement should be honoured, the Meletians, that is to say the majority of the council, would have none of it, for they had never expected that Meletius, by far the younger man, would die first. There was a violent outburst, and Gregory's appeal in the name of Christian unity, of peace, of the respect due to the venerable Paulinus for the probably brief remainder of his days, was met with vociferous hostility. There was a chattering as of magpies, he tells us, and the younger bishops flew at him like a swarm of wasps, while the older men did nothing to restrain them. For their part they urged that as bishops of the East their opinion was entitled to prevail, for did not the sun rise in the East, and did not Christ choose the East when he took our nature upon him? Gregory's retort that in the East also he was betrayed and crucified was met by the Resurrection, which had also taken place in the East; and thus the contest proceeded. There were proposals for a successor to Meletius, and apparently to Gregory too, and at last, it seems, he lost his temper. Probably inaudible amid the tumult, he passionately invited the assembly to admit every one of no matter what shade of doctrine to come and vote in it, or, if it liked, to cast lots.

He seems to have left the assembly then, and he never

returned to it. Illness kept him at home, a convenient illness he calls it, so presumably it was of that kind which has often saved men from awkward situations. He would have left his worldly duties at once but for the entreaty of his own small flock, who, in spite of the intrigues of foreign bishops, still loved their distinguished but unpractical pastor.

And then there occurred what Gregory regarded afterwards, if not at the time, as a heaven-sent solution of all his troubles. The instruments of heaven, as often, were peculiar: the anti-Meletian bishops who had not been present at the council had now decided that Gregory was implicated in its too Meletian leanings, rather oddly, since it was his support of Paulinus that had brought about his fall. But news travelled slowly in those days and their information was probably a trifle out of date. A party of them, including Theophilus the new bishop of Alexandria, Peter's successor, Acholius of Thessalonica,[1] and the Illyrians, appeared suddenly at Constantinople and claimed that, as Gregory was bishop of Sasima, his tenure of the bishopric of Constantinople was illegal, by the fifteenth canon of the Council of Nicæa which enacted that bishops could not be transferred from one see to another. Gregory says that they blew upon the proceedings of the council with the rough breath of the West, and that they had flashing eyes and sharpened their tusks like wild boars. There was great surprise at their intervention, and at the reasons they put forward; for every one had forgotten the fifteenth, as indeed many another canon of Nicæa, and Gregory had forgotten all about Sasima. But the facts were correct and could not be denied, and they were most opportune for Gregory's opponents in the council.

Gregory now had every one against him: the Alexandrians, the Illyrians, Rome, and both sides in the Antioch dispute. He had no support outside Constantinople, and in it only

[1] It is possible that Theodosius was tired of Gregory and originated the manœuvre to get rid of him.

[316]

his own flock, and even that was not undivided. The world, he felt, had no use for integrity of mind, for loyalty to the faith; it was time for him to go. He relinquished at once his throne and the presidential chair, and falling on his knees before Theodosius in presence of the court, he begged for his release; he had come, he said, to ask not money, nor marble panellings, nor rich draperies for the altar, nor places for his friends—the usual demands of bishops in those days —but his personal liberty. With no more desire perhaps than the council had felt to induce Gregory to retain his throne, Theodosius behaved at least with decorum and some imperial grace. He expressed the regrets that were proper but did not try to make Gregory change his mind; in a few days Gregory was gone.

One duty to himself, however, he did not omit: he delivered a farewell oration, the summit of all his oratorical works. In it he spared no pains to display to his public those gifts with which they were so ready to dispense. They crowded to hear him, of course, the faithful from the Anastasia, the general public, the riff-raff who cared for naught but a fine rhetorical performance, even the bishops of the council; and indeed they were not disappointed. The oration is full of everything which that age most valued in such a work. It has emotion, grandeur and elegance; it is sweetly polite, it is perhaps not very humble, for Gregory could claim that he had achieved the purpose for which he was called: he had found a small and wretched handful of Catholics and left them in possession of the second city of the world. And it has, unmistakably, the superciliousness of the man who cares nothing at all for the men who have ruined him, for their standards are not his and they cannot touch his soul. Finally he accorded his audience what they always expected, an exposition of the faith, that is to say a definition of the Trinity. Before this august and also incomprehensible theme the audience could give themselves up to Gregory's

rich melodies, his rolling cadences, and lose themselves in
a metaphysical counterpoint where the phrases seem to chase
each other, to break up, to scatter, and even disappear, only
to re-emerge triumphantly whole and in unison, just when
the confusion seems about to be complete.

'First let me run over the details', says Gregory in his easy
way. 'That which has no beginning does not consist in being
without beginning or being unbegotten, for the nature of
a thing lies, not in what it is not, but in what it is. . . . And
the Beginning is not, because it is a beginning, separated
from that which has no beginning. For its beginning is not
its nature, any more than the being without beginning is the
nature of the other. For these are the accompaniments of
the nature, not the nature itself. That again which is, with
that which has no beginning, and with the beginning, is not
anything else than what they are. Now the name of that
which has no beginning is the Father, and of the Beginning,
the Son, and of that which is with the Beginning, the Holy
Ghost, and the Three have one nature—God. . . .'[1]

And then, a long, almost lyrical farewell to the churches
of Constantinople, beginning with the Anastasia, his dearest
of all churches and a somewhat contemptuous farewell to
the 'mighty, Christ-loving city of Constantinople', with its
brilliancy that dazzles those who look at the surface; and,
finally, a brisk shaking-off of the dust of that perhaps too
brilliant city, with its passion for horse-racing and theatres,
and its very similar passion for things spiritual, which it
treats in far too sporting a manner. He had been thrown
overboard like Jonah to save the ship; he had been too quiet,
too spiritual, for them; and now for his country life, his
peaceful simplicity, and his God.

Gregory left his throne trailing clouds of glory, no longer
in eclipse. The throne itself he endowed with a new prestige;
thereafter much was expected of those who occupied it. For

[1] This passage is almost a quotation from the *Phaedrus*.

the moment a very plain, competent, ordinary person was appointed to fill it, Nectarius, who had been prefect of the city, a man of no very great personal distinction but of good practical gifts, which were perhaps what Theodosius and even the jarring bishops wanted. The council finished its deliberations very peaceably and produced six very commendable canons, all of which Gregory would have approved.[1]

As the council had presumably been glad of Gregory's fall, it should perhaps have shown some gratitude to the Alexandrians and Illyrians for their part in it, but gratitude was not a feature of ecclesiastical councils. No further attention was paid to the Alexandrians, and the relations of Alexandria and Constantinople were carried on thereafter in a jealous and acrimonious manner, with repeated attempts on the part of Alexandria to interfere.

There were some further excursions, amusing but unedifying, between East and West. Theodosius decreed the restoration of all churches to the Catholics, and received from a council at Aquileia a letter of thanks for this step, with a regret that the Catholics of the East were still so quarrelsome and disunited, and a recommendation that a further council should be held in Rome.[2] Eventually a joint council of East and West was summoned to be held in Rome, but the Eastern bishops failed to appear and wrote to the council to affirm doctrinal agreement with the Western bishops, adding that in other respects there was nothing that they could not settle for themselves just as well at home.

---

[1] Maximus was deposed. Consubstantiality was affirmed. The Creed of Nicæa was confirmed with an addition, the invention of the Cappadocian Fathers, about the Holy Ghost proceeding. The See of Constantinople was pronounced to be second only to that of Rome, which must not, however, interfere in the East; and bishops and metropolitans must in no circumstance meddle outside their dioceses.

[2] The Council of Aquileia was Paulinian in feeling and was also the victim of fresh intrigues by Maximus the Cynic.

IX

Gregory's brief and troubled excursion into public life was over. He seems to have been without regrets and remained on friendly terms with his successor Nectarius, to whom he wrote a good-humoured letter of congratulation: 'It was right that a royal city should have a royal figure-head, so the capital has received you with open arms, with your high qualities and your skill in oratory and all the gifts which heaven has lavished upon you. Me it rejected with scorn as the sea casts up flotsam and scum. . . .' To other friends he wrote very frankly and flippantly that he had escaped from the bishops as from the fires of Sodom. Now, if his intentions were sincere, he could seek that retirement which was the professed ambition of his life.

He returned to Nazianzus, where for some months, as a kind of self-imposed penance, he took a vow of silence. But this did not hinder him from writing letters and listening to those who wished to come and talk to him, a self-denying ordinance indeed, the reason of which he does not explain. But it cannot have been for long, for Nazianzus was bishop-less as ever, and as ever determined to have no bishop but Gregory, and the old game of hide-and-seek was resumed, just where it had been left off, with no less enthusiasm by either side. Gregory put forward candidates of his own in self-defence, and tried to manœuvre them into the bishopric, to the great offence of the Cappadocian bishops who should have been called to an election. There were appeals to the

Primate of Tyana and to the Prefect of Asia, and an exchange
of brisk and angry letters on both sides. There was a compli-
cating circumstance in a heresy called the Apollinarian, of
local origin,[1] which seized upon a number of the Nazianzenes
and elicited from Gregory, for the instruction of his own
candidate of the moment, two vast letters[2] on the nature of
Christ, in both its human and divine aspects, upon which
the Apollinarian heresy had gone very perversely astray.
These letters have been accepted by the Church in later ages
as a final statement upon a thorny subject. They delighted
the orthodox, but somehow failed to discourage the Apollinarians, and while Gregory was away taking the waters at
Xantharis, a local spa, they elected a bishop of their own,
and threatened Nazianzus with a schism. Gregory then at
last perceived that to shirk a responsibility may prove more
troublesome than to shoulder it; he faced the duty he had
evaded for so long and took the bishopric himself. The rival
candidates seem to have disappeared quietly, for if Gregory
would take his own Nazianzus it was not worth any one's
while to attempt to stand in his way.

Efforts were made, quite unsuccessfully, now that he was
bishop, to get him to Constantinople to the second Ecu-
menical Council there. 'I am of a mind to avoid all gather-
ings of bishops,' he wrote to a friend, 'for never have I seen
one that produced any useful result or composed any difference of opinion. Rather the trouble, whatever it was, was
aggravated.[3] For there is ever contention in them, and ambition and talking competitions, and people make accusations
against one another rather than come to terms. . . .' For this
council and its conduct Gregory evidently feared the worst,

[1] It had its origin at Laodicea, not far away, where an ingenious
bishop, Apollinaris, had indulged some unbridled speculations about
the nature of Christ, according to which the mind of Christ had never
been human, but had remained divine.
[2] Epp. CI, CII.
[3] 'Synods are mystical bear gardens. . . .'—Samuel Butler.

thinking it might resemble its predecessor, for he wrote to the heads of the Constantinople police, who were friends of his,[1] to preserve the peace among the jarring bishops, expressing the flattering wish that the bishops in their behaviour might emulate the dignity and public spirit of the police.

The story of Gregory and Nazianzus now seems to have reached the happy, the only reasonable ending; but biographers have many troubles, not least among them the too frequent obligation to record that the objects of their attentions have not behaved as they should. Too often a story which seems to have reached a neat and satisfactory conclusion must sink, in deference to the recalcitrance of human nature, into anticlimax at the last. Gregory did not spend the twilight of his days and die in glory upon the episcopal throne of Nazianzus: he occupied it, probably, for about a year. He could not be a bishop: to be a bishop inevitably made him ill, and he was ill, and the metropolitan of Tyana, his old friend Theodore, very soon received his entreaties to be relieved of his see. When these brought no reply (and Theodore's boredom at the communication can well be imagined), Gregory wrote with some vehemence to threaten that he would declare the see vacant and proceed to the election of his successor himself; and eventually he did in fact send Theodore his resignation. There was some dismay in Cappadocia, and a bishop who had not unnaturally written to Gregory to urge reconsideration was dealt with a little sharply: 'I thought I was entitled to an apology from you— so old fashioned and simple am I.[2] But you set no limits to your persecution of me, you have always some fresh provocation ready, and heap insult upon insult . . .', and again, 'Twice you have tripped me up, and twice deceived me (you know what I mean). . . . But just as you are master of your

---

[1] Letters CXXXV and CXXXVI. One of them, Modarius, was a Goth and also a Christian, an Arian most probably.
[2] Ep. CXXXVIII to Bosporius, bishop of Colonia in Cappadocia.

own opinions, so am I of mine. That troublesome Gregory will trouble you no more. . . . I will retire into myself. This I have determined, for to stumble twice upon the same stone is a thing, according to the proverbs, which only a fool does.'[1] Gregory made amends later for this acrimonious letter by defending its recipient, Bosporius, under a charge of heresy.

The resignation was at last accepted, and after some bitter bickerings, in the course of the year 383 a cousin of Gregory's, Eulalius, was elected his successor. Everybody, even Gregory, was satisfied at last.

[1] Ep. CLIII.

Gregory now had full lease of that leisure which he had always desired, and could realize his philosophic dream. He retired to the family property at Arianzus, where there was a garden and a spring and such amenities as philosophers like to have about them. The estate and its management could not annoy him now, for it was in the hands of trustees, administered for the benefit of the poor of Nazianzus, with, presumably, some allowance for his own needs. Here he could be secluded indeed, and that he was able to realize his dream of leisure is indicated by an enormous literary output, mostly in verse. There are a few orations also, and he collected Basil's letters and his own, and perhaps composed or finished the funeral oration for Basil, for which he had hitherto found no time.

There were interruptions, of course. He was appealed to by everybody on all manner of questions, personal and other, for advice, and for his interest with people in high places. There are letters of introduction, letters to officials begging for consideration, protection, or leniency to personal friends who were in trouble or in disgrace. Once, in an episode only vaguely hinted at in one of his poems,[1] Gregory had to flee before slanderous tongues; and once he was evicted by the unwelcome proximity of a relative called Valentinian, who came to live beside him with a troop of disorderly women, in the hope, it seems, of using Gregory's ecclesiastical pres-

[1] *Carmina*, xliii.

tige and blameless reputation as a cloak for his nefarious doings. The ladies became so objectionable that Gregory had to leave the field, temporarily at least, in possession of the enemy, though not before he had relieved his feelings in an excellent, most expressive letter.[1] By Eve, he says, he was cast out of his paradise. But, on the testimony of his enormous output of verse, there must have been sufficient peace in the paradise and, despite his ill health, he lived to enjoy it, from the election of his successor Eulalius, for at least seven years. He died, as Saint Jerome tells us, in the eleventh year of the reign of Theodosius,[2] when he was about sixty years old.

A will of doubtful authenticity has come down to us which may have been made by Gregory on his departure from Constantinople. In it he leaves the bulk of his property to the poor of Nazianzus, with some bequests, on a small scale, to a number of people, his freedmen, his lawyer, some distant relatives, and some of his slaves, who are to be freed under the will.[3] To his 'daughter' Alypiana, a lady well known for frequent and affectionate mention in his correspondence, he apologizes that he can leave her nothing but some clothing and effects of his brother Cæsarius, and to two other 'daughters', Eugeneia and Nonna, Gregory leaves not even an apology, for their lives are of 'ill repute, and they are not to make a nuisance of themselves to the executors, or to the Church of Nazianzus'. Further, in regard to his 'son-in-law', Meletius[4] (the husband presumably of one of the above-mentioned), Gregory adds that he

[1] Letter C.
[2] 389 or 390.
[3] Gregory is described in it as bishop of Constantinople, and the witnesses subjoined are bishops who might have been among those gathered at Constantinople for the council. The will is preserved in two Vatican codices.
[4] An unknown person, not of course the schismatic bishop of Antioch.

is wrongfully occupying property given or perhaps sold by Gregory to Euphemius, whom he has often reproached for weakness in submitting to this injustice.

Gregory's so-called 'daughters' have perplexed those who think that Fathers of the Church should have daughters after the spirit only, and who are ready to deny Gregory his sainthood for a possible paternal relationship. The acrimonious mention of Eugeneia and Nonna, and of the 'son-in-law' Meletius, who are cut off without a shilling and loaded with insults, does not accord with the character usually displayed by Gregory, who, when irritated, could speak his mind frankly enough in life, and did not need to take an unworthy revenge on offending parties by insulting them in his will from beyond the grave. Alypiana, whatever her degree of relationship, was certainly loved as a daughter; she and her husband Nicobulus and her children appear in Gregory's correspondence as constant objects of his loving interest and care. Eugeneia, to whom the will is so rude, is the subject of an urgent letter[1] to the metropolitan of Tyana, demanding protection for her interests in a lawsuit about her grandmother's property. If not his own daughters, the three women, Alypiana, Eugeneia, and Nonna, were perhaps his sister Gorgoneia's children, the youngest bearing her grandmother's name. Possibly the will is a forgery by some one who disliked Gregory or resented his 'daughters'. The great Cardinal Baronius[2] was uneasy about it, for he takes pains to establish its authenticity from internal evidence, without producing a very conclusive case.

Gregory has said often enough, more especially in his poetry, which is of the self-revealing sort, that he had neither wife nor child; that he had followed virginity and martyred the flesh, inspired by his childish, romantic dream in which the lovely virgins Chastity and Temperance appeared to him

[1] Ep. CLX.
[2] *Annales Ecclesiastici.*

in sleep. Once, in his verse, he says that his children all are dead and his friends departed; dream-children, perhaps, for the poem is a lament: all, all are gone, the old familiar faces. But, without going so far as Baronius, who roundly asserts that Gregory was a virgin from birth, we can ignore what he calls the 'passing shadow cast on Gregory's character by the daughters and son-in-law'; for the shadow, if any, is surely on the watch-dogs of celibacy and on those inquisitive puritans who indulge a sordid curiosity regarding the private lives of eminent men.

Ascetic himself, Gregory was no stern advocate of a harsh asceticism for others; his attitude to ordinary life was genial in the extreme. Marriage he was kind to, regarding it as not only a holy state, but a happy and advantageous one; and he had no misgivings, as had so many of the Fathers, as to the propriety of indulging in its lawful blisses.

'The happiness of your life is now secured,' he wrote to a young friend, whose wedding he was unable to attend,[1] 'the prayers of your parents have been answered . . . and I, unfortunately, must be at a distance. . . . Others then must invoke the powers of love (for gaiety becomes the nuptial feast) and describe the beauty of the bride . . . and . . . the bridegroom's handsome grace, and lastly, bedeck the bridal bed with complimentary addresses as with flowers.'

'I can well imagine what you are saying about me,'[2] he wrote to Procopius,[3] who had invited him to the wedding of his niece Olympias: ' "Here we are celebrating a wedding, the wedding of our lovely, darling Olympias, and we have a whole crowd of bishops to grace it, and you choose to absent yourself, you fine fellow, either shirking it or thinking yourself too good for us." Indeed, neither is true, my dear

[1] Ep. CCXXXI.
[2] Ep. CXCIII.
[3] This was not the Procopius who was *præfectus urbi* at Constantinople.

man . . . it is hardly nuptial or festal to have a couple of gouty old gentlemen hobbling about among the dancers, to be the sport of the whole company. . . .[1] As far as the wish goes, I am with you, I make merry with you and join the young people's hands together.'

To Olympias herself, in an admonitory poem on the same occasion, he recommended a prudent use of her connubial joys, and advised her to persuade her bridegroom to respect, perhaps, holy days and the festivals of the Church, just to keep him in mind of the superior claims of religion.

In a letter of rebuke to another friend, Verianus, who was attempting to separate his daughter from her husband with whom he had quarrelled, Gregory takes his stand not on principle, nor upon objections to divorce for its own sake, but on the cruelty and wickedness of separating two loving hearts. 'Far better is it to be a means to union and love . . . and this our excellent governor had in mind when he entrusted this case to me, for he knew I would not harshly or unfeelingly promote the divorce.' With Gregory of Nyssa, Basil's brother, he condoled upon the death of a lady named Theosebia, whom he calls the 'true and worthy consort of a priest, the most beautiful and glorious among all the beauty of the brethren'.[2]

Virginity he commended, as a good churchman; fornication and adultery he condemned, but with mercy. If a wife errs, let her not be cast out, but brought to a better way of thinking by a course of sensible punishments; her trinkets

[1] The Council of Laodicea had forbidden ecclesiastics to dance at weddings, apparently without success.

[2] Ep. CXCVII. The Benedictine editors have decided that this 'worthy consort of a priest' must mean Gregory of Nyssa's sister, and regret the handle given by Gregory of Nazianzus in this ambiguous phrase to those who favour marriage for the clergy. For the habit among ecclesiastics of living with ladies whom they called their 'sisters', see page 226 and *Codex Theodosianus*, XVI, 2, 44. See also Council of Nicæa, Canon III, on *mulieres subintroductæ*.

should be taken from her for a time, or her pleasurings cur-
tailed. And fidelity must be equal between the sexes, there
must not be one law for the woman and another for the man.
'A woman who practises evil against her husband's bed is
an adulteress and the penalties for this are severe, but if the
husband commits fornication against the wife he has no
account to give. I do not accept this legislation, I do not
approve the custom. They who made the law were men, and
so their legislation is hard on women.'

G regory claims to have regarded the making of verses as a form of asceticism, a penance; and so perhaps his enormous output in this kind should be credited to his ascetic rather than to his literary reputation. There are five hundred and seven poems, filling seven hundred long and closely printed columns in the Benedictine edition of the Greek Fathers. Unfortunately, as a French scholar, a devout admirer of Gregory, has felt obliged to admit, no one would think of selecting them for his bedside reading.[1]

Theology, moral homilies, prayers, the circumstances and adventures of his personal life, his relations with people and his opinions of them, everything, in fact, that was dreamed of in Gregory's philosophy went into verse in one form or another. Of form he was no mean master; metrically his verse is skilful and at ease. Hexameters, iambics, elegiacs, anacreontics, almost the whole gamut of Greek prosody was employed to express the diversity of his themes, without any misgiving that the subject might be unsuited to the form. His purpose, to show that Christianity was capable of providing a literature of its own equal to the great models of pagan literature, was not perhaps very successfully served; for to show that Christians could write verse did not also prove that they could write poetry.

Christian theology in hexameters has an incongruous sound to our ears, but the conjunction is not so disastrous

[1] Fleury, *Saint Grégoire de Nazianze*.

as might be feared. Mythology, which is after all theology
of a kind, is the theme of the best Greek poetry, and a
language which can express one religion has no inherent
unsuitability to another. Gregory, composing verses, could
not rid himself of the trappings of his Athenian education;
he drew freely and deliberately on the Greek poets and had
a vast resource in tags. Both language and metres must have
evoked in his contemporaries, as they do in ourselves, in-
effaceable memories. The grand epic melodies, the heroic
glamorous words are charged with associations that cannot
fail to awaken an answering thrill. All the most frequently
used words and phrases, words for light and darkness, for
spirit and shadow, for life, for suffering and for death, to
quote only a few of those most incident to a Christian writer,
trail the clouds of glory of their earlier, more inspired use.
The Gospel story itself acquires an epic ring; even the
manger seems the lineal descendant of some older, not un-
hallowed trough, that fed honey-sweet corn to the fleet and
glossy steeds of Diomed, or of Thracian Rhesus, or of Nestor
lord of horses. Of all this Gregory was perfectly aware and,
far from feeling that there was any profanity in using these
pagan trappings to deck the austerities of Christian theology,
he rejoiced that he could thus convert the glories of ancient
poetry to the service of the faith.

It is all most smoothly and expertly done. Adam and
Moses, and the personalities of Jewish and Christian theology, are surprisingly at ease in their unaccustomed dress.
But all the charm and all the music is in the borrowing.
Gregory is neat and scholarly, graceful and accomplished,
but he is never inspired; he escapes doggerel but never
achieves poetry.

Most interesting to posterity are the poems 'about himself'; a long autobiography, and some others dealing with the
events of his own life, precious, if somewhat emotional
records, from his own pen. Here there is genuine feeling, and

if the voice is a trifle declamatory it comes at any rate from the depths of the heart. And in the 'moral' poems, on such subjects as touched him closely, bishops for instance or false friends, there is occasionally a venom and a sting which save these works from insignificance and from the tedium of convention.

There are a number of trifling epigrams, epitaphs in elegiac metre, which tell us something of his friends and the people among whom he lived at various times. They have their historical interest, and in other respects are no worse than the bulk of the verses in that metre preserved in the Palatine Anthology.

Rhetorical in poetry, poetical in rhetoric, Gregory is at his best in his letters. Like all cultivated men of his time he practised, very deliberately, the refinements of the art of letter-writing, that sole gift of the Roman to the Greek. We possess over two hundred and thirty of his letters, selected partly by himself at the request of Nicobulus, his 'son' and protégé, from what must have been a mountain of material. Many of them are personal letters, in a variety of veins, letters of protest, teasing letters, angry letters, letters of introduction, in all a most remarkable monument to the friendships and to the personal relations in that circle of distinguished men to which Gregory belonged. Almost everybody who was anybody in the East at that time is to be encountered, in an atmosphere of intimacy that suggests old association from school or university days. Many of them were Cappadocians,[1] and the feeling is suggested that a common culture, membership of a ruling class all having similar responsibilities and interests, formed a bond among them. There was Basil, of course, and Gregory's brother Cæsarius, Theodore, a Nazianzene, ultimately bishop of Tyana, an intimate friend to whom Gregory could speak

---

[1] Libanius, the great professor, often teased Basil for continually introducing young Cappadocians to him.

out his mind.[1] There was Amphilochius, a Cappadocian, perhaps a relation of Gregory, who became bishop of Iconium, and was celebrated not only for horticulture but as a great ecclesiastical disciplinarian. There was Gregory of Nyssa, Basil's absurd brother, only too devoted to the art of rhetoric, as his writings deplorably show, and Nectarius, Gregory's successor at Constantinople, to whom Gregory showed no rancour, only the utmost geniality and good will. There were Sophronius and Procopius, prefects at Constantinople at various times, Saturnius, the consul in office at the time of the second Council of Constantinople, and Olympius, prefect of Cappadocia Secunda during Gregory's years of retirement. There are the rhetoricians Eudoxius and Themistius, the latter Theodosius' panegyrist who followed him about the empire with a panegyric ready for every great occasion, and Libanius the great Antioch professor, everybody's friend and most people's tutor, who receives the briefest of all the letters, a letter of introduction, a rather foolish epigrammatic *tour de force*.[2] And there is the tiresome Nicobulus, Alypiana's husband, who collected Gregory's letters, the usual hanger-on who dogs a great man's footsteps, flatters him, marries his niece or daughter, and gets money and introductions out of him. He gave up a lucrative position in the civil service in order to follow philosophy, and eventually left Alypiana a widow with very insufficient means and a family which included a further Nicobulus. 'You ask for flowers of the field in autumn,' Gregory wrote to him, in reply to his request for a collection of his letters, 'and demand of hoary Nestor that he should shoulder arms again. Fancy asking me for a smart literary display; it is now long since I renounced the pomps and vanities of the pen, nay of life itself. Still, it is a sweet task you have set me, no burdensome toil such as Eurystheus

[1] See page 305, note.
[2] Ep. CCXXXVI.

would set or Hercules undertake.' His request for a dissertation on the art of letter-writing drew from Gregory his famous epistolary essay: 'Letter-writers are of two kinds, some are too lengthy, some are too brief. Both are wide of the perfect mean, like archers who shoot their shafts short of the mark or beyond it. . . . The test of a good letter is its utility; it should not be long-winded when there is little to say, nor too brief when there is much. A letter must be simple, lucid, devoid of rhetoric, and it must have charm; it must not be without some adornment in the way of apophthegms, riddles, or jokes. They are to be used about as much as purple in weaving. Figures of speech we may employ, so they be few and above reproach. Antitheses and corresponding clauses we will gladly leave to the sophists, and if we do employ them let it be by way of a joke. My final remark shall be one which I once heard a clever man make about the eagle, that when the birds assembled and each came decked in his peculiar finery, the finest thing about the eagle was that he did not set up to be fine. This is of especial importance in letter-writing, to avoid superficial finery and get as near as possible to the natural.'

Gregory could write any sort of letter, flowery or neat, laconic or verbose; and as for angry letters, no one has ever written them better, they have a touch of flippancy that saves them from offensiveness. 'How fiercely', he wrote to Basil in the Sasima affair, 'you caper about in your letter, like a fiery young colt. It is not surprising that now that you have been raised to glory you should wish to show me how grand you have become, so as to raise your prestige in my eyes.' And, 'it is so long now that I have taken you as my guide in life, my teacher in the faith . . . and if I get any profit out of life, it is from your friendship and from association with you. . . . What I write now I write unwillingly, but still I must write it. . . . Do not be angry with me, or I shall be angry with myself if you do not give me credit for being prompted by good-

will to you in what I say and write. This was something
which a stronger mind than mine would have foreseen, but
I was too simple and unsuspecting to fear it when I wrote to
you. My letter annoyed you, but in my opinion your annoyance was neither reasonable nor just. . . .'[1] It is a scolding, but
a good-natured one, for which Basil should have been grateful, inasmuch as Gregory's provocation had been severe, and
his patience almost beyond justification. But Basil was never
grateful to Gregory, not even when Gregory, as often,
championed him in his absence, defending him against the
slanderous tongues which, in that atmosphere of general
theological suspicion, found plenty of congenial material to
set them wagging. All Gregory's epistolary inventiveness was
used to keep his friendship with Basil from disaster; there
were occasional quarrels, but never a permanent breach, and
the preservation of friendship with that touchy nature, that
fiery autocratic temperament, impatient of criticism, intolerant of any difference of opinion, was an achievement for
which Gregory must have the sole credit. Not that Gregory
showed weakness or cowardice; nor, indeed, was he very
conspicuously tactful. His great quality was an integrity
which must command respect; if Gregory protested, Basil
knew in his heart that Gregory must be right. Gregory's mind
was a fine instrument, which he kept from rough contacts
that could only spoil it for the delicate purposes for which
he intended it. He never submitted it to the domination of
any baser judgment or lowered its standards to any vulgar
necessity. In the affairs of the world and by its standards
he was a failure, because he refused to pay the price asked,
and generally paid, for worldly advancement. But in the
struggle to preserve his spiritual consistency against all
assaults and shocks, and against the more insidious dangers
of gradual blunting and wearing-down, he scored a conspicuous and, in the pages of history, a very unusual success.

[1] See also the letter to Basil quoted on page 291.

APPENDIX

Translations of a few of Gregory's Poems

Y

Epitaph for Euphemius[1]

Euphemius flashed upon our mortal gaze,
Brilliant as lightning, and as brief his days;
Beauty of mind and form together shone,
Illumined Cappadocia—and are gone.

The following translations in the style of the eighteenth century aptly convey the archaizing affectation of Gregory's verse:[2]

Hymn to the Deity[3]

Thee, peerless Monarch of the sky,
My soul aspires to glorify;
And swelling with immortal verse,
Immortal wonders to rehearse.
Through thee the tide of praise has rolled,
The seraphs strike their chords of gold
And wake the anthems soaring high
With inspiration's ecstasy,
Whilst Angels, quickened by thy glance,
Circle thy throne in mystic dance.
Through Thee, the seasons 'gan to roll,
Exulting in their Lord's control.
With golden flowers the starry train
Enwreathed the fair eternal plain.

[1] Epitaph XXXII.
[2] H. S. Boyd. Gregory of Nazianzus, *Select Poems*.
[3] *Carmina*, bk. I, sect. I, xxx.

Flashed high the Sun, in glory bright,
Looked forth the Moon with softer light,
The lovely shepherdess of night;
And born Jehovah's works to scan,
Uprose Creation's wonder, Man,
Uniting in his complex form,
Mild reason's calm and passion's storm.
Thou, oh my God, createdst all,
The highest heaven, this earthly ball,
Within thy breast the whole designing,
By Thy sole power each part combining,
At Thy command the work's begun,
At Thy command the work is done.

A Vision of Temperance and Chastity[1]

As once reclined in genial rest I lay,
A vision, sparkling with unclouded day,
Charmed my rapt soul, redeemed from low desire,
To glow with purer love, with holier fire.
Two virgin forms in snowy raiment dight,
Approaching near, enchained my dazzled sight.
Of equal age they bloomed, with equal mien
They moved majestic, and in each were seen
Those charms which all external arts out-vie,
The charms of unadorned Simplicity.
No gold their necks entwined, no emerald blaze
Shone on their radiant brow with fainter rays;
No silken vest their slender limbs embraced;
No gorgeous robe their humbler garb displaced;
No golden ringlets floating unconfined
Played with the breath of every gentle wind;

[1] From Gregory's poem on his own life, *De Vita Sua.*

And on their vermeil cheek no borrowed dye
Usurped the blush of health and modesty;
With maiden zone their simple vest was bound,
Flowed to their feet, yet trailed not on the ground.
Such their attire, a kerchief half concealed
Their blooming charms, and half those charms revealed,
And half betrayed the mantling blush that told
A heart by modesty's meek law controlled.
While their fixed eyes, to contemplation given,
Courted the earth, yet beamed like orbs to Heaven.
And as a rose-bud in its dewy hood
Shrinks from the gale too keen, or touch too rude,
So their closed lips in timid awe were sealed,
Unknown their will, their purpose unrevealed.
Wondering I gazed; for ne'er on earth was seen
Such perfect grace of gesture, form, and mien. . . .
A while they viewed me with maternal care;
And when I asked them who and what they were,
And whence they came, 'In us', they cried, 'you see
Mild Temperance and spotless Chastity!' . . .

Epitaph for Cæsarius[1]

If trees could mourn, and mourning, droop their head;
If rocks could chant a requiem o'er the dead;
If murmuring brooks and fountains as they flow
Could heave the sigh, and swell the tide of woe;
Fountains and trees and rocks would blend their tear
And weep Cæsarius, to each object dear.
All loved Cæsarius, sceptred monarchs gave
Their high applause . . . he sank into the grave.

[1] Epitaph XVIII.

[341]

Epitaph for Cæsarius[1]

In youth we sent thee from thy native soil,
August, and crowned with learning's hallowed spoil,
Fame, wealth, on thee delighted to attend:
Thy home a palace, and a king thy friend.
So lived Cæsarius honoured, loved, and blest;
But ah, this mournful urn must tell the rest.

Epitaph on Euphemius[2]

Euphemius sipped Castalia's honeyed dews
And wooed the Attic and th' Ausonian muse;
For him, their blended flowers were fully blown,
When o'er his head but twenty years had flown:
In youth's gay morn, in beauty's roseate bloom
He fell, and withered in the envious tomb.

Epigram from Gregory the Elder to his Son Gregory[3]

Small is the pearl, yet queen o'er every gem,
And Christ was born in lowly Bethlehem;
Thus small, yet precious, is the flock I fed;
Be then, my son, their pastor and their head.

[1] Epitaph XIV.
[2] Epitaph XXX.
[3] Actually composed by Gregory himself.

Gregory on his Retirement[1]

Surcharged with care, with heaviest anguish fraught,
A deep sequestered grove I lately sought,
Panting to find in sweet retirement's calm,
For every mental ill a lenient balm.
Vernal the air, and mild the murmuring breeze,
And sprightly birds that warbled on the trees
Seemed as they strove to charm away my woes
And lull my wearied bosom to repose.
On every bough the grasshopper was seen,
Unfolding to the Sun his robes of green.
Cheered by the blaze he soon essayed to sing
And bade the woods with merriest chirpings ring.
To lave my feet a gurgling fountain strove,
Whose streams meandered through the dewy grove
With gentle flow. In vain all Nature smiled,
My joyless heart no sounds of joy beguiled.
The feathered quire appeared to mock my woe,
To insult my grief the fountains seemed to flow.
Life's gloomy scene I pondered in my mind,
And thus I poured my sorrows unconfined. . . .

Epitaph for the Sophist Thespesius[2]

Though thou art dead, thy glory cannot die;
Thy deathless fame shall bloom eternally.
Sublime thy speech, yet ancient Athens cries:
'With thee no modern can divide the prize.'

[1] The first of his elegiac poems.
[2] Epitaph IV.

BIBLIOGRAPHY

I

PALLADIUS: *Lausiac History* (including the *Historia Mona-chorum*). Text and exhaustive study of the various extant versions of both works, and their history, by Dom Cuthbert Butler in Robinson's Texts and Studies.
  Translation: Lowther Clarke: *Lausiac History*.
  Various versions of the text in Migne, *Patrologia Græca*, XXXIV.
Vitæ Patrum. A collection of lives of the ascetics and others from various sources, both good and bad. Ed. E. Rosweyde. Migne, *Patrologia Latins*, vol. LXXIV.
Verba Seniorum. A similar collection by the same editor: Migne, *Patrologia Latina*, vol. LXXIII.
Book of Paradise. Syriac Text with translation and commentary by Sir E. A. Wallis Budge.
SOZOMEN: *Ecclesiastical History*, VI, 28.
THEODORET: *Ecclesiastical History*. Trans. in Library of the Nicene Fathers.
SOCRATES: *History*, IV, 23 (derived from Palladius).
ATHANASIUS: *Vita Antonii*.
JEROME: *Life of Hilarion*, *Life of Paul the Hermit*, and Ep. CXXV, Ep. XIV, and Ep. XXII to Eustochium (end).
JOHN CASSIAN: *Institutes and Conferences*. Migne, vol. XLIX. Trans. in Library of the Nicene Fathers.
SULPICIUS SEVERUS: *Dialogue*. Migne, vol. XLIX. Trans. in Library of the Nicene Fathers.
AMÉLINEAU: *Vita Pachomii. La Vie de Schnoudi et des Moines Égyptiens. Géographie de l'Égypte copte.*
Cambridge Mediæval History, vol. I.

L. DUCHESNE: *Early History of the Christian Church*, vol. III.
ANATOLE FRANCE: *Thaïs*. A novel based on Cassian's *Conferences*.
CAXTON'S *Golden Legend* contains many of the *Lives*.
CHARLES KINGSLEY: *The Hermits*.
FLAUBERT: *La Première Tentation* and *La Tentation de Saint Antoine* (with enormous bibliography).

II

VALERIUS ABBAS: Migne, *Patrologia Latina*, vol. LXXXVII.
J. H. BERNARD: *Pilgrimage of Saint Silvia*. Palestine Pilgrims' Text Society, vol. I.
M. L. MCCLURE and C. F. FELTOE: *The Pilgrimage of Etheria*. S.P.C.K., 1919.
M. FÉROTIN: *Le Véritable Auteur de la 'Peregrinatio Silviæ'*.
A. BLUDAU: *Die Pilgerreise der Ætheriæ*. Studien für Geschicht und Kultur des Christlichen Alterthums, Band 15. Heft i und ii.
W. HERAEUS: *Silviæ vel potius Ætheriæ Peregrinatio*. Sammlung der Vulgarlateinischer Texte, vol. I, 1921.
Z. GARCIA: *Etheria*.
J. H. BERNARD: *The Bordeaux Pilgrim*. Palestine Pilgrims' Text Society, vol. I. *Itinerarium Bordigalense*. Migne, *Patrologia Latina*, vol. XXXIX. Palestine Pilgrims Text Society, vol. I.

III

PELAGIUS: *Commentary*: Text edited with exhaustive introductory study by A. Souter in Robinson's *Texts and Studies*. Text and *Letter to Demetrias* in pseudo-Jerome: Migne, *Patrologia Latina*, vol. XXX. Fragments of Pelagius are scattered through Augustine's anti-Pelagian works. Biographical study by Garnier in Migne, *Patrologia Latinv*, vol. XLVIII.

MARIUS MERCATOR: *Commonitorium Super nomine Celestii* and *Liber Subnotationum in Verba Juliani*. Migne, *Patrologia Latina*, vol. XLVIII. This volume contains a collection of works about and against the Pelagian heresy.

ALEXANDER SOUTER: *Pelagius' Expositions of the Thirteen Epistles of Saint Paul*. Texts and Studies, vol. IX. *Pelagius' Commentary on the Epistle to the Romans*. Proceedings of the British Academy, vol. II. *Character and History of Pelagius*. Proceedings of the British Academy, vol. VII.

AUGUSTINE: *Anti-Pelagian Works*. Migne, *Patrologia Latina*, vol. XLIV. Trans. in Library of Post-Nicene Fathers.

JEROME: Letters CXXIV, CXXX, CXXXIII. Migne, vol. XXII. *Dialogue Against the Pelagians*. (Trans. in Library of Post-Nicene Fathers.) Preface to *Comm. ad Jeremiam*, bk. II. *Contra Jovinianum. Contra Joannem*. Also Letter XLV to Asella, Letter LXXVII about Fabiola.

OROSIUS: Migne, *Patrologia Latina*, vol. XXXI. *Historiarum Libri Septem: Apologeticus de arbitrii libertate contra Pelagium*.

VINCENT OF LÉRINS: Migne, vol. L.

INNOCENT I: Letters: in Jerome's Letters 135–7.

RUFINUS: Migne, *Patrologia Latina*, vol. XXXI.

J. B. MOZLEY: *Augustinian Theory of Predestination*.

H. ZIMMER: *Pelagius in Ireland*.

J. B. BURY: *Origin of Pelagius*. Hermathena, XXX, 26. *Life of Saint Patrick*.

T. R. GLOVER: *Conflict of Religions in the Late Roman Empire*.

E. C. S. GIBSON: *The Thirty-Nine Articles*.

W. BRIGHT: *Church of the Fathers* II.

C. P. CASPARI: *Briefe, Abhandlungen und Predigten aus dem letzten Jahrhundert des Kirchlichen Altertums.*

H. WILLIAMS: *Christianity in Early Britain.*

L. DUCHESNE: *Early History of the Christian Church,* vol. III.

W. BRIANT: *Age of the Fathers.*

C. OMAN: *Britain before the Norman Conquest.*

W. M. FLINDERS PETRIE: *Neglected British History.*

W. CUNNINGHAM: *Saint Austin.*

J. W. McCABE: *Saint Augustine and his Age.*

IV

GREGORY'S *Works* in Migne: *Patrologia Græca,* vols. XXXV, XXXVI, XXXVII, XXXVIII. Trans. of the principal orations and a few letters in Library of Nicene Fathers, Second Series, vol. VII, Wall and Schaff.

Life of Gregory. Migne, vol. XXXV.

C. ULLMANN: *Saint Gregory of Nazianzus.*

E. FLEURY: *Saint Grégoire de Nazianze et son temps* (1930).

GREGORY PRESBYTER: *Vita Sancti Gregorii.*

BENOIT: *Saint Grégoire de Nazianze.*

W. R. RAMSAY: *Historical Geography of Asia Minor.*

BASIL: *Letters.*

JULIAN: *Letters.*

LIBANIUS: *Letters.*

W. W. CAPES: *University Life in Ancient Athens.*

T. R. GLOVER: *Life and Letters in the Fourth Century.*

CARDINAL NEWMAN: *The Church of the Fathers.*

INDEX

z